"WHAT A BOOK IT IS . . . A MAJOR LEAGUE BOOK ABOUT LIFE IN THE MINORS. . . . We meet Jim Gattis, the Blue Sox manager, a man with the calm temperament of a volcano . . . Roy Moretti, a 30-year-old relief pitcher too good for the minor leagues, not good enough for the majors, who knows he ought to give up the game but can't bring himself to do it . . . the world's shortest starting outfield . . . a third-baseman who stops everything with his chest . . . a catcher who can balance a bicycle on his chin . . . and Roger Kahn, learning how the other half lives . . . We find these improbable men improbably involved in a pennant race, short of money, short of baseballs, short of bats— short of everything but the love for the game."
—*St. Louis Post-Dispatch*

"THIS BOOK READS LIKE A NOVEL. IT JUST SO HAPPENS THAT IT'S NONFICTION."
—*The New York Times Book Review*

"From his lyrical opening paragraph we know we're in the palm of a master's hand."
—*The Miami Herald*

For more CHEERS! please turn page . . .

Great Baseball Books from SIGNET

GOOD ENOUGH
TO DREAM

Roger Kahn

A SIGNET BOOK

NEW AMERICAN LIBRARY

SIGNET TRADEMARK REG. U.S. PAT. OFF. AND FOREIGN COUNTRIES
REGISTERED TRADEMARK—MARCA REGISTRADA
HECHO EN CHICAGO, U.S.A.

SIGNET, SIGNET CLASSIC, MENTOR, PLUME, MERIDIAN AND NAL BOOKS
are published by New American Library,
1633 Broadway, New York, New York 10019

First Signet Printing, April, 1986

1 2 3 4 5 6 7 8 9

PRINTED IN THE UNITED STATES OF AMERICA

For the ladies of the club, Liss and Joanne

1

The Nine-year-old Right Fielder

The first dream, full of innocence and sunlight, is to play the game. The dream shines, with that same eerie, morning light of promise, at Renton, Washington; along Spring Garden Road in Lincroft, New Jersey, and on West Arthur Street, Chicago. To play the game. To play the game superbly. To play with such a brilliant, sunlit, morning grace that the dream itself leaves you at length, like Caliban, able only to speak fragments. "The clouds . . . would open and show riches/Ready to drop upon me. . . ."

I remember versions of my small baseball fantasy from loving and faraway days when ball players wore uniforms of hot, baggy flannel and television existed only in the laboratories (and fantasies) of arcane electrical engineers. (Electrical engineers once seemed as arcane as alchemists.)

You could pitch, like Christy Mathewson, Van Lingle Mungo or John Whitlow Wyatt, and then the batters, aggressive, mean-spirited men—none seemed to have shaved this morning—quailed before your fast ball and your swift, snapping curve. Or you could hit. Now the pitcher became a foul, murderous brute who stared out of a storm-cloud visage. He knocked you down and cursed you with what people in baggy-flannel days, described, in studied loathing, as "foul epithets." You stood against his fast ball, his swift, snapping curve, and drove a long, high drive that climbed the sky.

After that long-sounding thwack and a blur of base runners, you were borne shoulder high by exulting teammates. In the crowd beyond, your father cheered and your mother brought both hands to her face, her cheeks glistening with pride. Somewhere else in the careful tapestry of the imagined throng sulked a regretful, baby-doll face. It was the girl who let you get away.

The ball players were seated along wooden benches, anchored to the floor, beneath two rows of orange lockers inside a stout, brick blockhouse of a building. Forty years earlier, W.P.A. workers had laid and cemented every brick. Only four of the players had so much as heard of the Works Progress Administration. "I either read it in history," said a catcher named Mark Krynitsky, "or my Dad, or *his* Dad, worked for the W.P.A. I don't know."

Light entered through two opaque windows backed by metal grills, and fluorescent tubes glared overhead. The team assembled in the weathered (some would add socialistic) brick was called the Blue Sox and they played their home games in the historic community of Utica, New York. Historic, but in a baseball sense obscure. Those sunlit boyhood dreams project you far beyond a drab clubhouse in Utica; you see yourself moving on winged spikes through carpeted, indeed hallowed, dressing rooms in Los Angeles or New York City.

Still, the Blue Sox were professionals. Their abilities resembled the skills of major leaguers far more closely than the enthusiastic fumblings you see among high school athletes. Professionals in a W.P.A. clubhouse.

Most would be earning $500 a month. Out of that they had to pay taxes, rent, living expenses and meals when the Blue Sox played at home. The cars they drove were small or old or both. But the good athletes, the ones who would turn out to be good, felt pride in their professionalism. Poor, unpampered, they *were* professional ball players, the job description that covered Mickey Mantle, Willie Mays and Steve Garvey. On this particular hot June day the manager was hurling forward a campaign, a personal crusade, to give these twenty-five young people, the Utica Blue Sox, a sense of their own professionalism.

I was sitting in the clubhouse not as an auditor, with an intrusive curiosity about the inner workings of a ball club, nor even as a journalist granted, as it were, a privileged pass from the manager in exchange for the promise of a favorable story. I was sitting there, bless my wallet, as a principal stockholder and president and chief executive officer of the team.

Since running a successful election campaign in the subsenior bunk at Camp Robinson Crusoe forty-five years earlier, I had not been president of anything. I took my motto from William Tecumseh Sherman: "If nominated I will not run; if elected, I will not serve." Aside from that, I don't recall ever being offered any kind of nomination for any kind of office across all those decades. As a writer, I presided over my prose. Typically, I stood as far from high office as Walter Mondale found himself one November morning in 1984. (Or farther yet.)

Now in the clubhouse in the warm June of 1983, I viewed my new-won presidency with resolute optimism punctuated by spasms—cellos playing in a minor key—of undressed and unarmored alarm. Those friends of mine who knew the least about baseball suggested that being president of a low minor league club would provide me with an ultimate toy, far better than my latest stereo set, more fun even than a black Mercedes sports car that an entrancing lady had once offered up as an adjunct to a romance.

Other friends, who knew somewhat more baseball—say,

for example, that minor league teams can go bankrupt—
put forth temperate forecasts. "Best way to look at it,"
said one of these, possessed of a dogged literary manner,
"is that you're taking over the *Pequod*. Now maybe you're
going to find that old white whale. But maybe you're
not."

My cherished Brooklyn Dodger friend Carl Furillo, a
veteran of twenty years of glorious professional ball playing,
took a colder view. "You're taking over a minor league
club? In Utica? You're president? You'll be lucky if you
don't have two ulcers by Labor Day."

Whaling voyager or ulcer candidate, I was at the true
beginning of the Adventure. Traditionally, of course, baseball seasons open in April. That is a marvelous month to
start, particularly in the North where some April days sting
with the afterbite of winter and others glow with summer
promise. That summer promise and the game of baseball
fuse.

But in the low minor leagues in upper New York State
April is no month to play professional ball. Spring rains
muddy the fields and the small grounds-keeping staffs are
no match for the elements of early spring. Besides, the
nights—and minor league baseball is a nighttime sport—
bite with winds curling coldly from the Adirondack Moun-
tains. In April local fans prefer beer, bowling or warm
living rooms to baseball. So this June day in this hot
clubhouse was the backdrop for a final preseason meeting
for the Blue Sox. We were beginning, we were all beginning, although by then the major league season was two
months old.

"Now listen up, everybody," the manager said. He was
a powerful six-footer, thirty-one years old, with straw hair
and a remarkably mobile face. He had firm even features
and a lantern jaw and sometimes under his straw-colored
hair the manager, Jim Gattis, looked like a movie version

of a grown-up Huckleberry Finn. Sometimes, later, when his blue eyes raged and his mouth set and his jaw jutted, Jim Gattis was a sadistic drill sergeant. Then he looked at his charges with equal measures of hatred and contempt. "Baseball," he would say, "is not like life. It *is* life. The games are a three-hour lesson in life every day."

Playing for Gattis would not always be pleasant. Careless work infuriated him to a point where I came to fear he might strike one of the Blue Sox. The young players were startled by Gattis' eruptions. Before the Blue Sox summer—variously an idyll and a tornado of a season—reached a molten climax, certain players would wonder if Gattis' single-mindedness did not exceed the bounds of reason and, perhaps, sanity. For his part, Gattis would speak of a generation gap. Ten years ago, he said, when he was twenty-one, everybody played smarter and harder, a hell of a lot harder, than young people played today.

Standing between the orange lockers, with young players docile and expectant on the bolted benches, Gattis declaimed orders for the season. (These would hold, unless I chose to fire him.)

"Don't go getting hammered," Gattis said. "You come to the ball park hung over, and it's going to show. In your roadmap eyes. You'll know. I'll know. That's not what you came to Utica for. To get hammered."

Two of the players, both relief pitchers, were smoking. Roy Moretti, a small John Wayne out of Victoria, British Columbia, liked Marlboroughs. Jimmy Tompkins, called J.T., a guitarplaying right-hander from Austin, Texas, who blanketed his appealing complexity beneath layers of cowboy charm, puffed a Barclay, which promised pleasure with low tar. The others looked at their spiked shoes—all black shoes on the Blue Sox, against the current trend that has ball players wearing spikes dyed to a pastel palette. Although many, including Jim Gattis, would get hammered on certain nights, no one responded about his individual right to drink. Low minor league players have no unions, no agents, no lawyers and fewer professional rights than an army corporal.

"What about drugs?" Jim Gattis said. "Our drug program here is simple. Do drugs and you're gone. See ya. You won't be around."

A light scraping of spikes sounded along the concrete floor. Gattis did not distinguish hash from pot or coke. Can you find a professional baseball team today without a group of casual pot smokers? I doubt it. Gattis doubts it too. But the rules a manager issues in these rebellious, sprawling, Grenadan, Reaganistic times, are, like John Keats's pathetic epitaph, writ in water. Still they are important. Without commandments, there would be no guideposts against which to stumble. Without established rules, young people would have no rules to break. Psychologists expand and enlarge this point, repackaging rules as "limits," and write monographs and books on the one-note theme. *Nothing frightens the young as much as anarchy.*

Agreed. Agreed.

Only once, to the best of my knowledge, did any of the Blue Sox smoke grass on any bus I rented for the team.

Neither Gattis nor I could testify with accuracy or specificity, should this issue ever come to court. While sweet smoke curled about the back of the bus, Gattis and I, in the two front seats, were getting hammered.

"I want to get to the signs that we'll be using," the manager said. He put on eyeglasses and was able, in his protean way, to look rather like a teacher.

"Okay. Now notice some of the things I do."

Baseball signs, as we shall see, are among the oracular mysteries of the game. I will, with exuberant pleasure, guide you through that particular Delphi as best I can, but for the moment let me simply offer two of Jim Gattis' chrestomathy of signals.

After much cap touching, ear tugging and miscellaneous fiddling with his person, Gattis' right hand moving downward meant that all signs were off. He could brush *downward* on his uniform shirt or knicker, brush *downward* along the skin of his left arm, but so long as he brushed *downward,* the message was the same. A wipe. In other terms, an erasure. Gattis was, in fact, a splendid pantomimist, and this downward motion could suggest a housemaid wiping a windowpane clean. He was such a splendid pantomimist that his movements in the W.P.A. locker room created a third-base coaching box on the concrete where he stood.

"Okay, everybody," Gattis said. "What's this?" He touched the bill of his cap above his left eye, moved his right hand to the upper quadrant of his jersey, touched the bill of his cap above his right eye and wiped his right hand down the left sleeve of his shirt. "What is it?"

The glorious rabble muttered in half a dozen voices, "Nothin'."

"Why nothing?"

"Because you wiped," said Don Jacoby, a compact, mustached, earthy twenty-four-year-old from north New Jersey, who flipped pancakes for a living during the eight months between minor league baseball seasons.

"Good," Gattis said. "You got it, Cobra. Very good. Now let's see what else you can get."

As Gattis spoke in an assertive high baritone, one of the ball players slipped from a bench and sat on the floor. It was hot, it was always going to be hot, in the Blue Sox clubhouse. The ball player, Daryl Pitts, of Los Angeles, let his head loll forward and closed his eyes. Gattis did not appear to notice. Someone nudged Pitts and whispered, "Stay awake."

"Hey, man," Pitts said. "I'm *real* awake."

The manager moved to a more complicated sign. He extended both his arms and his palms flashed upward briefly. He demonstrated how the flash would fit amid a flurry of ear tugs and sideways brushing of his hands.

Usually, in the New York-Penn League, when the count is two balls and no strikes, the batter is allowed to swing at the next pitch. Usually, when the count is *three* balls and no strikes, he is not. The arm-extended palm flash, Gattis explained, meant that the batter was to do what was *unusual*. "Everybody know what that word means? *Un*usual."

Pitts's eyes closed again. A teammate elbowed him awake.

"So when I give palms to you, 2 and 0," Gattis said, "it means take. Don't swing. But when I give palms to you, 3 and 0, the same sign, it means don't take, but swing. The same sign means two different things in two different game situations. Is that clear?"

Various nods and mutters of assent.

"Good," Gattis said. "I know most of you have been to college." His voice turned harsh.

"Pitts!"

"Yeah. Yeah. I'm here, Skipper. I'm right here."

Daryl, the count is 2 and 0. What do you do?" Gattis twitched through a set of fake signs, extended his arms with a palm flash and clapped his hands.

"I swing," Pitts announced with great confidence. He had guessed and he had guessed wrong. Other players began to boo.

"I take," Pitts said, waking up too late.

"Same sign," Gattis said. "The count is 3 and 0. What do you do?"

"I take," Pitts repeated. Two guesses. Two wrong guesses.

The booing built toward a crescendo.

"Let me run through this again," Gattis said.

Pitts was confused. He is short, muscular, lovable. He is also, as it will develop, always in debt, as befits a man who claimed that his alimony payments exceeded his monthly salary from the Blue Sox by three hundred percent.

After Gattis' repetition, he turned to Pitts again. "The count is 3 and 0." The manager flashed palms. "Daryl?"

"Take. I don't swing." Three guesses. Three wrong guesses. The season had not yet begun, and already Pitts was 0 for 3.

Other players smirked. A few laughed. "I mean I swing."

Gattis neither smirked nor laughed. The laugh lay in his gullet. Deadpan, he told the Blue Sox, "Look," he said, "these signs are pretty complicated. Maybe they're too complicated for all of us. So instead of using the ones that I've been showing, we'll just use voice signs this year. Like this."

Gattis cupped strong, hitter's hands about his mouth and bellowed over the heads of his players down the orange corridor of the W.P.A. clubhouse.

"Swing!"

"Steal!"

"Take!"

"Bunt!"

"Did everybody get those okay?" this fierce manager asked mildly.

Out of the roughly 1,250,000 young men who graduate from American high schools every year, no more than 500 are signed to professional contracts. The chances against your getting any contract at all, on the very lowest level, anywhere in organized baseball run about 2,500 to 1. A certain percentage of male high school seniors don't like to play baseball. Factoring that in, the chances improve to perhaps 2,300 to 1. The Utica Blue Sox call odds like that "awesome." "Awesome" was a word they especially liked along with "seed," which meant a line drive, and "yard," which meant a home run, and "really," meaning "I agree with you," or "Indeed" or sometimes even "Really."

The death of the baseball dream, with all its innocence
and sunlight, comes early to most. You have to be very,
very good to play professionally, even at a rudimentary
stage, and few young ball players are that—very, very
good. I lunched once with Hiram Haydn, a famous editor
of his day, and the talk about the structure of personal
essays moved forward without much excitement. I had the
sense in a restaurant called Cherio's, which was noted for
northern Italian cooking and martini glasses the size of
birdbaths, that Haydn was telling me things he had told
many others, many times before. He seemed to be boring
himself. Then suddenly he held his great martini glass
firmly and said, "You must know Phil Rizzuto."

I said I did.

"Well, how does a small man like that hit home runs in
Yankee Stadium? How in the world does he do it?"

"He's strongly built. He's stronger than he looks and
he hits most of his homers right down the left field line,
which isn't much more than three hundred feet from home
plate. It's a question of knowing how to pull the ball.
Making contact at the instant of maximum bat speed."

Haydn sipped his drink. "I played ball," he said, "when
I was growing up in Cleveland. Batted right-handed. Never
had power. Not as much power as that little Rizzuto, that
son of a gun. Then one day when I was in a pickup game,
I batted left for a lark. You know"—Haydn's mild gaze
vanished in remembered fire—"I just whacked that baseball
over the fence. And I realized that if I'd been batting
left-handed all along . . ." His voice dropped. The sentence died. He returned to discourse on essays after asking
if I was ready for another drink.

I have lived variations of this moment, with authors,
physicians, lawyers and bartenders. Layers of acquired,
mannered sophistication fall away to passion when they
talk of distant baseball dreams that failed.

For myself, I guarded dreams carefully. My father knew

baseball, played baseball and coached baseball. Dad mentioned that he had played third base for the City College of New York in the season of 1923, and years later, when I had the means to check old City College box scores, I decided not to verify what he said. He wanted me to believe that he had played college ball and I wanted to believe he told the facts. Who needed truth, with all her tedious footnotes, breaking in on admiration and love?

I wanted above all things to play professional baseball, but there were insistent early hints that Joe DiMaggio and I were made of different stuff. For one thing, I was always small for my age. For another, my throwing arm was suspect. Although in later years I reached a respectable level of competence in softball, we are talking hardball here. *Major league* hardball. I never came close.

My father's conversation was an intriguing babble of Berlioz and base hits, history and politics, detective stories and Gibbon, and anecdotes about athletes I would never see called Jigger Statz and Jake Daubert and Ivy Olson. We lived in Brooklyn, which my mother pointed out was a community that attracted the great musicians, Horowitz, Heifetz and Piatigorsky. My father enjoyed classical music, as he enjoyed most things, but he suffered as I did from the regional—*liebestod* seems the best word—*liebestod* erupting about the Brooklyn Dodgers. It was love because the rooting was fierce and naked and pure. It was death, because every September managers like Max Carey, Casey Stengel and Burleigh Grimes brought the Dodgers home in seventh place in an eight-team National League. But love was born again like hope, every spring, when cherry blossoms bloomed in the Brooklyn Botanic Gardens, half a mile from Ebbets Field.

After several unremarkable misadventures, I was enrolled in a private school named for the German educator who is credited with inventing the kindergarten, Friedrich

Wilhelm Froebel (1782–1852). Out of an early respect for
minimalism, the school was called simply Froebel Academy.

Late in the Great Depression, the directors of Froebel
engaged Carleton M. Saunders, M.A., North Carolina, as
the new principal. Mr. Saunders, a gangly man of perhaps
thirty-five, canceled afternoon classes on a cold spring day
in 1937 so that the upper school boys could travel, under
his supervision, to Ebbets Field, where the Brooklyn Dodgers
would open their season. I forget who won, but I do
remember that the opening-day tickets were cut in the shape
of a catcher's mitt and that all of us, even mouthy, disrup-
tive Donald Kennedy, were moved to unutterable delight.
After years of the severity of the previous headmistress,
Miss Olive Place, we had miraculously fallen under the
care of a headmaster who would take us to a ball game, *on
school time*. (Nor did we have to write an essay called
"What I Learned at Ebbets Field.")

Continuing his efforts at liberalizing a school that had
embraced the nineteenth century, Mr. Saunders proposed
certain changes in the curriculum. He wanted a science
program that acknowledged the existence of Einstein. He
didn't think it amiss if the upper school children read
works more challenging than *Balto, the Hero Dog*.

Mr. Saunders also observed that a large, pebbly field
behind Froebel Academy was underused. Froebel had no
formal sports program, nor any interscholastic teams. Now
Saunders began looking for a coach who would not tax the
school budget. In short, Saunders wanted a coach to work
for free.

My father, Gordon, a teacher, editor and polymath,
developed a fine and rather relaxed friendship with me
around the centerpiece of baseball. Whatever my father's
great concerns—high tariffs vs. free trade, his own career,
angina pectoris, Stalin's megalomania or the rise of
Hitler—he did not discuss such things with me. My father
and I played catch and went to ball games, sometimes to

Ebbets Field and more often to a kind of enormous sand-lot, called the Parade Grounds, where recruits had been marched about during World War I. I was no idiot, at least in my studies of baseball, and I learned from play, observation and my father's tutorials.

"You want to throw the fast ball high and tight.

"As a fielder, you have to get your body behind the ball.

"As an outfielder, do not run backing up. You turn early so that you run forward toward the point where the ball is going to descend."

This last is a difficult skill to perfect although professional ball players perform it routinely. At the Parade Grounds, my father and I watched semiprofessional teams representing Consolidated Edison, the Catholic Youth Organization and the Brooklyn Union Gas Company. Often, in these games, for which no admission was charged, an outfielder backed up awkwardly for a fly ball. Almost as often the fly fell to earth, a yard behind him. The position player most often guilty of this ghastly amateurism was the right fielder.

When I mentioned this to my father, he explained: "As a general rule, you put your worst player in right. That's because most of the hitters are right-handed and they'll usually hit the ball to left field, if they hit it. Right field is the position where the worst ball player has the least opportunity to do damage."

"But at Ebbets Field," I answered, "I've seen some terrific right fielders, like Leroy Watkins and Goody Rosen. Besides, you told me Babe Ruth played right."

"Do you want to argue?"

"No."

"The major leagues," my father said, "are a different kettle of fish. First, there are no bad ball players in the major leagues. All things are relative, but even the worst major leaguer is a good ball player. Second, good major

leaguers can hit to all fields. Right is every bit as important as left. It's even a little more demanding. A right
fielder has to have a stronger arm to reach third base with
a throw. But that's the majors. In amateur ball you put
your worst player in right. Next question."

I had no next question. I listened to my father's baseball
lore with full measures of affection and concentration. He
knew the game. He could hit a ball four hundred feet. And
if he used the Socratic method, with the persistence of a
youthful law professor, no one has ever spoken to me with
such kindness, concern, enthusiasm and love all at the
same time. When Gordon and I, father and son, walked in
our baseball moments, Caliban's gorgeous cloud rode lordly
above us, opening and showing riches ready to drop as
softly as the leaves. . . . "That when I waked I cried to
dream again."

After the Blue Sox players and I felt our way into
summer friendships, some asked about my children, my
thoughts about the press, my car. The black roadster was
gone with the vanished petals of the old romance, but I
still drove a Mercedes. Eight years old, a leisurely yellow
diesel, but a Mercedes nonetheless. For all my protests
that it was a good car, but nothing magic—"rubber and
metal, same as your 1968 Mustang"—the Blue Sox looked
at Big Yellow with a lust I thought would better have been
thrust upon a good (or perhaps not necessarily good) woman.

Then they asked, oh, question of unanswerable questions: "You're going to write a book about us, and I was
wondering, how do you write a book?" Some asked nothing at all. Ball players are performers, focused on their
own performances, and numbers of them are as insensitive
to other people's lives as this year's latest hyperactive rock
singer or next year's firm-bosomed, hard-eyed television
starlet who will move, so to speak, by vital parts to a vital
part.

But almost all of them, knowing that their baseball skills were extraordinary, would ask on one afternoon or another if I had once wanted to play professional baseball myself. Sometimes this was simple curiosity. Sometimes it was a way of making conversation with the club president. Sometimes it was a way of saying: "Hey, you may be boss here, but don't you wish you once could have done what I'm doing now?"

A decent WASP reserve was part of the unwritten curriculum at Froebel Academy and I found myself giving them a clipped "Damn right I wanted to play."

"What happened?"

"Great desire. Mediocre talent."

Jimmy Tompkins, a fine relief pitcher, who was twenty-four and had been released by an Atlanta farm team, said in his soft Texas twang, "Well, it looks like we my-ut be in the same boat. I've got a ninety-mile fast ball and where has it gotten me?"

"To the Blue Sox, J.T."

"But, Rog, don't you understand? There's not a soul in Austin who ever has *heard* of the Utica Blue Sox."

Barry Moss, twenty-nine, was a coach and designated hitter who had been invited to a major league spring training camp by Cincinnati. Unfortunately for Moss, the invitation came during the era when Cincinnati's roster flowered with so much talent that sportswriters referred to "The Big Red Machine." Moss tasted a spoonful of major league ambrosia and then was exiled to the Burger Kings of the minors.

"What was it you couldn't do well enough?" Moss asked me. "Hit? Field? Throw?"

"Kind of a combination of all three."

Barry, who had left a $60,000-a-year real estate business to play for the Blue Sox, practiced a fine reserve himself. Indeed, he might have been an honor graduate of

Froebel Academy. As it was, he simply met my eyes and nodded.

Certainly Jimmy Tompkins, Roy Moretti, Gattis, Moss and I, along with all the others, embraced variations on similar dreams. The dreams were as disparate as the ranging paths of boyhood, but unified by a common incompleteness. At treeless, barren Murnane Field, in Utica, New York, we were a long way from the playing fields that had felt the spikes of Johnny Bench and Carl Yastrzemski.

"You've been around," Jim Gattis said before even the telephone functioned in the clubhouse office. "Don't you ever ask yourself what the fuck you're doing in Utica?"

I forget how I answered and it doesn't matter. Utica and the season would bring us deep measures of pain and elation, humor and anger, and above all a sense of purpose. Not only Utica, but places named Watertown, Batavia, Newark, New York, and sweet Auburn, which is not the loveliest village of the plain. Indeed, Auburn is the site of the maximum security prison in New York State, a fortress gray as death that makes Attica appear to be a rose garden.

At about the time headmaster Carleton Saunders elected to introduce interscholastic sports to Froebel Academy a remarkable new family entered the rolls. They were German-Irish, middle class and Roman Catholic, an unusual mix for Froebel in an era when most middle-class Roman Catholics sent their children to the parochial schools that had sprung up about Brooklyn's scores of Catholic churches. Terry, a pug-nosed blond tomboy, became my sister's classmate in the third grade. Peter, a long-limbed little fellow, entered kindergarten. The mother, Katherine, could not speak above a whisper. Cancer surgery, which took her larynx and her voice, had saved her life. But Katherine's loss was lessened by the fact that her husband,

Walter Francis O'Malley, quite easily could speak for two, or ten or a legion.

Carleton Saunders took the measure of Mr. O'Malley, as best a schoolmaster could measure a man who had the manner of a feudal baron grafted onto the soul of a clerk at a failing bank. O'Malley became a Froebel Academy trustee, and his interest in Mr. Saunders' new athletic program was limited to ledgers. "If the older boys are going to play baseball," O'Malley said, "make sure the parents, not the school, pay for the bats and balls and gloves." Baron O'Malley never lost his ledger view of baseball. Along with a variety of other qualities, including courage, that enabled him to create the Los Angeles Dodgers, which evolved into a perfect fusion of himself. A Hollywood baron, such as Cary Grant, or a Culver City grocery deliverer, buying a ticket for the covered stands in center field, admired the Los Angeles Dodgers with equal enthusiasm. Walter would be hung in effigy on Flatbush Avenue as though he were a global tyrant, but he matured as a middle-class Brooklyn Catholic lawyer who dispatched his children to a school of Episcopalian haughtiness. At his death in 1979, he left an estate approaching $100 million.

Years earlier in Brooklyn, on a chilly March afternoon, Carleton Saunders arrived at my family's graystone, bay-windowed house, number 252 Brooklyn Avenue. The neighborhood was dominated by St. Gregory's Roman Catholic Church, topped by a campanile, that was in turn surmounted by a large cross.

No one told me Mr. Saunders was expected and when I answered the door and saw a gangly, stern-faced adult—the headmaster, the *darn* headmaster, the headmaster *himself*—all my school sins appeared as knives before my eyeballs. At nine I wavered between cold, rational atheism and a soft, ecumenical religiosity, combining Episcopalian chapel, the cross of St. Gregory's with a touch or two of Torah which I had picked up through a forgotten osmotic process. Mr. Saunders' appearance stirred panic and called for prayer.

"Good afternoon," Mr. Saunders said.

"Yes, sir," I said.

Mr. Saunders smiled. (I had never seen his predecessor, Miss Olive Place, smile. Her face is imprisoned in my memory as a joyless, openmouthed hymnal mask, suggesting sulphurous fires which burned—and still burn—in flashes of my ad hoc religion.)

> Cast thy burden upon the Lord
> [Miss Place sang in certain hope of resurrection]
> And He will sustain [two, three, four]
> Thee.

I sang along grimly and mostly dutifully. Froebel was a school for dutiful children. I did not sing for very long, however. At one chapel, Dexter Davidson, the music teacher, stood close enough to hear my tuneless treble. "You don't have to *sing* the hymn," Mr. Davidson said, with noncommittal tenderness. "If you just move your lips, silently, please, that will be satisfactory."

"I have an appointment with your father," said Carleton Saunders from the doorway.

My father, a stocky, strong-armed, loquacious man, appeared behind me in a blue sleeveless sweater Mother had knit for him. I cast my burden upon my father and began to perspire, in the gray sleeveless sweater Mother had knit for me. (At Froebel we learned that horses sweat. People perspire.)

"You can sit in," Mr. Saunders said, "if it's all right with your Dad."

"Homework finished?" my father said.

"Uh, no. I was reading that book you gave me by Christy Mathewson."

"At least he's told the truth," Mr. Saunders said. "I think we can let him up for a while."

Under my mother's firm direction, Dorothy, the housekeeper, served what Mother would later describe as high tea. Except for the requisite appearances by Dorothy, a master at the servant's art of moving soundlessly, the living room, with its lovely bay window and capacious brick fireplace, became a male redoubt. Given my mother's presence and personality—"presidential" and "stalwart" are appropriate adjectives—this did not happen every afternoon. Or ever again, that I recall.

It turned out that Mr. Saunders' arrival had nothing whatever to do with my schoolwork. He and my father had struck up an acquaintanceship—although they still addressed one another as "Mister"—and now Saunders wanted a favor. Would my Dad take over, indeed create, an interscholastic athletic program for Froebel? Begin with baseball, add football in the autumn and something else for the winter months, when the field was free of snow? Perhaps basketball or soccer? In addition to being de facto athletic director, would my father coach as many sports as he could? There could not be a fee in view of the general Depression economy and the specifics of Froebel's budget, guarded by that fiscal warrior Walter O'Malley.

Mr. Saunders was no longer headmaster but supplicant. "It would be good for all the boys, in my opinion," he said. "As it stands, we don't offer them anything after school but woodworking."

My father accepted the assignment at once and said that taking any fee would be unthinkable, even if a fee had been offered. He was working on a private project (which would become the popular radio program, "Information, Please") but, except for the professional demands on his time, he would indeed organize a program and be delighted to coach at every game he was able to schedule.

"I know you played college ball yourself," Mr. Saunders said.

"Third base," Dad said. "I covered a dime."

"I pitched a little," Carleton Saunders said. "I call my curve the ol' dipsy-doo."

"I dislocated a shoulder sliding head first into second," Dad said, "and my throwing arm never did come back."

"But I guess you could hit," Saunders said. "Third base is a hitter's spot, am I right?"

"Fast balls," my father said. "I never played against a pitcher who could blow one by me, after the first turn or two at bat."

"Maybe you'd like to hit against my old dipsy-doo."

Baseball was as serious to my father as it would be in a different time to Jimmy Gattis. Dad protected his conversation with Mr. Saunders from descending toward frivolity.

"Of course, I never had quite the experience of my friend Skater Sayer, who's a few years older than myself. Sayer can hit and he earned himself extra money playing for a semipro team on Sundays, in the days when states had laws against major league games on the Sabbath. One day Sayer found himself batting against a right-handed pitcher who threw so hard he couldn't be touched. Sayer struck out three times and grounded back to the mound. The right-hander's name in the line-up card was Pete Smith. Do you know who Pete Smith really was, Mr. Saunders?"

"No idea," Mr. Saunders said.

"Just Grover Cleveland Alexander," my father said, "picking up an extra fifty dollars for a Sunday afternoon's work."

Mr. Saunders' eyes widened. Alexander, nicknamed "Old Pete," was regarded as the finest pitcher who ever lived, after the incomparable Mathewson. (In 1916, Old Pete Alexander pitched sixteen shutouts for the Philadelphia

Phillies. Neither Sandy Koufax nor Bob Gibson, the best pitchers I have seen, ever equaled Old Pete's record.)

"I'm sure you'll be a great help to the boys," Mr. Saunders said, recovering from the greatness of Alexander. But I had seen awe in the headmaster's eyes. *Awe* for a ball player. "On any day you can't make it to our field," Mr. Saunders said, "I have a young man named Red Duff who can keep an eye on the boys, make up the line-up, things like that."

I possessed no wisdom at the age of nine, but I had shown enough sense to sit silently, without spilling my tea, during a conversation between grown men. Listening to Carleton Saunders and my father talk about the game, over Dresden china in the bay-windowed living room, I found a way toward a boyhood Holy Grail: the door that led into the world of men.

The door was marked in letters that any Froebel boy could read. The letters spelled a single word.

Baseball.

"Bend your knees.

"Keep your body behind the ball.

"Snap that throw, don't push it.

"Nice try, son, but you played every hop right except the last one."

My father's exhortations carried above the workout noises in the spacious gravelly field behind Froebel Academy. Baseball brought communal joy to the little school and the after-school boys' woodworking program had to be discontinued. Attendance dropped to zero.

The field itself was laid out within a rectangle. Left was quite deep, with obstacles, in the form of swings and seesaws thirty feet beyond the outfielder's usual station. Center was deeper yet, with a wall of red brick, one side of a carriage house, no longer in use. In his occasional turns at batting practice, my father hit high drives against the center field wall and when he did the sequence of sounds thrilled us all. First came the hearty smack of a bat solidly striking a baseball. Then, after we followed the ball in flight, we heard the duller but even more impressive thump of the baseball slamming into the faraway brick wall. Nobody else could reach that wall. None of the boys came close, nor could Carleton Saunders, whose old dipsy-doo turned out to be a pretty damn good curve ball when he didn't throw it in the dirt. (Of course, any curve is a pretty damn good curve when you are throwing to boys of grade school age.)

Right field—Siberia, as far as I was concerned—was short, as indeed right at Ebbets Field and Murnane Field in Utica were short, allowing for different levels of the game. It was backed by a high cyclone fence that protected the grounds of a massive Victorian home that rose near Froebel Academy on Prospect Avenue.

I associate not only joy but also shock and agony and disappointment with the coming of baseball to Froebel. My father and Mr. Saunders, now not only headmaster but a sometime batting practice pitcher, began calling one another Gordon and Carl. That intimacy, a humanizing of two powerful figures, unnerved me. Saunders' first name was supposed to be "Mister" or "Sir." My father's first name was "Dad." Reacting in the quixotic ways of privileged and spoiled private school children, we ball players decided never to use first names among ourselves. It would be simply Kennedy, Denzau, Shumway, Kahn and, later, nicknames as nasty as we could invent.

My father ran disciplined workouts. He said no horsing around and he meant no horsing around. If you horsed around, behaved clownishly or began to wrestle with a schoolmate, he barred you from that day's workout and required you to sit on the rear steps of Froebel, forlorn, pounding your glove and forbidden to play catch. If you didn't shag flies, you didn't hit. He had only a limited kind of power over all the boys except myself, but his strong baritone and those high line drives he pounded against the red brick wall created authority no one challenged. No one except "Fats" Scott, a minor misfit in our midst who said he had actually enjoyed woodworking.

One of the senior boys addressed Kennedy, Donald Kennedy, the president of the Froebel fifth grade, as "Pose-oh." Kennedy, who wore glasses, swung hard and usually missed the baseball. He would then freeze in his follow-through, holding, as it were, the pose. Ergo Pose-oh.

Kennedy detested the nickname but had neither the wit nor the physical strength to challenge senior boys. What he could do was pin nicknames of his own on his peers.

We were standing together, well in front of the left field seesaw, waiting for fly balls one April afternoon, when Pose-oh turned to me and said, "You look like an Izzy."

"I don't get you."

"Izzy. The name, stupid. Your first name ought to be Izzy."

"Well, it isn't," I said.

"Maybe it wasn't," Pose-oh Kennedy said. "But it is now."

There was no stopping the damn thing. From then on I was Kahn within the Frebel building but Izzy or Iz on the ball field. Twice I fought with my fists in a wild effort to destroy Kennedy's nickname, which others, even my buddy Bobby Denzau, picked up mindlessly. I lost one fight. The other was adjudged a draw. But on the ball field, any ball field, nicknames, coarse, punishing and sometimes ethnic, spring up like dandelion shoots. Excellence with your fists or at the game itself alters but does not purify the turf. Al Rosen, a skilled boxer in his youth, heard "Jew bastard" scores of times during his distinguished baseball career. Sandy Koufax's superlative pitching for the Los Angeles Dodgers in the 1960s won him the offensive nickname "Superjew."

Bob Veale—Robert J. Veale, Jr.—forty-nine-year-old pitching coach for Utica, is a black man whose physical strength is a minor baseball legend. We had purposeful talks about ethnic humor during our Blue Sox summer. Neither of us believed, even for an instant, the cliché that distinctions of race and religion dissolve magically as soon as ball players step between the lines and go to work. We both enjoyed some ethnic joking and, without ever having to spell out matters, we understood the applicable rules. I could tell a Jewish joke. Veale could tell a black joke. Self-mockery was acceptable. Mocking others, or other groups, was not.

(Once, when Veale was building a bull-pen pitching mound, he snapped, "Damn it, I need a hoe." Then, to a small audience of young white ball players, he added, "And that don't mean a woman.")

"Izzy" humiliated me. My parents' Eleventh Edition of the Encyclopaedia Britannica, which I cherish to this night's writing, showed only two Isidores in history. Isidore of Alexandria, "one of the last of the Neoplatonists," had views that alienated the administrators of a school from which he was "compelled to resign" toward the end of the fifth century. I know how the Alexandrians forced out that Isidore. Someone said to him in terse classical Greek, "Take a hike, Izzy."

The other one, Isidore of Seville, became an archbishop. Then, in the large red leather volume, you moved on to "Isinglass," a corruption of the Dutch word for "sturgeon's bladder," which got twice the space of both Isidores combined. Izzy was not a distinguished nickname. It meant, quite simply, "Jew."

For all his authoritarian manner, my father elected to ignore the muttered "Izzy." The others used the name softly in his presence, but still they used it. Perhaps my father recognized, in the manner of mature coaches, that his power was limited. If he forbade Izzy to be barked toward me on the field, it still would be whispered at me in the locker room.

Perhaps. But in our brief time together Dad spoke often about the gutter anti-Semitism of his own boyhood. Although his speech to me was free of obscenity—he would sometimes refer to hell as "the hot place"—Gordon Kahn did explain with infinite distaste such words as "kike," "mocky" and "sheeny."

"Where do they come from?" I said.

"I don't know about mocky. Kike is probably Slavic. Sheeny comes from a kind of cloth, not very good cloth, that Jewish tailors were supposed to have sold during the Civil War." My father sighed and looked uncomfortable. "These are not words worthy of serious study," he said.

He had heard them so often as a boy that his own father enrolled him in boxing classes. Later, one of his friends told me, grinning, "He must have learned the lessons well because, when a West Pointer used a bad word in the presence of your mother, your father decked him with a single punch." How often I wished my father would hammer Pose-oh Kennedy in the protruding Scotch-Irish teeth and shatter the mouth that called me Izzy.

But my father likely believed that learning about anti-Semitism and coping with it was part of the ritual of growing up, even for an indulged Anglo-Catholic Semite in the private school of Friedrich Wilhelm August Froebel, Walter Francis O'Malley and Carleton Saunders. At worst, he was wrong. At best, he was teaching a lesson out of his own past in which such demons as Adolf Eichmann and Josef Mengele were inconceivable.

Curiously, my father was not an outstanding coach. I say curiously because he was a remarkable teacher of botany, mathematics, economics, Brahms and the history of the game. Jim Gattis and Barry Moss were outstanding batting instructors, so schooled and articulate that even after forty years of auditing baseball coaches I found myself learning fine points from each. So did the Blue Sox players as they soon would show.

"Pull the ball," my father told me, and it was true that numerous ball players, Mel Ott, Hank Greenberg and Lou Gehrig among others, enjoyed dizzying success as pull hitters. My own circumstances at the age of nine were somewhat different.

My father had diagnosed me accurately. I was what is now called a "contact hitter." This describes someone whose swing usually makes contact with the baseball without driving it a great distance. Larry Lee, of San Luis Obispo, California, was a good contact hitter for the Blue Sox. Lee, a black-haired, seemingly fragile infielder, who was still studying toward a degree at Pepperdine College, struck out only eighteen times in Utica's seventy-nine games. He also hit few home runs: three.

I never hit with power. In no place where I played baseball or softball, and the geography runs from East Hampton to Santa Monica, is there a stone engraved: *R. Kahn once hit baseball from home plate to this distant point.*

"Pull the ball," Dad said. "Just hit it between the third baseman and the base and you'll be fine. Don't try to hit for distance. Pull the ball. Place the ball. I'll tell you about Wee Willie Keeler when we get home."

Charitably, that was passable grade school coaching. It was certainly better than some Little League miscoaching I heard imposed on one of my sons when he was nine. Uncharitably, it is really not coaching at all. Pull the ball! Fine. Place the ball! Better yet. But dealing with reality, not hypothesis, how do you do either? Or, using a cover-all word Casey Stengel employed with febrile love, how do you *execute?*

One dictionary defines pull in its baseball sense as "to

hit in the direction one is facing when the swing is carried through." (Loose, but that is definition number 11, under the same word, pull.) Briefly, a right-handed pull hitter hits to left field, the direction toward which his body is shifting at the instant when bat and ball meet. A left-hander, similarly, pulls to right. But baseball seldom is simple enough for brevity.

Pulling is a matter of bat weight, stance, stride, timing and the concerted interaction of body parts all the way from the ankles to the head. My father never fractioned batting into its components. He may not have known how to do it. Alternatively, he may have wanted the boys of Froebel, including his son, to feel first the spikey wonders of the game. Intense instruction can work against such feelings. Even the finest coaching, overdone, becomes nagging after a while.

I liked to swing the heaviest bat that I could lift. If they were going to call me Izzy, then I would cast myself as Samson. This aberration—the skinny-Jewish-kid-heavy-bat aberration—stayed me, like jungle rot, for almost twenty years. Then, swinging light bats, I became an effective dead-pull hitter. By that time my father was dead.

Accepting our little family's tradition, I decided to play third base. At a Froebel level your ability at third coincided with willingness to take pain. To block hard smashes, you had to keep your glove low. It is easier to move a glove up than to stab a glove downward. But what happens when your glove is low and the baseball finds a pebble and hops high? Pain. Pain is what happens. The baseball strikes you.

Given decent reflexes, you get your face out of the way. Given a decent regard for the future of mankind, you learn—without coaching—how to protect your genitals. I evolved a crouch in which I held my right forearm in front of my groin, like armor. Still I had to take smashes in the forearm, wrist and chest.

As a nine-year-old I harbored no fantasy that I would start Froebel games at third. We all understood, Kennedy, Denzau, Fats Scott and the rest of the fifth graders, that starting was the province of senior boys. Then the juniors had to be worked in. At nine, we were backup ball players, which, if imperfect, was a darn sight better than being no ball player at all.

"Gentlemen." Dad's booming voice stopped practice and drew us into a panting circle. "I've scheduled our first game. We are playing our first game, an away game, against Adelphi Academy this Friday afternoon."

We cheered. My father looked beyond us and let the moment make its tuneful sound.

"I think I've prepared you well. Unfortunately I have a professional commitment for this Friday, which I'm not at liberty to reveal. Red Duff will handle the actual game."

Fats Scott and several seniors booed.

"None of that," my father said. "You are to give Red the respect that you give me and Mr. Saunders. Red is in charge. He will report back to me. Now get back out there on the field."

The radio program, "Information, Please," was proceeding from just another random Depression scheme to make more money into something that the Red Network of the National Broadcasting Company and a *sponsor*, Canada Dry, took seriously. NBC, a mighty fortress in those days, operated not one but two radio networks, which were labeled arbitrarily, independent of politics and mood, "Red" and "Blue." That Friday my father had to meet with people named Franklin Pierce Adams and Clifton Fadiman, and I wanted to play at least three innings of third base at Adelphi field.

A band of terror runs through competitive sports. It seems to deepen in inverse proportion to the skills of the players. "If you're afraid, you shouldn't play the game,"

Stan Musial told me with great assurance in 1957. Of course. If you can hit like a young Musial, there is almost nothing to be afraid of. But, at Utica, Gattis questioned not only the intensity of certain players but also their courage. During the many afternoons when Don Jacoby, a .389 hitter, had trouble fielding hard smashes at third base, Gattis actually shouted, "Coward!" Jacoby, a rugged, mustached Italian stallion—the name was originally Giacobetti—paled with rage, ignored the shout and missed the next ground ball.

Branch Rickey had the best technical baseball mind in history and phrased ideas and exhortations with enough eloquence to qualify as the game's Winston Churchill. (Rickey could have out-orated any twentieth-century American President except F.D.R.) He once graced me, on a day when his only son lay dying, with an analysis of the bands of terror that run through competitive sports. He seemed happier that morning, as we sat on a leather couch in the lobby of an elderly Pittsburgh hotel, to discuss fright on the fields of baseball, rather than touch the unfathomable dread that drowned his heart.

"The good ball players," he said, "the great ones, are never afraid of the baseball, at bat or in the field. You might as well ask if an oak is afraid of the rain."

The old man raised massive eyebrows in thought and rolled a Cuban cigar between thumb and forefinger. "But I would be more of a fool than I have been to suggest that the great ones never know fear, as if greatness were a bejeweled shield against emotion. If you contemplate, as I have contemplated for half a century, the element of fear in our very difficult game, you may discover a kind of progression. At least, I have."

Two men passed us saying something about the uses of vanadium in the manufacture of steel.

"First, the ball player is afraid of making a fool of himself, in the full view of friends, who are his teammates, and strangers who are watching the game. The sportswriters and the fans make too much of the idea that hitters are afraid of being beaned. No! Few real hitters are ever beaned. Was Cobb? Was Ruth? Was Robinson? But in getting out of the way of a fast ball at your head you lose all dignity. Your bat goes one way. Your cap goes another. You sprawl in the dirt. Loss of dignity. That bothers all of us who are worthwhile.

"A pitcher can make a hitter look ridiculous by throwing a fast ball behind the hitter's neck. He can also make a hitter look ridiculous, before the crowd, by striking him out with a change of pace thrown at the knees. Then all the grandstand gasps, and grandfathers tell their grandchildren, 'I could have hit that pitch myself. It was a slow ball.' Am I being clear on the distinction between physical fear and the greater baseball fear of looking inept?"

I nodded and took notes.

"Now, the second element is looking ridiculous before yourself. Take what I said about the crowd and grandfathers and apply it to self-criticism. A cagey pitcher, or a tricky ground ball, just might make me look as if I were not a ball player but . . . but a mill hand or a plowboy. Very well. Before a worthwhile person's merciless self-scrutiny this issue holds the elements of fright. In his heart, did Ol' Pete Alexander know if he was a great pitcher—which he was—or an epileptic drunk, which he was also?

"Are you with me still?" Rickey said.

"Yes, sir."

"Finally, and least important, is the fact that a batted or a thrown ball can hurt you, or someone else's spikes can cut your legs. This is seized upon by certain sportswriters and broadcasters because it is obvious. I impute no malice. But remember, young man, it is dangerous to spring to obvious conclusions about baseball or, for that matter, ball players. Baseball is not an obvious game."

He seemed finished but made no move to rise. He was going to a hospital when our conversation was done. Rickey would not truly be able to converse with his son at the hospital because Branch Rickey, Jr., a diabetic who drank, was already comatose.

"Have these few remarks made your flight purposeful? Will your editor be pleased?"

"Thank you, Branch."

"Ah-rerr." The subdued cry burst from Rickey's chest. "He's gone, my friend, he's quite completely gone. Thank you for listening to me. The most that he has left is forty-eight hours."

Branch Rickey, Jr., called "The Twig," was dead within the day.

But *his* son, Branch Rickey III, employed as farm director of the Pittsburgh Pirates, would appear in Utica twenty-three years later, a bland Rotarian of a baseball man, who confessed without shame that he had not read Murray Polner's fine and detailed biography of his grandfather.

"I'm scared, Dad."

"Why are you scared?"

"Red Duff won't play me against Adelphi." (Or perhaps I was afraid Duff *would* play me against Adelphi.)

"He may play you, but that will be the way he'd play any other fifth grader. If the game is lopsided, one way or the other, and the senior and junior boys have had their chance."

"But . . ."

"Don't 'but' me," my father said. "The topic is closed."

That Friday we rode a yellow school bus to Adelphi field, which offered turf and rolled clay as opposed to Froebel gravel. Adelphi, benefiting from a baseball program of long standing, put Froebel Academy to rout. By the fifth inning, Red Duff was pulling out seniors for juniors. It was one of those wretched children's games where everybody on both sides gets to play. In the seventh inning Pose-oh Kennedy replaced a junior at third base. In the eighth, at last, Red Duff called my name.

"Yes, Coach."

"Get in there."

"But Kennedy's at third."

The score was 19–5 against us. "You can't play third," Duff said. "Get out to right."

Trembling a little, I trotted to Siberia. Right field, where the worst players were consigned. The day felt cold and I felt cold. Then why were my palms wet?

An Adelphi scrub singled over the second baseman's head and I stopped shaking long enough to field the ball on a high hop and throw it to second, also on a high hop. "Good play," called Bobby Denzau from center field.

It didn't matter. Denzau was my friend and always nice. But if I got to hit . . .

If I had to hit . . .

Red Duff had arranged the batting order so I did *not* get to hit.

Sometime that summer, when I was still nine years old and taking tennis lessons from my father, the dream of playing major league baseball expired. This came with neither tears nor mourning. My father assured me, in an impersonal, loving way, that I was far from being the poorest ball player at Froebel. I was, indeed, "pretty decent" for my size.

But I was not the best ball player either and I believed then that the majors were a peak, like Parnassus, reachable only by the most gifted, like Apollo. I would continue to believe that until the Utica summer, when I discovered that some of the most gifted ball players have to play in the minor leagues, because of politics or personalities or simple mistakes made within major league organizations, which to this day leave important decisions in the hands of contemporary Red Duffs.

"It was good for you, going out to right," Gattis told me in a dark bar.

"Bullshit, Jim," I said in a mild tone.

"You didn't *like* it," Gattis said, "but you still have fun at the workouts and you do okay. You had to deal with a failure. Okay. I don't write myself, except privately, but I know not every book you write gets to be a number one best-seller."

"Good book, Jim. You don't set out to write a best-seller. You set out to write a good book well."

"And you don't always make it. You can't always make it, any more than you can make it with every girl you love, with every marriage. But I guarantee you this. I guarantee it. You cope with failure better today because of what baseball and that coach, dumb as he was, forced you to cope with when you were nine."

Ordering another round, I was not certain of something. Gattis, a manager of profound knowledge, limitless commitment, a calculating manner and a temper of blue-white flame, was earning $750 a month to run the Blue Sox on the field. He'd had his own dreams as a towheaded muscular Little League star in North Hollywood, California.

I was not certain whether he was talking about me or about himself.

Athletes are always playing with English vocabulary and they describe cut-down day—when some are demoted or released—in colorful ways. "Watch out for the Turk," they say. Or, "I'm layin' low today. I don't want to meet the big guy swinging the ax."

The team that would become the Blue Sox was organized across three tryout camps and was pretty much set before I got to Utica. That means that just before opening day we only had to break the dreams of one young man.

He was a pitcher named Keith Gaynor, strong, black-haired, intelligent and, through family follies I never quite untangled, the offspring of a prosperous Miami lawyer named Don Feldman.

Gaynor looked good enough to make the team, but not to star, in his first efforts at Murnane Field on June 14. Then he flew to New York and drove into the Long Island suburbs where his grandparents were celebrating their fiftieth wedding anniversary. On his return, looking like an advertisement for Alka-Seltzer, he retreated to the room we had secured for him at the Utica Econo-Lodge.

"Where's Gaynor?" I asked big Bob Veale in the lobby.

"Sufferin'," Veale said. "He's feeling all this pressure, his career and his family and stuff, so he's gone and got himself an attack of the hemorrhoids."

"You tell the trainer?"

"Hey, man, I don't need no trainer. What I do need, if you'd oblige, is some Remy Martin."

"We're in Class A, Roberto. You better learn to like beer. How is the kid?"

"I got him some Epsom salts and I told him to squat in a hot tub. I could really fix him up, if it's okay."

"What do you mean?"

"When I was pitching for the Pirates, we had this doctor, Finegold. He didn't get along with Clemente, but he was okay. One of the guys had hemorrhoids and I watched Finegold cut them out. You spread the cheeks. Or you get somebody to hold the cheeks apart. You take a little scalpel, or even a single-edged Gem blade, and just take a tiny slice and the hemorrhoid is gone. You press in with gauze. That stops the bleeding."

"You want to do that?" I asked Big Bob.

"Don't want to. Just telling you I can, if you care about your pitcher. Ain't nothing in the world that I can't do, after I've seen it done one time."

I said I appreciated Veale's demythicizing surgery.

"All those big docs, they make big bucks because they

hide the truth. They won't let people know simple things is simple.''

I decided to leave Gaynor alone in the tub and to buy Veale his Remy Martin. "You see," Bob said, in Oscar's Bar, "the boy is nervous and bad nerves comes out in different ways in different places. With this boy, the bad nerves comes out around his ass.''

"The hell with that," I said. "What do you think of his nerves on the mound?''

"Ain't my decision, is it?" Veale said in a basso that startled the bartender.

Gattis joined us. "I got to tell the kid he's gone." He grimaced. "The bad thing," Gattis said, "is that he took off during important workouts and blew a night's sleep to go to a party. It doesn't matter what kind of party. I'm not saying he went to an orgy. It means the party was more important to him than being fit for an important workout, and I don't want ball players like that. We sure as shit won't have the best talent—and I'm not sure how much I like this team—so we better have the most intensity, desire. Or else we might as well all go home.''

I invited Gaynor into my office the next evening, after he had heard the terrible news. There is always time for kindness. Barry Moss joined us. Since Gaynor's eyes were wet, I instructed an assistant to fetch a bottle of red wine from a counter top in the kitchen of the waterless trailer that was our front office.

Silence held us until the drinks came and the Lambrusco warmed our spirits.

"It hits you in the heart," Keith Gaynor said.

Moss nodded.

"This was my last shot," Gaynor said. "I wasn't even sure I still wanted to try for it, but my father said to give it another year. He told me, 'Don't go out a quitter,' and I haven't.''

"Damn," Barry said, "you just had a bad tryout stretch. You just didn't have enough pop on the ball."

"Yeah, but I was blasé. I went to my grandparents' party. I think underneath I was saying, 'I'll just do the best I can,' instead of saying, 'I got to make it. It's my *life*.'"

Gaynor's young face showed long creases of dejection, but his eyes appeared to be drying. He drank another paper cup of wine.

"But now that this has happened," he said, "I don't feel blasé. I'll never separate the game from my heart. No way. I've had my chances in the minors and I pitched in Venezuela, but it's over now, isn't it, Barry? You're my friend."

"I am your friend, Keith, and, yes, it looks that way. It does look like it's over."

"I mean I know that no more than three in a thousand ever make it to the bigs, but it's over for me. I mean, I won't be a Blue Sox." Gaynor shook his head, eyes moistening again. "I love the game," he said. "It's a real sad night in Utica."

Gathering himself, Gaynor rose. "I'll be playing Sunday softball for the next fifty years. Maybe I'll open a sporting goods store. Hey, I don't want to depress you guys."

"It's all right," Moss said.

"You probably want a snack," Gaynor said. "I got to get back to the Econo-Lodge and pack." He put his wine cup down beside my in basket and then, to show Barry and me how little, how truly little, he was hurt, Keith Gaynor walked away from the trailer office and away from the Utica Blue Sox and away from professional baseball, snapping his fingers, as though in joy.

Barry Moss normally held his head back, with a slight upward tilt, at the top of a confident posture. He had blond California good looks. He could hit a baseball more than four hundred feet. He was intelligent and perceptive and, except when playing ball, earned a comfortable living. Moss had a lot to be confident about.

"So this is how it is?" I said.

'You didn't know?"

"I knew in a way as a writer and I knew in a way as a child. But it's different now. We're all *inside* professional ball. I guess what I meant to say was, 'So this is how it feels.' "

"It feels bad," Moss said. Barry's posture had changed during Gaynor's pain. He sat on a wobbly brown second-hand couch, his customary uplifted head down so far that his strong chin touched his chest.

"In the cliché of my generation," I said, "this isn't the way it's supposed to go. The kid trying out comes out of a coal mine or a mill. When he doesn't make it, he has to go back to a wretched little company town and a job that takes twenty years off his life. But Gaynor, that's obviously a middle-class fellow."

"I'm a middle-class fellow," Moss said. "Upper middle class. But I don't believe that makes being cut any easier."

Outsiders described Moss as laconic, but he was not. He conducted himself with a decent reserve. This was going to be important for a player-coach, particularly on those nights when Jim Gattis' emotions broke loose and you could see the manager clear to his nerve endings.

Barry was the fourth of five children sired by Abner Moss, a gynecologist with a large and fashionable trade. (The elder Moss delivered Bing Crosby's last three children and, practicing the privileges of a free economy, later purchased Crosby's large home in North Hollywood.) Barry grew up with Episcopalians, piano lessons and culture, a kind of Froebel boy in Southern California. But his deepest passion was baseball, and he succeeded at it. He succeeded at a junior college, then at Pepperdine, and got a $10,000 bonus to sign with the San Francisco Giants' system, before being acquired by the Cincinnati Reds. When he was twenty-five, the Reds invited him to their major league spring training camp in Florida.

"I was an outfielder," Moss said, "and that was the problem. The Reds already had outfielders, plenty of good ones. George Foster, Ken Griffey, Cesar Geronimo and backups like Dave Collins and Champ Summers, and behind them a second wave that would be playing in Triple A. The Reds made a kind of option deal and sent me over to the Toronto Blue Jays' camp in Dunedin. Florida. Three weeks later I broke an ankle and the Reds released me."

We were sitting close together—my office was roughly eight feet by six—but Moss was far away. "Logic told me the release was something to expect, but all the same I was hurt and shocked and angry.

"The end of the world is a little drastic, but being released sure is an end of *something*. Your opportunity to play in the major leagues. If that's been your goal since boyhood, and it was my goal since boyhood, it's a real crusher, like it was to Gaynor.

"I had my aspirations," Moss said. "They didn't come true and I'm going to be thirty years old this November. I feel it's a situation in my life that's incomplete. I feel I came up short, and it's unsettling. It's frustrating having to go through it in my mind."

"There's a team party at a place called the M. & O. Grill."

"Then let's go," Barry said.

I turned out all the lights in the trailer, remembering that the year before the Utica Blue Sox had been unable to pay the last $1,500 of the bill due the Niagara Mohawk Power Company.

Bob Veale looked resplendent at the M. & O. in a fitted blue blazer with a gold crest aglitter near a lapel. "You gonna get those moth eggs out of your wallet, Mr. President, and buy your pitching coach a Remy Martin?"

"I thought the tavern was throwing the party," I said.

"Right," Veale said, "but, like you said, we're in Single A. Only the beer is free."

Gattis, in a sports shirt and slacks, was sipping scotch. "I worry about this team," he said. "I look at what we have, over and over, and I just don't see enough power. Hell, I got to stop worrying. I feel like singing. Barry, could you play that piano over there?"

"I could," Moss said.

"But you won't," Gattis said.

"You got it," Moss said. Then, quietly to me, "I hated my piano lessons as a kid. All I wanted to do was run away from that piano and play ball."

"Big Bob," Gattis said, "you gonna sing with me."

"I might be induced."

"You start."

In his stately baritone, Veale began:

> "Pack up all your cares and woe,
> Here I go,
> Singin' low,
> Bye bye blackbird."

Gattis joined him with a pleasant tenor.

"Sing," Barry urged me.

"I don't remember when I last sang in a saloon."

"Hey," Barry said. "Listen up. You didn't get cut. I didn't get cut. We're still Blue Sox. This is the time to have fun."

Somewhere else a jukebox, fed by the quarters of our underpaid young players, was blaring the theme from *Flashdance* and then a ghastly song called "Maniac" (and pronounced very loudly May-ay-ay-ay-niac). Our new quartet, anchored by Veale, overwhelmed the electronic rock.

Barry's voice was better than mine but not so good as Gattis' tenor. "We're the .500 quartet," I said. "Half of us sing on key."

"Market us," Gattis said.

We ran through songs from *Oklahoma!, Camelot* and *My Fair Lady,* and I bought more Remy Martin for our indispensable bass baritone.

"Did you ever hear Paul Robeson?" I asked Veale.

"Heard *of* him," Veale said. "What black man hasn't? But personally I never knew the dude."

Then Veale sang "Ol' Man River" and the rest of us stood silent, the better to appreciate Veale's Utica thunder.

"You don't know me very well," Gattis said, "but I guarantee, as this season goes along, you're gonna hear I'm so damn into baseball that I'm crazy. . . ."

"Ease up there," Barry said.

"No, I got to get this out. What I'd really like to do," Gattis said, "is work a piano bar. Just sing and play for the people."

"Really?" Moss said with a gentle sarcasm. "That's really all you'd want to do?"

"Oh, listen," Gattis said. "I'm not going to lie to you guys. Maybe I'd like to meet the girl who is the foreplay champion of the world. Lotsa foreplay. Lots and lots, and good and slow. But I mean, if you play piano bar, you don't hurt anybody. You don't have to tell Keith Gaynor he's through, and you bring people some pleasure and some happiness." What a line Gattis had uttered. *The girl who is the foreplay champion of the world.*

I grabbed a muscled arm. "That's what we're going to do this summer," the retired nine-year-old right fielder promised the manager "We're not putting a damn piano bar on second base. We're going to play good baseball, winning baseball, and that's what will bring people pleasure."

"I hope so," Gattis said, suddenly nervous. He turned,

"Hey, Bob. Hey, Bar'. We got a twelve-thirty curfew; did I tell you guys that?"

"You told us that," Moss said.

"Well, then we got to start clearing the ball players out of this bar. We got a ball game to win tomorrow."

2

The Pursuit of the Quarry

"I don't mean to be rude, but can I ask you a question that might *seem* rude?" My interrogator had shoulder-length blond hair, a somewhat worried look and a manner that ranged from girlish vulnerability to Utica gamine toughness. Joanne Gerace was thirty-one, single, attractive, Catholic, liberated and one of only two women to be employed as a general manager in American professional baseball during 1983.

"Try your question," I said.

"You won't think I'm rude?"

"If I think you're rude, I'll tell you that you're rude. If this thing is going to work, we've got to get along, even in the mornings."

It pains me to describe the Blue Sox trailer, as it would pain me to describe a mud flat. The structure was a rectangular eyesore of indeterminate age that had been purchased by some previous management group and placed on concrete blocks—so that it would be level—about twenty yards behind the bleachers at Murnane Field. One door wouldn't lock and had to be secured with a backing of plywood boards nailed to a wall. A small front room, curtained off, housed a mimeograph machine, an old refrigerator and a sink. The sink was merely a prop; there was no running water in the trailer. A central room was broken off into a front counter section, where fans could buy tickets, behind which stood two desks for staff people. Behind them a plywood partition—more *damned* unpainted plywood—screened off Joanne's desk. Then there was a small bathroom, from which the fixtures had been removed and which we would use as a countinghouse for each night's receipts. Finally, my own office lay in the back behind a sliding door which did not close tightly. In a burst of fanatic egalitarianism, I decreed that we would not buy a large air conditioner for the trailer, or even a small one for my office. The players' dressing room had no air conditioning; we would put up with the same conditions that they did.

Joanne, standing near my desk, pressed her lips together, sighed in a resigned way and said, "Well, what does a president do?"

"Mostly," I said, "he avoids nuclear war with the Soviet Union."

Joanne blinked. I had made a New York joke. I was in Utica.

"Seriously," she said.

"I'd say, Joanne, that if everybody else—the concessions people, Gattis, Veale, the grounds crew, the ticket takers, and all the other employees—do their jobs perfectly, the president doesn't do a whole hell of a lot."

Joanne shook her head. She was dissatisfied but reluctant to press me harder. One thing a ball club president can do is fire a general manager, for cause or merely on whim.

Someone has described a minor league franchise as being as stable as a balloon in a tornado. Hyperbole rules that statement but the recent history of Utica baseball had been tempest-tossed, windy and indeed cyclonic.

A Toronto farm team called the Utica Blue Jays materialized at Murnane in 1978, taking its nickname from both the parent club and an old Phillies farm that had played good baseball in the Eastern League during the late 1940s. (In 1949 engineers ran a New York State Thruway ramp across the infield of McConnell Field, the old ball park, and the original Blue Jays vanished, leaving Uticans to muse about the values and priorities of civil engineers.)

In 1980 the Toronto management weighted the new Blue Jays with seventeen Latin-American ball players. Utica is an old-line industrial city, a kind of giant mill town, peopled by the children and grandchildren of Polish and Italian immigrants. Their identification with Spanish-speaking teenagers was limited. The ball players felt uncomfortable in a community with no beans, no rice, no coconut oil. Attendance fell. The team played badly. The Blue Jays went out of business. A rubble of unpaid bills was all that remained.

Miles Wolff of Durham, North Carolina, then organized the Blue Sox as an independent team, relying on a small talent company called Texas Star Baseball to supply the players. Texas Star signed young ball players: young ball players nobody else wanted. The rules of baseball are written to benefit the major leagues and independent companies can't sign anyone until the last major league farm system has made its final selection. Wolff would be the more or less absentee president.

The ambient discipline was less than military. Gattis was thrown out of one game for uprooting first base and scaling it over the right field wall. Managers within a major league system seldom behave that way. They do not advance in large organizations unless they show reasonable self-control. The front office was a cacophony of disrupting voices. Three general managers quit or were fired in the two seasons before Joanne Gerace was appointed. Indeed, on opening day, 1983, I would hear from a stockholder that I was to fire Gerace at once, or else.

"Or else what?" I said.

"I call a board of directors meeting right now," said the stockholder, assuming a power he did not in fact possess.

Shout, fire and punch were the orders of too many Blue Sox days. An experienced clinician would have prescribed warm baths.

Wolff, the most professional, if not the most forthright, of the people in the management crowd, is bespectacled, thin-armed, mild-mannered, shrewd and tough. After majoring in history at Johns Hopkins, he found work as a public address announcer at some forgotten Southern ball park and set his sights on more demanding goals. He has since written two published books, including a novel, and created a substantial baseball world for himself. By the time I met Wolff he was president of the Durham Bulls, plus a rookie league team in Pulaski, Virginia, and had founded a weekly newspaper called *Baseball America*, which reports on the minor leagues and colleges. He was also president of the Blue Sox, a job he said he didn't really have time for and would be happy to turn over to me, on receipt of some cash, as his lawyer would presently specify.

To the Utica ball players, the great debacle of 1982, the year before I arrived, was the team bus purchased by one of Wolff's assistants. As the players tell the story, the bus was always breaking down (on the New York Thruway at 3 A.M.) or losing its brakes (on the downward slope of an Adirondack mountain when the sun was in the driver's eyes). This nameless, unloved vehicle was a school bus, without air conditioning or a rest room and, worse yet, in its faraway prime, it had been an *elementary* school bus. "That means," Barry Moss said in his dry way, "that the seats were designed for very little people."

To Wolff, the debacle was the Utica club's 1982 balance sheet. He had agreed by contract to cover certain debts left by the Latin Blue Jays and then found, he claims, that the new company, formally Utica Baseball, Inc., was stuck for $20,000. "That sale contract," pointed out Moses Goldbass, of Utica, whom I engaged as the team lawyer, "was not exactly drawn up by Oliver Wendell Holmes." The previous team attorney, Joseph Dacquino, was no longer available for consultation. He had been found dead in his office with adhesive tape over his mouth and a bullet hole in his head. (You would hear rumors from time to time that a Mafia don reigned in Utica. Content as I would become in new friendships with the Democratic mayor, Stephen Pawlinga, and the Republican congressman, Sherwood Boehlert, I neither sought out a godfather nor did I find one.)

It was a lane of many turnings, as we shall see, that finally led me to Miles Wolff's sales pitch. The books he presented were confusing both to me and to a professional accountant and in time I would suspect, without being able to prove, that the Blue Sox could not have opened the 1983 season without my investment. But Wolff is a man who combines the manner of sincerity with great slickness and I can still hear the soft sell he made at last, as I can hear echoes of a particular auto mechanic assuring me that if I did not buy a new camshaft *today* my entire family would ride about in deadly peril.

"The picture," Wolff insisted, "is really pretty good for you. Substantial metropolitan area. Colorful manager. And we've finally gotten all those old Blue Jay debts out of the way." (He had not.) "If you do your work well as president, the Blue Sox can have a very positive future."

In my trailer office I told Joanne, "One thing this president is going to do is keep a close eye on the books."

"Do we have a margin?" she asked. "Do we have enough to finish the season?"

"We have a margin that covers everything," I said, "short of a flood that wipes away our field."

My eye fell to a copy of the New York *Times* on my

desk. A group of Columbia University scientists, the *Times* reported, who maintained that they could forecast weather by studying the growth rings of trees were predicting that 1983 would bring us the wettest summer since Noah.

What *did* a president do? I had been whipping myself with that question across most of the eight months it had taken me to find a ball club I wanted to rescue and run. I had known four outstanding baseball presidents, but they all seemed to do different things in different ways.

Wesley Branch Rickey, the old Methodist spellbinder, directed teams with matchless brilliance and a parson's penury until the years overtook him at Pittsburgh near the end of his journeys. I remember asking in 1954 if a wretched Pirate team was going to improve.

"I know a rosebush is going to bloom on the eighteenth of May," Rickey said, "and do it pretty nearly every year. And it's all green today and three days later it's in full color. Well, I don't control a baseball club's development the way nature controls a rosebush."

Others believed that he did. Behind the silvery oratory you found a man who had worked decades of observation and analysis, introspection and experiment, into an infinitely detailed, wholly coherent approach to winning baseball.

Rickey believed passionately in the importance of speed. Why?

"Because speed is the one element in baseball that is equally important offensively and defensively. Willie Mays making an over-the-shoulder catch and Jackie Robinson stealing home both are employing their God-given speed."

He wanted his pitchers to throw their curve ball overhand. "The break is then straight down—what schoolboys used to call a drop—and it's equally effective against left-handed hitters and right-handed hitters. All the other curves favor one side or the other."

There was not an aspect of baseball, from a batter's swing to a pitcher's psyche, that Rickey did not explore ceaselessly. He knew how to sell tickets and hot dogs, grasped press relations and promotions and, with that Churchillian tongue, he relished sharing his theories, particularly when a sympathetic (and preferably syndicated) columnist was taking notes.

Rickey grew out of a literally dirt-poor childhood on a southern Ohio farm where everyone grunted and strained under a weary life and turned either to intense religiosity or hard drinking in mankind's common quest for hope. His own metamorphosis from farm boy to baseball capitalist led Rickey to believe that poverty was a virtue when combined with discipline, Christian faith and sobriety. Unfortunately the line between frugality and stinginess blurred and Rickey could be downright nasty when someone challenged his checkbook.

He signed Ralph Branca off the Bronx campus of New York University and was particularly pleased when the collegian began to win. But he offered Branca only $3,500 to pitch for the 1946 Brooklyn Dodgers. After all, Rickey was paying Pete Reiser, a former National League batting champion, $8,000, no more.

When Branca wrote a courteous letter asking for an additional $1,500, Rickey reacted as though he had been assaulted. He stopped speaking to Branca and muttered that the young pitcher had more greed than character. He took his team to spring training without Branca, leaving Ralph to borrow $100 from a brother and make his own way to Florida. After three days in a verminous motel, Branca was granted a brief audience with his employer. Rickey then forced an apology and signed Branca for the original $3,500.

Aside from making money for himself and his clan, Rickey's genius lay most deeply in his skills as a scout. He could size up a ball player and project the athlete's future more accurately than anyone who ever lived. He then signed the good ones for the smallest sums possible. Later he taught them technique and taught his assistants how to teach technique. Finally, he comforted his athletes with homilies and kept them in a servile state with tiny paychecks and occasional outbursts of anger. As a general rule, a servile ball player is a hustling ball player. Rickey's players hustled like the wind.

Bill Veeck, a Chicagoan from an upper-middle-class background, was by contrast innately generous, even lavish, even extravagant. Once when we were talking sports with an editor at the old Toots Shor's restaurant in New York, the editor attempted to pay for a round of drinks by placing a fifty-dollar bill on the bar.

"I'm the host," Veeck said.

"It's my turn," the editor said.

"It's never your turn when I'm the host."

"I insist."

"Oh, you insist?" Veeck picked up the fifty dollars and shredded the bill between strong fingers. Veeck paid for all the rounds, and the editor had to get down on all fours to retrieve the molecular particles of his money. (I suspect Veeck would have made a fine literary agent.)

Like Rickey, Veeck was a superb talent scout and, unlike Rickey, he sparkled with a sense of fun. He gave away live lobsters as ticket prizes, designed scoreboards that erupted with fireworks to celebrate a home team home run and, in his most famous stratagem, employed a midget named Eddie Gaedel to pinch-hit for the late St. Louis Browns. The midget walked on four pitches which, if memory serves, were high.

Because his promotions were so extraordinary, Veeck's approach was often misinterpreted. He liked baseball and circuses, ball players and laughter, but most of all Veeck liked to win. "I'll give you my real formula," he offered once.

"Go ahead."

"The objective is to have a winning team with great promotion. Second best is a winning team with poor promotion. Third, but only third, is a losing team with great promotion. And last, of course, is a losing team with no promotion. I never had one of those. I never will."

One does not associate a sense of fun with that formidable field marshal, George M. Steinbrenner III. With some justification, Steinbrenner is maligned for inconsistency, arrogance, insensitivity and cruelty, which he directs at his staff, his ball players, journalists and secretaries. (By his own semantics, Steinbrenner is not president of the Yankees but managing partner. The title is misleading. George does not manage. He dictates.)

But, at a certain remove from each day's Bronx hysteria, you tend to appreciate the man's accomplishments. He assumed command of a Yankee franchise that had gone to weed as a subdivision of CBS. The old Yankees offered still older memories—Ruth, DiMaggio, Mantle, Maris—as a backdrop for underqualified major leaguers with names like Horace Clarke. Against persuasive arguments to move, Steinbrenner kept the franchise in the Bronx. He adjusted better than anyone else when the current era of free agency began and spent large amounts of money very wisely. Good-bye, Horace Clarke. Hello, Reggie Jackson. By inviting models, actors, industrialists, politicians and newspaper executives into the South Bronx, and providing limousine service for his most prestigious guests, Steinbrenner recreated the illusion that Yankee Stadium was a pleasant and fashionable place. This is no small trick when you consider that the right field bleachers abut one of the dreariest slums in the United States.

He is a conglomerate character, who works in shipbuilding, horse racing and finance as much as he works in baseball, but despite an increasingly irritable press he has succeeded. Trying to summarize Steinbrenner in a recent book, Dick Schaap, the television journalist, made a curious analogy to *Macbeth.* The scene at Yankee Stadium, Schaap wrote, was like the final scene in *Macbeth,* where the stage is littered with bodies. Actually, at the end of *Macbeth* the villainous hero's head is on a pike, but no corpses, not one, lie on the stage. There seems to have been confusion here between the conclusions of *Macbeth* and *Hamlet.* Still, knowing George and knowing television journalism and knowing Schaap, I get the point. The man who saved the Yankees for New York is motivated by vaulting, imperial ambition.

When a more gifted writer, Ed Linn, published an unauthorized portrait, Steinbrenner engaged the lawyer Roy Cohn to sue Linn for $10 million, charging libel and defamation of character. A counterclaim, inevitably, might allege that George had no character to defame.

People like Rickey and Veeck never litigated with the press. They were not reluctant to *manipulate* the press, which sometimes rebounded. But a lawsuit, with all its raucous braying, seemed somehow beneath them. There is no loftiness to Steinbrenner. He attacks, fires, terrorizes and says pridefully, "I sure as hell wouldn't want to work for me." Although the man is a moderately liberal Democrat, the nickname that inevitably found him is "Der Fuehrer." Still, Horace Clarke is gone and Steinbrenner's Yankees have made money as surely as they make noise.

Somewhere, perhaps in no more obscure a publication than *Life* magazine, I read a remark about the famous existentialist Jean Paul Sartre. "The little, wall-eyed Frenchman knew it all." (The reference is to the tumult of Europe in the 1930s and '40s.) Although I don't believe that Walter Francis O'Malley read a single line of Sartre's work, the *Life* comment on philosophical omniscience echoes through my brain when I remember this extraordinary adventurer, this self-proclaimed Brooklynite who was born

in the Bronx, this professional Irishman whose roots were
half Germanic, this busy, bespectacled, cigar-chewing po-
litico who built the strongest empire in baseball.

The convergence of my father and O'Malley at Froebel
Academy did not endure for many years. Work in radio
and teaching forced Gordon Kahn to abandon his unpaid
job as director of athletics. The sports program, like Froebel's teams themselves, went into an extended slump.
Eventually, but on schedule, I graduated, listening to a
pretty senior named Janet Arpert sing, "When You Come
to the End of a Perfect Day (and the end of a journey,
too)." It pleased O'Malley, during his eighth and final
decade, to insist that he had handed me a diploma at
Froebel's commencement exercises in St. Bartholomew's
Episcopal Church in Brooklyn. He had not; he did sit on
the dais while I recited An Old Athenian Oath to an
audience of parents, mostly impatient for me to finish so
that their own graduating child could get on with his
number.

Ambition moved O'Malley, as powerfully as it moves
Steinbrenner, but Walter cloaked his drive in the hearty
trappings of geniality. He was not, however, going to end
his days as trustee of an obscure private elementary school.

He practiced law out of a modest office in the Lincoln
Building on 42nd Street and, although it embarrassed him
to admit it in grander, later times, he specialized in collections. Pressed, on a triumphant Dodger day, O'Malley
insisted that his specialty had been admiralty law, which
has a more distinguished ring to it than "dunning." (I
don't believe he ever owned so much as a dinghy.) He did
live for a time in Brooklyn, seven blocks south of Froebel
Academy, and he insisted he had purchased a season box
at Ebbets Field, because "I could get a better location for
myself and my law clients there than I could at the fancier
places, the Polo Grounds and Yankee Stadium." Not all of
O'Malley's assertions can be checked and he once warned

me about that in a smiling, indirect way. "Only half the lies the Irish tell," he said, "are true."

He did represent a client called the Brooklyn Trust Company, one of whose assets or liabilities was a mortgage on Ebbets Field. The Dodger management was neither retiring the principal nor paying the interest. Fine, said George V. McLaughlin, a Dodger fan and president of the bank. We can carry the bastards and, besides, what choice do we have? For a Brooklyn bank to foreclose on the Dodgers and evict men like Dolph Camilli and Pee Wee Reese would be a public relations catastrophe. Imagine the tabloid headlines:

BANK HURLS THE DODGERS INTO THE STREET!
GRANDMOTHERS, CRIPPLED CHILDREN NEXT!

Since at least the presidency of Andrew Jackson, most American banks have been subject to varying degrees of government supervision. In 1942, after the Dodgers had won a pennant and broken their all-time attendance record, a New York State bank examiner ordered McLaughlin and the Brooklyn Trust Company to collect "at least the interest" that the Dodgers owed. The banker engaged Walter O'Malley, the noted admiralty lawyer who specialized in collections, to see "what the hell is going on with the Dodgers' books."

O'Malley investigated and came back with horror stories. After sellouts, large sums were being trucked to a company vault in canvas bags. Either nobody, or too many people, counted all those dollar bills and all that change. The team was grossing $2.5 million, $3 million, $4 million. With the Dodgers' laissez-faire bookkeeping, and the employees' busy hands, no one could really tell. But money was vanishing from the canvas bags in something between a leak and a torrent. (One minor official, whom O'Malley would fire, immediately purchased a large Florida motel. He claimed he had made the down payment out of several years' savings. His salary had been a hundred dollars a week.) Although the Froebel old-boy network was tiny, it worked with sufficient power so that O'Malley was comfortable sharing indiscreet stories with me. He never told me all that he reported to the Brooklyn Trust Company. He simply recounted the result. Someone on the bank's side obviously had to get inside the Dodgers' organization, someone firm and trustworthy who could read a ledger. Someone, in short, like Walter Francis O'Malley. Supported by the bank, O'Malley was appointed counsel to the ball club, replacing the able, but absentee, Wendell L. Willkie. Further, McLaughlin's bank lent O'Malley a significant sum, probably $250,000, so that O'Malley could purchase a quarter interest in the franchise.

For eight years, eight summers with the length of eight long winters, O'Malley watched cash ebb and flow, paid the mortgage, and built alliances among the other stockholders. In 1950, the year Branch Rickey's contract as Dodger president expired, O'Malley was ready to move. With two other stockholders, he fired Rickey, assumed the presidency himself, and bought Rickey's twenty-five percent of the team for $1 million. (O'Malley was so furious at the price Rickey exacted that for the next few seasons any Dodger employee mentioning Rickey's name was fined one dollar.) Then, as other shareholders withered or died, O'Malley purchased their interests until, at length, he owned a hundred percent of the Dodgers. "That's a good way to stop arguments on the board of directors," he pointed out.

In 1955 O'Malley hired the designer Raymond Loewy to build a model of a domed stadium that was to replace Ebbets Field. He wanted to construct the superstadium over the Brooklyn terminal of the Long Island Railroad, so that the Dodgers could draw as many fans from suburbs as they attracted from the borough of Brooklyn. Robert Moses, New York's intransigent power broker, refused to issue the necessary permits. Thwarted on the Atlantic Coast, O'Malley packed up his family and his ball club after the 1957 season and moved to Los Angeles. There, on four hundred acres donated by the city fathers, he built Dodger Stadium (for $22 million) and with it the most successful sports franchise in the nation.

"I had some moments," he said once over a luxurious luncheon at a Los Angeles restaurant called Perrino's. "Moments of concern, if not downright worry. I thought I'd get pay TV going out here, but the movie people blocked that. I had to scramble a bit to arrange the financing for the new ball park. Our first year here, the ball players didn't perform very well, but they came around. We won the World Series the following season."

By the time of our lunch—1977—the Los Angeles Dodgers were setting attendance records almost every year. "We win," O'Malley said, "but other teams win also. The key is making the ball park a pleasant place, a place where a fellow would want to take a girl. Almost everything falls under the category: a pleasant place. Good parking, landscaping, planting flowers around the entrances. Clean rest rooms."

"Walter," I said, "nobody ever went to a ball park because the bathrooms were clean."

"No," he said, "but a dirty can will sure as hell keep them away."

I would remember that at Murnane Field in Utica, particularly in the later hours of our most successful promotion, cheap-beer night, when it became easier for our fans to drink beer than to get rid of it.

"With all your success," I said to O'Malley, "how do you keep everybody motivated?"

He sipped a daiquiri and chuckled. "I notice that, when the chairman of the board gets into his office at eight-thirty on the morning after a night game, the rest of the staff tends to do the same."

"I've never heard you talk technical baseball."

"That was Rickey's specialty. I've let it go at that. I don't go into the clubhouse, either. That's the manager's turf in a logical chain of order. I tell the reporters that at heart I'm just a fan and they seem to believe me. But I know a little more about the game than I bother to admit to the press and I've been smart enough to retain all our best baseball people, even the ones that Rickey hired."

Then two odd things happened. First, O'Malley insisted that I pay for the lunch. "Over the thirty-five years I've known you, counting Froebel days, you've never once picked up a tab for me." He made a joke of this later, but he was solemn as a priest on Good Friday. I paid. Then, as the brandy—*my* brandy—came, I asked if he ever wondered what had made the old Brooklyn Dodgers such a special team.

O'Malley used his stubby cigar as a pointer. "Begin with the names," he said. "Weren't those marvelous old names?" He stirred the air with his cigar. "Pee Wee Reese. Jackie Robinson . . ." He paused. The cigar froze, motionless before his face. "Hey," said the most successful of all modern baseball executives, "what the hell were the names of the other ball players?"

Distinct similarities link Rickey, Veeck, Steinbrenner and O'Malley. Energy. Intelligence. A feel for finance. A sense of adventure. A willingness to risk. Long hours. Hard work. Ego. But for each similarity you can find differences, sweeping all the way from individual character to style.

O'Malley and Rickey were patient. Veeck and Steinbrenner are not. Veeck and O'Malley appeared to enjoy the cut and thrust of dialogues with the press. Rickey and Steinbrenner, in the same circumstances, preferred monologues. Veeck is a consistently warm and compassionate man. The others had strong tendencies to bully.

Only Steinbrenner, the moderately liberal Democrat, would succeed as dictator of El Salvador. Only Rickey could have substituted for Billy Graham as public address announcer for God. Only O'Malley could have thrived as the political boss of a moderately corrupt metropolis. Only Veeck could run a circus, an art gallery, a bookstore or a Sicilian opera company.

But Utica . . . *I* was in Utica . . . with a ragtag ball club, a shaky front office and a cash flow that would have made O'Malley weep.

"You knew all these executives?" Jim Gattis said in my small rear office in the trailer. "You actually knew them?"

"I had drinks with all of them, except Rickey, who was dry."

Gattis smiled his strong-jawed smile. "Well, before this summer ends," he said, "one day you're gonna ask yourself what the hell you're doing in Utica. I guarantee it." Then he was gone, to run a Blue Sox practice and, falling to earth, I went to work.

I could not turn on the lights at woebegone, lively Murnane Field on June 15, 1983. The previous season's regime had left that unpaid balance of $1,500 at Niagara Mohawk—the electric company. To this huge utility, drawing power from the misty roar of Niagara Falls, my intense young Blue Sox, Gattis, Moss and all the rest, represented merely one more deadbeat account.

"What do we have to do to get the lights working?" I asked a chilly telephone voice at Niagara Mohawk.

"Pay last year's bill in full."

"Fine."

"In addition, we will require a deposit of $3,000 for this season."

"So the total to turn on the lights is $4,500?"

"That is correct."

A check for $4,500 would cut the Blue Sox bank balance almost down to change. (I had some emergency savings of my own, of course, but I was hoping to save these for other bills, such as the children's tuition and the next quarterly statement from the collector of Internal Revenue.) "To whom am I speaking?" I said in my most formal executive tone.

"This is Number Seven."

"Do you have a name, Number Seven?"

"All you need to know is Number Seven." The voice was metallic, soprano female, but sexless in an Orwellian way. How would O'Malley have handled this? I wondered.

"You realize that this is the Blue Sox calling. Utica's baseball team. *Your* baseball team."

"We know about the Blue Sox," Number Seven said.

What color was her hair? Did she ever go to games? Did Number Seven watch sunset glow, know lust? O'Malley would have braked the fantasies and paid the bill. (But first he would have haggled.)

"You're putting heavy financial pressure on the team," I said. "Can't we negotiate on the deposit?"

"It's a computerized estimate," Number Seven said. "When can we expect your check for $4,500?"

No power, no lights. No lights, no games. "In maybe fifteen minutes," I said.

"By the way," said Number Seven of Niagara Mohawk, about to violate a spate of company rules, "good luck to you guys this season."

Damn, I thought. I moved too fast. I should have ordered Gattis or Moss with their blond Western good looks to date Number Seven. Negotiate further over margaritas.

But no. That wouldn't have worked. Nobody could date the power company's computer.

Besides, I had other things to do, such as measuring the Mohawk Valley town called Utica.

*   *   *

You hear contradictory slogans around the city of Utica, New York, which sits in rolling lowland just south of the Mohawk River, the New York State Barge Canal and the New York Thruway, in a valley that was once notorious for wars between white settlers, or invaders, and the local Indian tribes. The Chamber of Commerce distributes handsome lapel pins, with gold letters, announcing grandly from a rust-colored background: Utica Has It All. On the less ebullient side sounds the voice of Frank Pryzbycien, a professor at Mohawk Valley Community College, who calls his illustrated book of history and architecture *Utica. A City Worth Saving*.

Utica does offer a great deal to a minor league club, including a history of organized baseball dating at least to the Utica Mutuals and the Pastime Club, who played in the 1860s. It also suffers from afflictions common to Northeastern industrial cities: unemployment, an exodus of the young, decline. During the last three decades Utica's population has shrunk by about a quarter from 100,000 to roughly 75,000.

The city is a feast to the historian if not the eye. Utica traces from a Mohawk Valley redoubt called Fort Schuyler, built in 1758, and from forgotten stagecoach runs to Albany (1795) and from the crude, vital, bickering bustle that was America in the nineteenth century. A wanderer can still discover relics of the Erie Canal, an absolutely astonishing ditch, just fifteen feet wide, that ran all the way from Albany to Buffalo and cut freight shipment time, across most of the breadth of New York State, from twenty-eight days to five. Like Amsterdam, Herkimer, Syracuse, Rome and Ilion, Utica was a canal town in the days (1830) when the Erie Canal was the largest single employer in the state of New York.

> I got a mule and her name is Sal,
> Fifteen miles on the Erie Canal

The songs of Irish immigrants who worked along the towpaths, prodding mules or actually pulling barges, still echo in American folk music. But after a useful lifetime the Erie Canal was replaced by a wider, more sophisticated piece of engineering prosaically named the Barge Canal and opened in the early days of World War I. Unfortunately for the bargemen and possibly for Utica, the new canal arrived in the heyday of railroad transportation and at a time when highway trucking was beginning to grow toward its growling, eighteen-wheeled future. You can see motorboats cruising the Barge Canal these days and once in a while, if you look at the winding waters for a long time, you spot a tugboat nudging a long, low barge.

Just to the south, Utica and its past worth saving lie all about. Union Station, the last of the grand depots built by the New York Central Railroad, offers space, remnants of grandeur and marble columns that define one school of Greek Revival architecture. A walker in the streets discovers homes built in an extraordinary variety of styles: Federal, Romanesque, Spanish, Bungalow, and, sadly, Tarpaper Slum.

The Stanley Performing Arts Center on Genesee Street is home to the Utica Symphony Orchestra and also rents its marquee, at twenty-five dollars a day, to anyone who wants to read his name in lighted plastic. The facade is less formal than Lincoln Center's, and the marquee may cry out in jubilation:

> Happy Birthday to Poo!
> From Her Foo. Aug. 25!!

Underneath, a small poster promises an autumn pops concert featuring works by Gershwin, Tchaikovsky, and John Williams, who composed the theme for *Star Wars*.

Utica has been a bonanza for sculptors; statues grow as thick as Norway maples. Baron Friedrich Wilhelm von

Steuben, Nicolaus Kopernik, Christopher Columbus, General Casimir Pulaski and James Schoolcraft Sherman, Vice-President to William Howard Taft, stand in stone on sturdy plinths through winter winds and roasting July noontimes. Within the city limits the wanderer finds a ski slope, complete with chair lift; a zoo; the Munson-Williams-Proctor Museum of Art; three bars where women, stripped to G-strings, jiggle their bellies and their breasts, a thriving red brick brewery called F. X. Matts; several two-star Italian restaurants; scores of saloons that serve the spicy Polish sausage called kielbasa; and at least two kosher delicatessens. But you do not see new high-rise construction anywhere.

Utica began in pre-Revolutionary times as a way station on the American journey west. You left New York City, navigating north on the Hudson River, and at Albany, in the young Blue Sox phrase, "you hung a left." That carried you onto the Mohawk River, which in turn carried you a hundred miles west past Utica-Fort Schuyler. After a short portage you entered Wood Creek, which led you to Oneida Lake and into two more rivers and finally Lake Ontario. You could continue through the Great Lakes, proceeding over water halfway to the Pacific Ocean.

When the Erie Canal was completed in 1825, Utica's future blossomed like Branch Rickey's rosebush. One Moses M. Baggs, who had run a tavern near Jason Parker's stagecoach station, expanded his place into a large, squat red brick hotel. The Baggs Hotel survived until 1932. According to Professor Pryzbycien, guests at the Baggs included Lafayette, Aaron Burr, Andrew Jackson, Abraham Lincoln and Charles Dickens (who must have been miserable in a provincial canal town, but who, it is said, traveled anywhere any time, if the fee was right for reading from *David Copperfield*).

The population of Utica grew steadily: 2,972 in 1820;

44,007 in 1890 and about 100,000 in 1948. After that came stasis and more recently decline.

Mills were the prominent industry; indeed, an adjoining town is called simply New York Mills. The mills made towels, tablecloths, and one brand name, Utica Mohawk sheets, became nationally famous, at least to brides and wedding guests bearing gifts. The factories attracted Polish and Italian immigrants; there was ample work in Utica, New York, and if the winters battered you with snow, springtime came slowly and seductively with maple and birch joining spruce and pine in green communion. Moved by hope, Italian immigrants kept planting Lombardy poplars although the poplars, frozen through February, would die by summer or at most look like threadbare trees.

Neighborhoods developed and survive. Corn Hill. Central Genesee. East Utica (Italian) and West Utica (Polish). Successful businessmen built stately homes with such high-sounding names as Fountain Elms. At the turn of the century city fathers hired Frederick Law Olmsted of Boston, the most renowned landscape architect of the era, to design a park as he had done with such success in Brooklyn and with Manhattan's Central Park. Olmsted's Utica Park remains on the south side of town, above a boulevard called Memorial Parkway, which offers reasonably stately homes and the Parkway Deli, featuring Manny's Famous Cheesecake. Parkway, which curls east-west, and Genesee Street, which slants north-south, are the most imposing avenues in Utica. Murnane Field lies close to a dangerous corner where Parkway and Genesee meet, near Faxton Hospital, Our Saviour Lutheran Church, Leisure-Hour Hot Tubs, a cut-rate movie house and Peter's Parkway Diner, which advertises "Eat at Pete's, Where the Blue Sox Eat!"

Mostly, though, Utica consists of blocks, acres, miles of working people's homes. The sense is that of a middle-aged lady who has labored all her years and known success but now is fighting time. The finery, the Sunday-go to-meeting best, shows traces of elegance. It also reveals patches.

Decline is a familiar story now with Northern industrial cities. Mills moved south, away from the costs of union contracts. People moved southwest away from winter gales. The Utica unemployment figure in 1983 was 10.3 percent. At least three of our Blue Sox employees, competent and diligent people, came to the club directly from welfare rolls. And even the glum unemployment statistic is deceptive. It does not include all the young people who have simply left.

This, then, is a minor league American town, a Single A town, capable in theory of supporting a baseball team three notches below the major leagues. More than a century ago the Utica Pastime Club, organized in July 1860, drew crowds of 500 to 700 for a schedule of forty games. According to the long-dead Utica *Telegraph*, admission was ten cents.

Had Utica's fortunes developed differently; if Utica, not Rochester, had become the home of Eastman Kodak and the birthplace of Xerox, Utica could have supported a Triple A franchise with a steady, rousing traffic of talent to and from the major leagues. If Utica had withered like Haverhill, Massachusetts, it could have supported no professional baseball at all.

My journey to Utica took me into the back rooms, as it were, of organized baseball, where I met some good men and several others with the ethics of pool hall hustlers. It led me to Geneva, New York, Cooperstown, New York, St. Petersburg, Florida, Columbia, South Carolina, and Malibu, California, and came in time to feel like a circumnavigation of the United States. It began quite literally on a sidewalk of New York City.

I had left my apartment late of a mild spring evening in

1982 and bought a pack of cigarettes. I would discover, in a few unnerving moments, an unpublicized collateral risk of smoking.

As I was about to open the door to the comfortable, overpriced apartment building where I lived, I heard a faint sound. This would turn out to be sprinting feet in crepe-soled shoes. A force I did not see hurled me face forward to the pavement and suddenly hands clutched an arm, a hip, my chest. Other hands clasped over my nose and mouth.

I thought in confusion, but not fright, that some jock friend was playing a game with me, making a blind football tackle on the street. Only when I tried to breathe and could not did I realize that I was being mugged.

I saw a wide-eyed face. I heard a voice, low and breathless. "Yell, man, and you goan be one dead motherfucker."

Another calmer voice said, "Careful. We doan wanna choke him."

The hands came off my nose and mouth, and anger replaced confusion. "Get your fucking hands off me," I said.

Something jerked my head backward and one of the muggers delivered a practiced punch to my Adam's apple. After that I could not have shouted. The throat punch turned my voice into a rasp.

"Just take my money," I whispered. I resented the rough hands on me, this sudden intimacy with strangers, hoodlums.

"We got yo' money, man. We maybe goan let you live. But if you git up 'fo' we gits 'round the corner, you one dead motherfucker."

"Let's get outta here," the second mugger pleaded.

They fled on silent crepe-soled muggers' shoes, bearing my wallet, seven dollars in cash and a gold watch I had been given for making a speech to the alumni of the New York University Law School.

When they had vanished I arose and assessed the damage. No watch. No wallet. No doorman! God damnit, where the hell was the doorman? Where was anybody?

Be calm, I told myself. You're alive. I felt a slight discomfort swallowing and a vague, toothache-like pain on the lower right side of my neck. Anger charged back. I spend all my life working and two no-good fucking bums . . .

Be calm.

Two fucking bums.

They're probably broke and desperate.

Yes, and welfare covers that.

Be calm. And get yourself off this naked, dangerous street.

After I entered the lobby the doorman emerged from the bathroom, where he had run to hide. "Did you see what just happened, Peter? Where the hell were you?"

"Please, mister. I have a new baby. Can't take a chance."

I must have berated him at length, although your sense of time blurs for the moments after you have been assaulted.

I rode an elevator to the seventh floor. Nothing was changed in the apartment. An ocher Persian rug, a mirrored wall, an antique grandfather's clock offered the silent greeting of familiarity. Nothing was changed except, *Jesus Christ,* I could have been killed.

Then what? A bustle of insurance people and executors. A suitable disposition of the ocher Persian rug. The children . . .

Abruptly, I began to sweat. I filled an old-fashioned glass with scotch and reached for a cigarette. The pack, in the breast pocket of my jacket, was crushed by the impact of my fall. But it was still there. I had been mugged by nonsmokers.

The scotch felt good. I began turning on lights. It wasn't

such a rarity, getting mugged in New York City, but who in the world gets himself mugged on East 86th Street, on what reporters call "New York's fashionable upper East Side," with doormen supposedly keeping the peace, and police?

Police!

I had forgotten to call the police.

A woman's voice answered the number 911. She heard me out and said, "If you go downstairs now, a police car will meet you."

"You expect me to go downstairs again tonight?"

"A police car will meet you, sir."

"Tell the cops to call me on the house phone when they get here."

"Sir." She was developing that basic civil-servant tone of righteous annoyance. "They'll meet you in front of your building in five minutes."

I walked to a window, determined not to leave my apartment or to unlatch any of the three front-door locks until I saw a squad car actually park in front of the building canopy in the street far away under me.

Two policemen ushered me into their sedan with an aloof concern. The blue and white automobile felt as secure and protective as a heavy tank. We rode four and a half blocks to the intersection of York Avenue and 82nd Street.

"Have you got them?" I said.

"We think so."

"What are their names?"

"Galloway and Davis."

In time, Davis, the boy, drew a short sentence, and Galloway, my chimera, turned out to be a six-time offender. He was dealt three years in prison. It pleased me to see the criminal justice system work in my behalf, but the incident clung to me, a violent dream of death, lit by blazing colors, purple and red. For the first time in my life

I began to look over my shoulder as I walked. My sleeping pattern changed and I would find myself awake at 5 A.M. Worst, a certain innate confidence had been battered as roundly as my throat and neck.

On missions of journalism, I had wandered into dangerous corners of New York, slum neighborhoods where murderous drug dealers ruled. I might have been tense, but I always moved with a sense of invulnerability. The old Froebel Academy ball field macho held. I could take care of myself. Now conscious and unconscious memories of the mugging tore at me with bestiary claws. My city, New York, the capital of the world, with all the libraries and museums, ball parks and theaters, cloud-capped towers and seductive terraces, writers and diplomats and painters and professors and gorgeous, worldly, witty women, was, in the end, a pesthole. Besides, my neck hurt.

My swollen windpipe healed within a week, but the muggers, in jamming me to the pavement, had bruised a nerve in the neck. My right hand started tingling with fierce pinpricks. The neck pain shrank and swelled but never went away. Medical advice was as contradictory as it was expensive. I had to wear a cervical collar. I needed surgery. Had I tried massive doses of B vitamins? Whatever, I could no longer sit and work at a typewriter. That particular posture was excruciating. It would be half a year before all this, at length, subsided. During my convalescence the ball club idea appeared, like a rainbow.

Sunlight broke across an oval Cape Cod pond with delicate mellow softness. Quiet was the order of the day. Two men sat back in beach chairs, watching a boy fish gentle waters from a bank where stalks of dune grass stirred. They spoke, as was their wont, not of the blessings of the day, but of baseball.

"Did you ever want to manage a team?" asked Jay Acton. He is soft-voiced and white-haired at the age of thirty-three: lawyer, writer, editor, literary agent, friend.

"Not much. I just wanted to play."

The Cape light, with its suggestions of ease and comfort, simplicity and grace, kept me worlds away from the new violence of New York and the clamor of a professional baseball park.

"Could you manage?" Acton said. "Would an organization hire you?"

"Probably not. To manage in one place, you first have to be fired somewhere else. Look at Billy Martin. Look at Whitey Herzog. Look at Stengel."

"Own?" Acton said. "Would that appeal to you?"

"The Dodgers are not for sale."

"I'll bet," Acton said, his voice rising in enthusiasm, "that we can buy a minor league club somewhere."

"And lose," I said, "as much as we can raise."

Sitting up straight in his beach chair, Jay proposed a division of efforts. I was to search the minors for a ball club. He would concentrate on financing. He eased back in his lounger. The idea had come swiftly, without a single twinge of labor.

The conventional summary of baseball, which Walter O'Malley liked to utter, holds: "It's too much of a business to be a sport and too much of a sport to be a business."

This passably witty maxim obfuscates and deceives anyone who takes it seriously. Wit, from the tongue of O'Malley, was often a tactic designed to confuse. At the very least, baseball is a duality. There is the game and those who play for pride and ambition, dreams and hope and fame. Then there is the commerce freighted with jarring and vulgar (to me) discussions of tax depreciations and bottom lines. I know this is romantic, but baseball-money talk hits my ears like trombones blaring out of key. I don't like to be informed on what a great catch or a .380 batting average is worth in cash, deferred benefits and agent's commissions. Odd. Incongruous. Alien to current ways. But the last romantic moment may be a high line drive to left.

The contemporary class of sportswriters tells us tirelessly of agents, owners, contracts and salary figures in the millions of dollars, all of which increases our tendency to think that baseball was more sporting and less venal in certain good old days. This perception is illusional. The old days were not notably good for working ball players. Any intelligent reading of baseball history presents us with a swaggering cast of rapscallions and scoundrels, with both hands on the helms of ball clubs from the earliest times of professional baseball.

To me, at least, the ball games were so much more interesting than the business side that I never took the business very seriously. Tightwads and outright charlatans in high places were the stuff of sardonic anecdotes, nothing more. I had never labored for any of them. I enjoyed the illusion that the game belonged to nine-year-old right fielders and poets. In short, as I began to explore a baseball venture with Jay Acton, I was naive.

I telephoned friends at the Los Angeles Dodgers—who with the Orioles and the Mets had an outstanding minor league system—wondering if they would laugh at my shopping for a club. Nobody did. Someone suggested something might be worked out for me with Lethbridge, in the Pioneer League. But Lethbridge lies in the province of Alberta and I wanted to move into more traditional baseball country than western Canada. "We have a Class A farm in Lodi, California," Al Campanis, the Dodgers' general manager, said, "but that might not be ideal for you either. We own the Class A team at our spring training base in Vero Beach, Florida, so naturally we send most of our best A players there. It's possible that Lodi could finish in last place."

This turned out to be an Everest of candor. The Lodi

Dodgers not only finished last in the California League in 1983 but finished last twice. The California League split its season into two. Lodi trailed the North Division both times.

Eventually, after canvassing maps and telephoning two dozen contacts, my focus turned to the New York-Penn League, which stretches, more or less, along the old canal route from Utica to the industrial city of Erie, Pennsylvania, east–west, and from Watertown, New York, to Jamestown, New York, north–south. Most of the bus rides appeared tolerable. Most of the towns had lively baseball traditions tracing from the nineteenth century.

"Welcome to the minor leagues," said the merry tenor voice of Vincent M. McNamara, a dapper leprechaun of seventy-one who has been president of the New York-Penn League since the 1940s. "We're going to enjoy having you and you're going to enjoy us. Have more fun than you ever did in your life. I've read your books. I played some ball myself. Shortstop. Picked ground balls off infields with chunks of coal where there was supposed to be grass. I'll bet our fathers would have liked each other. Listen, other leagues will sweet-talk you, but believe me, you belong with us."

McNamara is a league president of great charm and decisiveness. His annual salary, I later learned, was $3,000. (Welcome to the minor leagues, indeed.) He rules on disputes between clubs, directs the umpires, and runs league meetings with a benevolent despotism that is both fierce and charming. I would have occasion, before autumn, to appeal to McNamara on two issues. He ruled against me both times but I never questioned his sense of fairness. McNamara did not see himself as ruling *against* me. He saw himself as ruling *for* the league.

"Now, listen," said his peppery voice on the telephone. "Why do you want to buy an old team? That's like buying a secondhand car. You pick up a whole mess of somebody else's headaches. Start fresh. That's the idea. Start fresh. We're expanding from ten teams to twelve teams right now, and I've got a little spot picked out for you that's perfect. You may have heard of it. It's called Cooperstown.''

According to baseball legend, the game was invented on a ''dirt field in the picturesque upstate New York village of Cooperstown by a local youth named Abner Doubleday, who went on to become one of Lincoln's generals during the Civil War.'' According to most historians, baseball antedates Doubleday's birth in 1819. Variations were played during Washington's presidency. Further, the sport was not invented by anyone. It evolved, from English games of stick and ball—cricket and rounders.

Withal, the legend seems harmless if inaccuracy can ever be said to be harmless, and Cooperstown is now the site of the National Baseball Hall of Fame and Museum. The village is also the home of a nice little ball park, called Doubleday Field, where major league teams play an annual Hall of Fame game in memory of an invention that did not occur.

McNamara was still talking in overdrive. ''Now the mayor of Cooperstown is the guy you want to contact. He's a baseball fan and his name is Harold P. Hollis. Got that written down? Harold P. Hollis. I'll get you his number. Say, you really knew some great old guys, Furillo, Robinson, Hodges.''

''We were all friends,'' I said. ''Mr. McNamara . . . ''

''Call me Vince.''

''Well, now to get this franchise for Cooperstown, don't I have to pay the league a franchise fee?''

''Very little,'' McNamara said. ''In this crazy economy a Penn League franchise is one of the very best buys you can find. Why, some existing franchises sell for many times what we ask. Then you'll need a major league affiliation—we oldtimers call it a working agreement—and I'll be able to help you out with that.''

I marshaled my courage. "How much is a franchise?"

"What I told you. Very little. Fifteen thousand dollars."

"Plus what the team loses," I said.

"Now don't be thinking that way," McNamara said. "You should be thinking how much the team is going to make. I've been in this business since I was a boy, picking up grounders in the coalyard. You've got to think positive. We'll take care of you."

On Christmas Eve, McNamara called my home. "I'm off to mass now," he said, "and I wanted you to know this: I'm going to say a prayer for your success."

Beyond prayers, I needed a crash course in the realities of minor league baseball. As recently as the 1930s, minor league teams were predominantly independent local operations. Businessmen in, say, Olean, New York, rounded up the best talent in the Olean area, bought franchise rights for perhaps $1,000 and joined a league. They then had to purchase uniforms, balls and bats, find a manager and rent the local ball park, which was typically owned by the city recreation department.

For revenue, the operators drew largely from three sources. Attendance. Concessions; that is, the sale of hot dogs and beer. Finally, the operators sold the contracts of their better ball players to teams in higher-classification leagues. These are the minor leagues of myth and memory. The best from our town takes on the best from your town while we drink beer and watch with pleasure on a Sunday summer afternoon.

Branch Rickey single-handedly shattered such relaxed pleasures in the name of efficiency. During the mid-1930s, when he was running the St. Louis Cardinals, Rickey created the first modern baseball farm system. He devised a kind of conglomerate.

Working through scouts, major league teams—Rickey's and those directed by his imitators—signed young players and dispatched them to any one of a large chain of minor league teams, which the major league club kept stocked like so many trout ponds. Local owners were happy to be relieved of their baseball payrolls. True, they lost the occasional windfall for a wonder boy, but wonder boys were as rare as . . . well, as rare as Joe DiMaggio. (The San Francisco Seals sold DiMaggio's contract to the Yankees for $25,000 in the Depression year of 1935.)

The strengths of the Rickey system were characteristic strengths of effective conglomerates: cohesiveness and intelligent direction from on high. From the major league standpoint, it was just about perfect. You taught all your managers, coaches and scouts a consistent point of view. You signed your players at the age of eighteen for very little money and, provided your farm system produced as it should, you were spared the expense of buying a DiMaggio from a clever minor league operator for all that cash.

At one point in the 1940s, when Rickey was working in Brooklyn, the Dodgers owned or maintained working agreements with twenty-two minor league teams. Thus Rickey controlled the progress of about six hundred young baseball players. The best, people named Snider and Campanella, found their way to Brooklyn. The worst were dropped and written off. The players in between, marginal major leaguers, were sold for a great profit to less efficient organizations, such as the Chicago Cubs.

The farm system, an idea whose time had come, swept the old small-town minor league baseball into history with Nineveh and the dead ball. Local operators had little to say on the talent they would field, and boys raised in Olean found themselves breaking into professional sports at Pueblo, Colorado, where they had to wash their own laundry for the first time in their lives. At least two commissioners railed against the Rickey system. Kenesaw Mountain Landis saw the end of local teams with local players as "dooming the minor leagues." Ford Frick spoke with more passion than clarity about baseball "eating its own young." To no avail. If something works, it works. By 1983 the Utica Blue Sox was the only independent minor league baseball team functioning in organized baseball.

As their price for player development contracts—for meeting the minor league team's baseball payroll—farm directors, a breed that sprouted in every major league office, began to impose conditions. In essence, they insisted that minor league baseball imitate major league baseball in significant ways. They liked ball parks with major league dimensions. (Murnane Field at Utica, with its ultra-short right center field, made visiting farm directors look bilious.) They loved large crowds, not purely to keep the minor league team solvent but to acclimate athletes to the sounds of hoots and cheers. As farm systems thrived, farm directors became more assertive. Routinely today farm directors tell minor league managers whom to pitch, and for how many pitches and on what night.

And here is where the major league replication ends. Major league ball is a sport played to win. Minor league ball is a sport played to develop major leaguers. The shade of difference approaches mislabeling. When one of our Utica pitchers won two games in three days, a rival manager—Art Mazmanian—said to me, "I'm not allowed to use our kids like that. The big club is afraid a hot prospect might hurt his arm."

"How do you feel about that?" I asked.

"I take orders. I'm a good soldier," Mazmanian said.

In essence, the farm club exists to ripen talent. If it wins games in the process, so much the better. But the fan, who buys a ticket to see the home team win, will seldom see the exciting win-at-any-price baseball that is offered by the major leagues. The minor league game may be thrilling, but the thrills are by-products of research and development. The 1983 Blue Sox, nobody's farm team, were unique. We played primarily, overwhelmingly, to win.

*   *   *

The directors of the New York-Penn League would meet, Vince McNamara informed me, in the banquet room of the Chanticleer Motor Lodge, in Geneva, New York, on Sunday, January 8. There they would have to approve my application to operate at Cooperstown, "a mere formality," McNamara said. Major Harold P. Hollis would attend the meeting and we could get to know each other over coffee.

Acton and I flew to Rochester, rented a car, drove to the Chanticleer Motor Lodge and found ourselves in a chilly room with walls of turquoise cement block. I don't care for the kind of fifth-rate prints of Impressionist paintings that hang on the walls of small motels. That was no problem at the Chanticleer Motor Lodge. The turquoise walls were bare.

In the morning, after a communal league breakfast, McNamara moved briskly through a full agenda. Fourteen owners and league officials sat docilely, making motions when McNamara requested motions and discussing the schedule, promotions and the price of baseballs ($28.50 a dozen, from Wilson Sporting Goods). McNamara spoke briefly of Acton and myself as men who cared about baseball, who were reputable and could be trusted. "Will somebody move for unanimous approval for Roger Kahn to operate a franchise in Cooperstown?" he said.

Moved. Seconded. Approved. Simple as that.

"You're in," McNamara said, smiling. "You're an owner."

"If somebody had told me in 1952," I said, "that I'd be in Cooperstown ahead of Pee Wee Reese, I wouldn't have believed it."

Grins from the older owners, who remembered the great Dodger shortstop.

"I have to remind all that this has been an executive

meeting," McNamara said, "which means we don't discuss what went on with the press."

Unanimous nods of assent. Then Mayor Hollis and I drove to Cooperstown, where the next morning we read, in the Oneonta *Star,* a complete and accurate account of everything that had transpired during the league's off-the-record executive meeting the day before.

It was not, I learned quickly, even remotely as simple as that. Doubleday Field is a pleasant green-walled ball park but it offers neither lights nor a clubhouse. The lack of lights would mean a lack of attendance. The absence of a clubhouse meant that major league teams would decline to issue me a player-development contract. Hollis, a hearty seventy-six-year-old retired newspaperman, said there was no real cause for concern. He had a secret financing scheme that he would be happy to explain to me, covering the necessary improvements.

Cooperstown is a lovely and historic summer resort, in wooded hilly country, situated on Lake Otsego, famous in James Fenimore Cooper's *Leatherstocking Tales* as Lake Glimmerglass. Hollis showed me the ball park, which was frigid, the batting cage, which was closed, and the Hall of Fame, which was dark. No lights are turned on at the Hall until the first paying customer enters. January 9 was a cold, slow day for baseball and it was eerie seeing a flesh-colored statue of Roberto Clemente in semidarkness. That evening Hollis would preside over a meeting of the Cooperstown trustees, whom I would address.

A minor league club generally exists as a three-way partnership. The major league team supplies players, coaches, manager and a trainer. The owner-president provides the budget for operating costs (bus, hotel rooms, balls, bats and telephone bills), sometimes with additional help from the parent club. The community supplies the permanent facilities, such as the ball park, the clubhouse and the lights, for a modest rental fee. Before you move into a town you had better have in place all the facilities that you hope to get. Once a minor league club is actually functioning, playing its games, the politicians figure that they have you and your money and why invest another dime of city funds? In minor league baseball, as in romance, the courtship phase is when you can best demand gifts.

Hollis was a Democrat. In the previous election he had beaten Rexene Ashford, a surgeon's widow, by two votes, supposedly because many Cooperstown conservatives were discomforted by Ashford's strong feminist tendencies. But the village trustees, who included Mrs. or Ms. Ashford, were solidly small-town Republican. In my scurry to learn the labyrinthine ways of minor league business, I had insufficiently weighted the adversarial ways of party politics. I walked into the town hall and the meeting of Republican trustees with Hollis' Democratic hand on my left shoulder. The Republicans looked at me as though I were trying to sell copies of Jimmy Carter's memoirs at full list price.

I considered my notes and began to talk. "Minor league baseball would be a happy development for so famous and so historic a place as Cooperstown. Since so many of your tourists come to visit the Hall of Fame, an evening with a professional game would be a perfect completion of their days. The village would get publicity in every newspaper that covers the minor leagues and beyond that . . .I have some figures here on how much revenue a Class A team can generate. . . . Personally, I don't expect to take any money *out* of Cooperstown. I expect to bring money *into* Cooperstown. . . . I don't have to tell you about tradition. . . . Great game, baseball. . . . Gifted ball players. . . . Family entertainment . . . Clean . . . Wholesome . . . Fathers and sons . . . Mothers and daughters . . . Oh [to myself], shut up."

As with Lincoln at Gettysburg, my words drew no applause. The Republicans continued to eye me icily on this cold January night. Rexene Ashford remarked that her home was situated behind the left field fence. "Aren't home runs going to hit my roof and break my windows?" she asked.

"It would take a tremendous drive to clear the wall by that much," I said. When with politicians one becomes political, by which I mean you do not tell all of the truth all of the time. The Ashford home would be fairly safe during games, since it would take a long, long drive, just down the left field line, to bruise the house. But in batting practice, when hitters crank up against medium-speed straight balls . . . Well, if Rexene wasn't going to bring up batting practice, I wouldn't either.

"But you said you were going to provide gifted ball players," a male Republican trustee said. "Aren't gifted ball players capable of hitting tremendous drives?"

"The answer is yes," I said.

Next morning, full of assurances that the trustees would come around, Mayor Hollis drove me to the Amtrak station in Rensselaer, New York.

Each major league farm director with whom I spoke insisted that an on-site clubhouse was an absolute essential to a professional ambience. There was, in fact, no sense speaking further until the village of Cooperstown had contracted to build one.

"What are they talking about?" Mayor Hollis asked me over the telephone.

"The word they use is 'facility.' We need a decent clubhouse facility, like other clubs have in the New York-Penn League."

"I hope they're not looking for any Taj Mahal," Hollis said.

"No Taj Mahal, Harold. Just a clubhouse, with lockers and hot water so the ball players can shower."

"This village can't afford any Taj Mahal," Hollis said with a severity I had not heard from him before.

I priced lights for Doubleday Field, modern halogen lamps which the New York-Penn League and major league farm directors prefer to older, dimmer incandescent bulbs: $105,000. That could be paid to the lighting company over five years. I relayed the numbers to Hollis. He became vague and began talking again about his mystery financing scheme. He would be visiting New York City soon, the mayor said. Perhaps we could lunch. Perhaps I knew a banker.

It was February. The man from the light company called and said that it was time to start sinking footing for his poles if I expected to illuminate Doubleday Field in 1983.

I telephoned Hollis. Lights were questionable for the moment, he said, although definite for 1984. That should not concern me, however. We could play our home games in the afternoon and attract spillover crowds from the Hall of Fame. The Hall drew 120,000 visitors during the New York-Penn League season, which would provide a secure base for the new Cooperstown team, provided that people who had wandered among the ghosts of Mathewson and Cobb then wanted to pay to watch anonymous Class A players.

I checked with several farm directors, including Steven Schryver, a bright, precise, driving man of thirty-three who works for the New York Mets. Nelson Doubleday, a descendant of the general, is board chairman of the Mets and the idea of putting a minor league team into Doubleday Field appealed to Schryver. (Newspapermen wrote that it appealed to Doubleday as well, although neither he nor I was talking to the press at this plenary stage.)

"I'd say," Schryver told me, "that we'll wait a year for lights, so long as the 1984 guarantee is firm, and so long as you can afford to operate in the daytime. Where do we stand on the clubhouse?''

"The mayor says he's had plans drawn. I haven't seen them.''

"Plans mean nothing," Schryver said. "People walk in here with blueprints all the time. What means something is a shovel turning earth.''

"Just don't expect the Taj Mahal," I said.

When Hollis appeared for lunch in Manhattan he seemed absolutely confident. I relaxed as the mayor spun out the financing plan for Jay Acton and Thomas J. Heckman, an experienced banker who had agreed to interpret Hollis on our behalf.

As befits a mayor, Hollis drew an expansive portrait of the fame and glory of the community he represented. "Everybody in America knows Cooperstown," he said.

Drinks arrived. Hollis sipped a manhattan. He wanted to start something called the Cooperstown Baseball Foundation and sell stock, at $10 a share, in each of the fifty states, until he had raised a total of $300,000. This would throw off roughly $30,000 a year in interest, which could go toward defraying some of the Cooperstown ball club's expenses and provide funds for local amateur baseball as well. Hollis leaned toward Heckman and began speaking with great intensity. Acton looked at me and shook his head slightly. "Every state has different laws governing the sale of securities," he said quietly. Jay smiled without mirth. "He's talking about offering $300,000 in securities and running into legal bills of $300,001.''

With a second manhattan, Mayor Hollis became animated. His talk moved from stocks to bonds to debentures with great speed. I sat back, secure that Tom Heckman, a vice-president of the Irving Trust Company, was assimilating Hollis' scheme, based on his own thirty years of banking experience.

As coffee came, Mayor Hollis fled. I did not understand

how a national sale of debentures, designed to throw off $30,000 in interest, would pay for a clubhouse, much less lights, even if Hollis found a lawyer in each of the fifty states who was willing to work for the greater glory of Cooperstown without a fee. Well, at least Heckman was there. Tom would understand. Good old Tom. Been a banker for years and years.

Heckman spoke my name quietly.

"Yes, Tom?"

"Did you understand what the hell he was talking about?" Heckman said.

I next (and last) saw Mayor Harold P. Hollis at another New York-Penn League meeting in the banquet room of the Chanticleer Motor Lodge. (This time my cement block walls were tan.) The date was February 27 and I felt, alternately, that I was making progress into a tangled Mato Grosso and that I was running very fast on what the late Fred Allen called a treadmill to oblivion.

McNamara convened the meeting and asked if there was any new business.

Mayor Hollis raised his right hand. It was 11:57 A.M. Hollis said: "The village of Cooperstown withdraws its application for a franchise in the New York-Penn League."

Joanne Gerace, who was there representing Utica, told me later that my face turned ashen. I remember thinking, So this is how a knife feels in between the shoulder blades. Then, son of a bitch. I've been mugged twice within a year.

My work, Acton's work and McNamara's efforts on our behalf had provided Hollis with a winter's amusement. But nothing more. If, as may have happened, the Republican trustees would not appropriate money for a Democratic mayor, or if they simply did not want the glorious tumult of minor league ball in their staid community, then why in the world hadn't Hollis told me?

He had not, I thought, had the courtesy to forewarn me that he wanted to pull out. Besides, the New York-Penn League application wasn't his anyway. It was mine. The baseball people around the room fell silent. Damn, I thought, Hollis does control the ball park. Even in anger and shock, I recognized reality. No ball park, no team. I sipped black coffee. Hollis avoided my eyes.

McNamara found a pretext briefly to adjourn the meeting. He walked to my side and whispered, "Don't worry. I'll set you up in Pittsfield or Gloversville. I'll find something. Don't worry."

As I sensed at once, in my noontime gloom, none of these choices would work. Joanne has a strong Neapolitan-mother strain and—we had chatted a bit at the earlier league meeting—she joined me for a drink. "I'm worried about you," she said. "You don't look well."

"Nobody looks well," I said, "sitting on a shaft."

She made a sympathetic, clucking sound and lifted a glass of red wine. "To better days," she said. "Have you thought of coming to Utica? I know my bosses there are looking for new investors."

"I've only thought of Cooperstown, damn it," I said.

"Still mad at that mayor?"

"Mad is too mild a term."

"He's just another politician," Joanne said. "Maybe he thought he could get *you* to lay out $200,000 for the clubhouse and the lights. Then he'd have been a hero in his town."

Maybe. I will never know precisely what Mayor Harold P. Hollis had been thinking, if anything. Reporters, who had been trying to follow my adventures, now telephoned at the rate of five a day. "Hollis did his best," I told them. "I have absolutely nothing against him."

I was showing early symptoms of becoming a professional baseball man. I was lying to the press.

*   *   *

Finding the right minor league team had become an idée fixe to both Acton and me, and each man's enthusiasm fed the other's. When Acton devoted himself to his established business ventures and appeared to forget baseball, I became the prodder. "Come on, Jay. Anybody can run a literary agency. We've got to find a team." The thrall of baseball worked on both of us in ways that were powerful and relentless.

Why didn't we simply follow up Joanne Gerace's advice to look into Utica? I had been listening (and probably giving too much credence) to a sort of conventional wisdom spouted by people working within organized baseball. Independent teams, Steve Schryver of the Mets said, played a fraudulent game. They used old players whom nobody wanted, proven failures, to put an edge on it.

Most of the twenty-six major league teams knew what they were doing. Even a skeptic would concede that. Consequently, every young player in America worthy of being signed to a professional contract *was* signed by a major league organization. What did that leave for an independent? "Nothing worthwhile," Schryver said. I imagined an independent team of bald thirty-five-year-old beer bellies.

Another sound baseball man told me to be careful not to confuse fiction and fact. In stories for young people that were popular thirty years ago, a farm boy is always throwing a round stone. He throws it at a location just visible from a two-lane blacktop road. There an old Ford coupe rattles up a slight incline. The boy continues to throw round stones very hard. The Ford coupe overheats. A man steps out of the car, opens the hood and looks up with a leathery, kind face. Who is that leathery, kindly, Ford-driving man? Just Samuel S. Scout from an independent team. That's who. He notices the boy throwing round stones. The Ford radiator fizzes. Sam Scout walks slowly away from the car, a look of wonder brightening the

leathery, kind face. And that, across a hundred thousand
words of juvenile prose, is how Baseball Billy Barton gets
himself signed to pitch for the Beaverville Bearcats. (Up
music, prepare sequel. *Baseball Billy Barton Makes an
Unassisted Triple Play.*)

"It simply doesn't work that way anymore, if it ever
did," Bill Veeck said. "With all the hundreds of major
league scouts, and the new computers, every good farm
director—not that all are good—has a file on every good
prospect in the country. They work with high school coaches
and American Legion managers. The problem isn't discov-
ering prospects anymore. The problem is signing them."

Finally, independent teams, by certain nasty strands of
evidence, have practiced wretched business ethics. The
unpaid bill is an accepted staple of the minors, more
prevalent even than beer stands, but I heard horror tales
about independent clubs that truly were disheartening. A
team had run out of money, could not buy balls and had to
forfeit games. A team had been unable to purchase enough
uniforms to dress its full roster all at once. A team called
the Co-Pilots in Newark, New York, about thirty miles
east of Rochester, had failed repeatedly to pay the players
meal money for their trips. The players responded by
slashing the tires and stealing the side mirror from an old
car that belonged to one of the owners. According to
people in baseball organizations, running an independent
team was moving into a neighborhood beyond redemption.

After McNamara's efforts failed, Schryver stepped forward as campaign manager for a forty-five-ish man named
Herbert Wishengrad, president of the Columbia Mets of the
South Atlantic League. Wishengrad was introduced as a
fan and businessman—"somebody you have to like"—who
had become a member of the *nouveau riche* by marketing
the cardboard cups in which a particular brand of yogurt
was sold. Jay and I agreed to Schryver's suggestion that

we dine with him and our shiny new prospective business partner.

Wishengrad, a heavyset, nervous man, wore an expensively tailored suit and peppered the evening with baseball trivia questions. "I've just put $150,000 into fixing up Capital City Stadium in Columbia," Wishengrad announced. "There hasn't been any baseball there for years, but the setup now is going to be fabulous. You can be president. I'll be chairman of the board. I'll work out the business stuff with Jay Acton here. Who was on base when Bobby Thomson hit that home run?"

"Clint Hartung and Whitey Lockman," I said.

"The sportswriters have been kind of dogging us," Acton said. "We've been getting a lot of press."

"I've read the stories," Wishengrad said.

"Well, when we make this deal and release it," Acton said, "Roger is going to get a lot more publicity than you."

"Don't worry about that," Wishengrad said. "I'm strictly a businessman. Publicity means nothing to me. Who was the last switch-hitter to win the Most Valuable Player award?"

"Vida Blue."

In the general organizational structure, the Columbia Mets, Herbert Wishengrad, chairman of the board, were positioned four notches below the New York Mets, referred to in traditional baseball argot as "the big club." But big is not synonymous with good and in the Mets' case the big club was still showing the effects of an old regime, which had put a money manager in charge of operations. The broker, whose name was M. Donald Grant, practiced dour frugality against the reality of rising player salaries. This led to uninteresting, losing teams in Queens, while a few miles away George Steinbrenner spent millions and restored pennant-winning baseball to the Bronx.

The contrast was not lost on New York's fans, who are both multitudinous and sophisticated. The Mets were second rate and second best in a city that loves mostly (and sometimes only) a winner. Then in 1980 Grant supervised the sale of the Mets franchise to a group headed by Nelson Doubleday, the publisher, for a sum reported in the press as $21 million. The broker, having done his brokering, vanished from the sports pages. The publisher now owned a franchise in a prime market, but he had purchased a big club that was a shambles.

Underneath, baseball men told me in the winter of 1983, the new Mets organization was performing well. It would be another year before results blossomed in windy, tacky Shea Stadium, but the Mets farm system was already moving toward the standards of the superb systems run by the Dodgers and the Baltimore Orioles. The farm chain ran in order from Tidewater (Triple A, a Norfolk, Virginia, area team) to Jackson, Mississippi (Double A) to Lynchburg, Virginia (fast Single A) to Columbia (medium-speed A). Lower yet, but still strong, as the Blue Sox and I would discover, was Little Falls, New York, of the New York-Penn League. At the bottom the Mets operated an instructional team in Bradenton, Florida.

All of the Mets minor league players not committed to schoolwork—a total of 148—were assembled in late winter at a large, concrete motel in St. Petersburg, Florida, named the Edgewater Beach. (I never found a decent beach near the Edgewater. Good beaches, on the Gulf of Mexico, lay more than ten miles away.) The Edgewater was a classic minor league motel, without bellhops, two-star dining or room service.

The trip was important, Steve Schryver suggested, so that I could see the Mets' training methods at first hand. I agreed to go, but I boarded my flight with modest expectations. The ritual of spring training dates at least from the first decade of the century, when John McGraw annually gathered the New York Giants at Marlin Springs, Texas, and marched them each day along the railroad tracks from some forgotten hotel to the local ball park, where the team worked out. Training methods have undergone relatively little evolution in eighty years. Everyone does calisthenics. Infielders pick up ground balls. Pitchers jog and throw. Sportswriters take notes in the sunshine.

One premise behind all the workouts and the strings of exhibition games that follow supposes that it takes a professional athlete at least six weeks to reach a physical level where he can play baseball every day. John Lardner splintered this approach once in a witty magazine article called "The Great Spring Training Nonsense." The true justification for spring training, Lardner wrote, was that it attracted all those note-taking sportswriters. They tended to cover workouts and meaningless games with great enthusiasm because they felt greatly enthusiastic about traveling to Florida armed with bathing suits and expense accounts. They wrote hundreds of thousands of words about rookies and veterans, which their newspapers printed and which loosed the torrents of spring in the arteries of baseball fans up north. The fans then went forth and purchased tickets. Spring training, Lardner insisted, was an exercise in promotion, rather than conditioning.

I subscribed to this view myself over a score of years. But after a day or two of shuttling from the Edgewater Beach to the Mets minor league complex, I realized suddenly and belatedly that my experience and my own iconoclasm were focused on major league spring training. I was in the minors now. I had better forget Lardner's classic attack. There were ball players aplenty on the bare and treeless plain where the Mets' four diamonds were situated. Neither sportswriters nor publicity men anywhere shuffled into sight under the bright Florida sky. The sense was of a work camp, not a carnival.

Schryver and his staff of coaches and minor league

managers had a hard job to do every day. They had to evaluate, instruct, occupy and sometimes discipline 148 young men, most of whom looked alike to me on the four diamonds. They were all wearing uniforms marked "Mets." The staff organized the players into squads and broke baseball down into a variety of component parts in specific drills. Later the farmhands played highly organized games against one another.

Each twilight Schryver gathered the managers and coaches into a conference room for an hour of discussion. Only when the day's analysis was done were the baseball men free to make their retreats to dog tracks or saloons.

I joined them some nights and listened to high-tech talk about inside-out swings and the rotation of sliders. After a bit of this and a few drinks, the baseball men would relax and begin to tell stories. Grady Hatton, a visiting Houston scout, is a sixty-year-old Texan who had good years long ago with the Cincinnati Reds, then moved to the Boston Red Sox and finally wound down with the Chicago Cubs. "Do you know what a role model is?" Hatton asked one night. "Well, my role model was Ted Williams and I thought it was just the greatest thing ever when he hit a home run and then retired. What a way to bow out of the big leagues, with a home run.

"So in 1960 with the Cubs I hit a ground ball past the pitcher. Damn ball must have bounced nine times before it made it to the outfield. And know what? I announced my retirement. I retired on a single up the middle."

A little humility clutched me. Beyond the humor and fellowship, these people had been organizing and evaluating baseball talent for years. I had been *writing* about baseball. The distinction made me feel like an invading amateur.

"How much technical baseball input will you expect from me at Columbia?" I asked Lou Gorman of the Mets one day.

"Well, we weren't counting on any," Gorman said. "That's the manager's job. But any input you can provide will be appreciated."

"Suppose I think someone should be cut or moved up?"

"Talk to the manager. Talk to us. We'll work it out."

I experienced a little relief and a lot of ambivalence. My *baseball* power was, to give myself the best of it, advisory.

"Learn," Vince McNamara would tell me a dozen times in the summer ahead, "because as long as you keep learning you never get old."

I learned in St. Petersburg, Florida, in 1983 that minor league spring training is far from nonsense. It is an indispensable preliminary to a winning farm system, which in turn and in time feeds the big club.

"I'm not putting you down," Lou Gorman said. "It's just that we have this system and if the manager and the coaches can't do the baseball work we replace them."

I must have frowned. Gorman asked me how I felt.

"I shall reign. I shall not rule," I said. "I feel like Queen Elizabeth wearing a warmup jacket."

Every baseball season begins with hope. Winter has passed. We have all survived, and even in the Northeast the ice is gone from the ponds. Willows show a hint of color. The spirit quickens with the promise of June roses. Besides, on opening day, even the worst team has not yet lost a game.

The New York Mets, who would finish the 1983 season in last place and then, incredibly, lose their club professional, Tom Seaver, began with a merry party on April 5. The setting was a huge tent, erected behind the center field bleachers at Shea, and every guest was given a pennant, of blue and white and orange, which announced bravely: "Now the Fun Starts." The whistles of a calliope piped amiable old songs and a fashionable and political collection of New Yorkers ambled from cocktail bars to hot dog stands and back. Pretty usherettes bustled about in bright costumes. This was as stylish as baseball gets to be.

At game time I quit the tent and climbed into the bleachers where I watched Seaver defeat Steve Carlton and the Philadelphia Phillies, 2–0. Then I drove from Queens to South Carolina, to settle into my dimly defined role as president—but neither chief executive nor baseball boss—of the Columbia Mets.

Negotiations between Acton and Wishengrad had gone smoothly in a guarded way. I was to purchase all the baseballs the Columbia Mets used, an expense of about $7,200 over the 144-game season of the South Atlantic League. Then I was to deposit a hefty sum into an escrow account. "If everything were ideal," Jay said, "you'd simply buy stock, but what do we really know about this Wishengrad?"

"He's talking about a future partnership with me for a Double A team in northern New Jersey."

"And then?"

"We start a major league franchise in the Meadowlands."

"Terrific," Jay said in a flat tone. "Your money will be safer in an escrow account." Then our conversation turned from business to romance. After several years of love and courtship, Jay Acton and Rose Sedgwick had decided to marry. My own honeymoon with the Columbia Mets did not last quite as long as their idyll on that most magic of islands, fair Bermuda.

The idea of an author with a sports background expending his own money to buy into a club was unusual enough to draw consistent press attention. (Before the summer ended, *People* magazine, *USA Today*, and even the New York *Times* ran accounts of my adventures with the Blue Sox.) The reporters fell into two general categories. The older ones, after requisite small talk and some questions on how a minor league team was run, asked if I wasn't afraid to lose a fortune. The younger reporters, after *their* requisite small talk, asked me how one wrote books and sometimes said, "Can a young writer find a publisher these days?" The resulting stories were generally accurate, informed and supportive in a dry, wondering way. The scheming, devious, seditious press that U.S. Presidents dream of in their dyspepsia either does not exist on sports pages or did not appear.

Then, in mid-April, a reporter named Mike Celizac telephoned from the Bergen (New Jersey) *Record*. We talked for twenty minutes about the ways of baseball and baseball books. On April 17 the *Record* published Celizac's account under the heading: "Kahn's Kids of Summer." The story was readable, well paced and included one error that seemed to me to be trivial. I said I had "bought *into* Columbia." Celizac wrote that I had bought the franchise.

Late the next afternoon the telephone rang again, bringing down on my left ear the wrath of Wishengrad. Gone was the trivia foilsman. Wishengrad's diffidence was blown to Timbuktu. Celizac's story had not mentioned his name, Herb shouted. His friends were laughing at him in his own hometown. His daughter felt humiliated. The story mentioned Acton's name, all right, not his, and now he could not get Acton on the phone. Where was Acton, anyway?

"On his honeymoon."

"I'm degraded in my hometown," Wishengrad screamed, "and that son of a bitch is off somewhere getting laid. You're fired as president. You're through. I'm starting a legal action against you and Acton for fraud."

A solution to the newspaper error was a correction. (Celizac would print subsequently that Wishengrad was chairman of the board.) But what was my salvation from a partner given to ungovernable rage? I suppose writers, for all their complaining, live amid shelter and privilege. I am not even certain that writers complain all that much. Except when they try their hands with Hollywood producers, writers function in a climate of civility or, at the worst, amnesty. The most demeaning critic, the snakiest book packager had never abused me to my face. I sat in the rented apartment on the scrub-pine outskirts of Columbia and tried to remember when someone had spoken to me in the style of Wishengrad Vulgate. Then, being a twentieth-century American, I called a lawyer.

"Have you been physically barred from the Columbia ball park?" asked Sanford J. Schlesinger, who would later invest in the Blue Sox. "What's it called?"

"Capital City Stadium, and no. The phone call just happened."

"We have a threat, not an action," Schlesinger said from a book-lined redoubt nineteen stories above Madison Avenue in New York. "Legally the best thing would be for you to go to Capital City Stadium and have two big Southern troopers throw you over the fence."

"Funny, Sandy. Anyway, the cops wouldn't do it. I buy them beer after the games."

"I'm not being funny. I'm explaining the legal difference between a threat and an action. You can't sue somebody just because he gets mad."

"Well, I don't feel I can work further with Wishengrad."

"That may be an emotional problem, not a legal one. In which case you've called the wrong office."

"And, further, he's talking about suing Jay and me for fraud."

"But you're not fraudulent," Schlesinger said, "and neither is Jay. Is the team winning?"

I thought of how a ball club executive must surely encounter death. Lying in intensive care, he hears a doctor whisper, "Your heart seems to be stopping. But, by the way, is that big first baseman going to hit?" *Fin. Mort.*

"The team isn't winning yet," I told Schlesinger. "They will. Right now they're playing .500 ball."

"Ignore the phone calls and enjoy the games," Schlesinger said. "That's my legal advice."

When I interrupted Acton's Bermuda honeymoon, Jay took a less Martian perspective. "If Wishengrad is going to abuse you—and me—this thing won't work," he said. "And if he drives you out and breaches our contract we'll sue him for every yogurt cup he owns."

"He's shattering the climate," I said, "if that scans."

"Why not stick around until Wishengrad shows up?" Acton said. "Then, if he doesn't come around, we'll have to see about a lawsuit." Jay began to muse on his warm island. "We have a book here that he may damage. There's movie interest in your adventures. How does a suit against Wishengrad for $5 million strike you?"

"A tolerable number," I told Jay.

In the end, nobody sued anybody. Wishengrad did call Acton to say, "When Kahn comes back, I'm imposing another condition. He has to pay for some more of the running expenses."

"Herb," Acton said, "there are no more conditions. He isn't coming back. And we won't be treated this way."

Wishengrad whispered and blustered for some time until at length he ran down, like an unpleasant windup toy, and Acton could hang up the telephone with courtesy.

Steve Schryver, who had been acting as an honest broker, remarked that Wishengrad was intense. That was how Wishengrad was. And it was best to give him his due. He, not I, had invested in refurbishing Capital City Stadium.

Lou Gorman, a beefy man, full faced, contained and profoundly affable, was more direct. "People read about giant egos, Steinbrenner and Ted Turner, coming into major league front offices, but egos like that are exploding in the minor leagues as well. We seem to get more and more of them every year. Steve and I deal with them all the time." Gorman brightened. "But listen, I'm sure I can set you up with another ball club, run by a solid fellow named Calvin Falwell. He's a relative of the Moral Majority minister, Jerry Falwell, but that won't be any problem. You and Cal Falwell will really get along.''

"Where does he operate?" I asked.

"Lynchburg.''

Quite aside from the Moral Majority, I told Gorman, I didn't care much for the sound of that town's name.

By all the signs and portents, Jay Acton, at his ease in pastel Cape Cod light, had given birth to a great gobbling turkey. His idea was determined not to fly.

Self-doubt eased into my paneled study and my brain. For years I had been handled with delicacy by editors and literary agents. I was a writer—in Hollywood English, "the talent"—and, without my efforts, editors would have nothing to edit, nor would agents have anything to sell. They both, in effect, were paid to worry about my typewriter and my sensibilities. Tantrums had become alien to me. I heard them only from children and underfed dogs.

But, I wondered, looking at debacles back to back, perhaps all this concern had softened and—dare I think it?—spoiled me. Maybe I had lost the flexibility, the toughness and the healthy paranoia one needs to function in a world of people like Harold P. Hollis and Herb Wishengrad.

Damn, I thought, Walter O'Malley would have devoured them each as an appetizer and afterward not required so much as a toothpick. But I wasn't Walter, which was just as well. Walter was dead.

Jay put forth a dogged kind of cheer. "We're getting great on-the-job training," he insisted. "It'll pay off." I saw small lines appear on his long face, stress showing through a restrained New England manner.

April had come. May was approaching. Tra-la, tra-lay, "the lusty month of May." I heard Julie Andrews' lusty young voice in *Camelot*. Sports pages were caroling baseball stories.

"Oh, somewhere in this happy land, the sun is shining bright."

But we still didn't have a team.

"There's always Utica," Acton said.

The Utica Ragtags, I thought. They had not become independent on ideological and practical grounds, like the thirteen colonies two hundred years before. They were independent because no major league organization wanted to claim them. Even the Falkland Islands were being claimed. Nobody wanted the Utica Blue Sox.

"Doesn't the challenge grab you?" Acton said. "Winning a pennant with an independent team?"

The challenge did *not* grab me. At most it touched me, made me willing to listen further.

After the Wishingrad episode, Jay had begun quietly looking into the business side of the Blue Sox. He concluded that the team franchise needed $20,000 to open its gates. I don't mean here to impute bankruptcy. Wolff might have had that much in private accounts.

Acton proposed that I invest $15,000 and become president. He and Sandy Schlesinger would invest the other $5,000. Putting my on-the-job baseball training to use, I asked, "Can anybody fire me as president in Utica?"

No, Acton said; he had taken care of that, in an enactment of his own on-the-job training. I would be accountable only to a five-man board of trustees. I would appoint three: Acton, Schlesinger and myself. People on Wolff's side would appoint the other two. The arithmetic was irrefutable. Sandy, Jay and I were a unit. In any dispute, the board would at worst back my position, 3–2. (As it developed, we did not have a single dispute until opening day.)

Fine. I would have job security, like a subway motorman in the Bronx. Next I wanted a measure of the people with whom I would be working. The man from Texas Star Baseball lives in Topanga Canyon and he suggested that we get together in Los Angeles. He would fly Manager Jim Gattis in from Tucson. And we could talk things through.

I booked myself into the Chateau Marmont, a hotel that Hollywood people call "the New York writers' place." The Chateau is an appropriately absurd Hollywood landmark, where I had once heard Boris Karloff, the most terrifying of all Frankenstein monsters on film, bleat indignation at a bored room clerk because he had been given a parking ticket. ("Eat the cop, Transylvanian," I wanted to say.) I am comfortable at the Chateau. The place gives me a sense of home-field advantage, and I booked Gattis there as well.

Jim, who has two or three personalities at the very least, presented a cornucopia of charm when we met in the highceilinged lobby, near an ebony grand piano. "You look like you're in pretty good shape," Gattis began. I inhaled, tightened my stomach and said, "Good morning."

After graduating from Santa Barbara State in 1970, Jim Gattis, quarterback, third baseman, English major, was drafted in the first round by the Atlanta Braves. He was a fine hitter, not all that fast afoot, and obviously an outstanding prospect. Then two years later a fast ball fractured his skull, cruelly ending his chances of advancing to the major leagues.

"I have played a little ball," I said. Then, giving Gattis his due: "But not in the same class as you."

"Maybe so. But you don't have to walk around with a steel plate in your head. I'll bet you played the game pretty well and had some fun."

This was Gattis, the charmer, in an open-throated polo shirt and slacks, talking to the prospective club president, the possible boss. That summery California day we drove first to a seaside restaurant where we drank fruity rum cocktails called scorpions. Chunks of pineapple floated at the top. A hangover lurked at the bottom.

"If I'm going to take over the club," I said, "we'd better talk about the rules."

"I know you're going to write a book," Gattis said. "That doesn't bother me. It doesn't bother me at all."

"First," I said, "in my role as president, I'm going to try and stay out of your way. You're in charge of the players. If I don't like the way something is handled, I'll tell you one on one. But there won't be any public second guessing, the way Yankee managers get second-guessed by Steinbrenner."

"Baseball is a game of second guessing," Gattis said. "My own brothers second-guess me."

The talk moved easily to the game and women and fathering and divorce and what divorce (and ex-mates) do to children. Gattis had a small blond son named Luke, who clearly was one of his greatest concerns. His own father had died when he was nine and Gattis contrasted his upbringing with the boyhood of Barry Moss, who had played ball with him in a North Hollywood Little League twenty years before. "My family, what was left of it, had to struggle," Gattis said. "Our television had a small black and white screen. Real small. Barry's father is a rich doctor. Real rich. I remember going from my house to Barry's house, when we were kids, as going from this real small black and white TV to a giant color set."

"You know the minor leagues don't pay," I said. "You know the minors are still a black and white TV world."

"I know that maybe better than you," Gattis said. "Look, after I got married and divorced, I settled in Tucson and I've got some businesses there, but it's a battle. One year I found out Volvos weren't selling around Tucson. Not at all. But out here, in Beverly Hills, the Volvo is a hot car for people who can't afford a Mercedes. So I borrowed some money from a friend and bought a Volvo in Tucson for $8,000. Then I drove it here and sold it for $11,000. I must have done that with six or seven cars. It was a living. I could make my child support payments for Luke. But it's always been that way for me, this struggle, if you know what I mean.'' Baseball was Gattis' joy, his discipline, his drug.

We drove on to the Malibu campus where Pepperdine would play the University of California at Davis. Gattis introduced me to Barry Moss, who seemed quiet, contained and friendly.

The buildings of Pepperdine, designed in a style of Bakersfield Seville, rise among clean green hills behind the ball park. Straight ahead, beyond the outfield, lie tranquil beach and the calm, immense Pacific Ocean. The crowd was small but very pretty and for the most part wearing hot pants of peach and purple and virgin white. It was a dreamy setting for sunbathing and voyeurism, but Gattis watched both ball clubs with intense professionalism. He liked Pepperdine's center fielder, Ralph Sheffield. (In time, Sheffield would play for us in upper New York State and suffer the pangs of geographic shock.) I began to feel that we could live together.

''The Utica ball club should be a contender,'' Gattis said. ''We'll have something like eight players back from last year, when we finished second. Not a winner necessarily, but we should be competitive.''

''Did you ever see Murnane Field?'' Moss asked. ''You might want to show up with a wheelbarrow and a shovel.''

''Bad?''

''Dangerous,'' Moss said, smiling without much mirth.

Later, after a very fast ride toward downtown Los Angeles, I ushered the men into Tommy Lasorda's office in the catacombs underneath Dodger Stadium. The Dodger manager is a cheerful, chubby, determined pear of a man whom I have known for almost thirty years. Lasorda threw out his arms and clutched me in a warm Abruzzi embrace.

When the hugging was done, I made introductions. ''Tom, you've managed in Class A ball,'' I said.

"I've managed everywhere and for $5,500 a year while bringing up two kids."

"Well, Jim Gattis here is going to manage Utica in Single A this summer. Got any counsel for him?"

The hugger vanished and Lasorda became a serious baseball man. "Listen," he said to Gattis. "At your level most of the talent everywhere is pretty much the same, except for a few super prospects. Now what you want to do is figure out how hard every manager is working his guys. Then work your guys just a little harder."

Gattis was listening intently, as a convert before a monsignor.

"Then figure out how hard every other manager is working and *you* work just a little harder than anybody else."

We went upstairs and watched the Chicago Cubs upset the Dodgers, 3–2. The crowd at Dodger Stadium was slightly over 46,000. In Utica that summer our total attendance for all our home dates would be 42,779.

There is no visually attractive approach to Murnane Field. It is set on a naked flat in a corner of southwestern Utica, without so much as a single tree to grace the scene. From one angle, you first see Murnane across a high school football field, observing the back side of the metal outfield wall, which cries for shrubbery and paint. From another side, Rose Place, you see slabs of plywood fixed to a wire fence, screening the playing area from those who have not bought tickets. Approaching the main entrance, you enter a dirty and rutted asphalt parking lot. The sentry box, where the ticket takers work, is faded blue.

I walked in on a chilly late May morning and tramped across the infield to deep shortstop. The infield dirt was dark, rutted clay. Every ground ball would be an adventure. There were no covered stands, only steep, naked bleachers behind first base and no seats at all on the left field side. Weeds were growing tall beyond third base. I remembered the manicured field at Pepperdine and the calm beckoning ocean beyond it. At Murnane I felt a sense of an ill-kept diamond set in the middle of an abandoned junkyard.

"We'll have everything fixed up in a few days," Joanne Gerace promised. "It'll look real nice."

So this was my ball park. After all the joyous times at Ebbets Field and Fenway Park and Yankee Stadium, I was assigning myself to work in an elephant graveyard.

"A little paint and some weeding," Joanne continued.

She stopped. "Bad, isn't it?"

I attempted to cheer myself by closing my thoughts to the drying mud and shaggy weeds. I imagined athletes performing on this wasteland.

"These fellows I hear are coming back," I said. "Hendershot, Jacoby. Moretti. Coyle. Are they really major league prospects? How good are they?"

Joanne stood on her high heels in the infield and thought for a while. Then she said, "They're good enough to dream."

3

Diamond in the Rough

We would open on Sunday, June 19, playing an afternoon game against the Watertown Pirates at a new ball park set in an old fairground, eighty-three miles north of Murnane Field. Although Watertown is familiar to summer tourists as the last major way station to the Thousand Islands, I knew little about the place, except that once in a while, on bitter winter nights, it achieved notoriety by recording the lowest temperature anywhere in New York State.

From that date, June 19, until Friday, September 2, the New York-Penn League schedule did not offer a single day off. Not one. The players were supposed to play every day (or mostly every night) and I would have to work at my modest presidency every day and every night. There are no banker's hours in the minor leagues.

"You had better like writing if you intend to be a writer," Harold Rosenthal told me years before when we both worked for the New York *Herald Tribune,* "because you're going to spend an awful lot of time at a typewriter." You had better like playing baseball if you're going to become a professional ball player, because you will play and practice, practice and play, until the game becomes a job and after that the job becomes the touchstone of your life. Nothing in my previous experience prepared me for the way a single baseball season, lived from within, rather than observed from without, takes possession of your spirit. Beyond reason, the team becomes an extension of your essence, your values, your competence, your very manhood so that, also beyond all reason, certain victories become more than victories and make you feel that for all your faults you are profoundly a good and formidable man. Conversely certain losses would throw almost all of us into silent wells of despair. We had not simply lost a game; we had failed. White-faced and grim, each man felt isolated and even worthless simply because another ball club had scored more runs.

A winning streak lifted us toward a mindless manic state. A losing streak would choke from us all humor. "It's a lithium league," I remarked once to Gattis. "We're all becoming crazy manic-depressives."

Gattis nodded. "And remember," he said, "we're only playing a short season."

Ladies in baseball have lately won attention as journalists assigned to cover ball players in locker rooms where (surprise) many ball players loiter while naked. A female magazine reporter, aged twenty-five, remarked after covering recent World Series clubhouses that her mother, aged fifty, had asked her only one question. "How many peckers did you see?"

I laughed, as I was expected to do. (The reporter never gave me the number.) But stories of this sort create a sense that women in baseball are lecherous voyeurs. Some indeed may be, but my own experience argues against this sort of soft-porn generality.

At any rate, I had several women employed at Utica. Like Joanne Gerace, Penny Lacey, entitled director of marketing and public relations, was a sincere and hardworking sort who served the Blue Sox because it was the best job she could find in town. We paid her eighty dollars a week and modest expenses.

These two ladies found yellow curtains for my trailer office. They moved in the ancient wobbly sofa. They even painted over a wretched-looking palm tree, etched on my longest wall, with a good bland "ivory-cream."

I found for myself a white clapboard house, at 1917 Bradford Avenue, in a blue-collar neighborhood with little driveways that separated the buildings without cutting off the sounds of blaring television, a family spat, or lovemaking. Helped by Penny, I negotiated with a secondhand store called Upstate Furniture and stocked the house with necessary pieces. Six rooms for $398.

One would not have hosted a party for Mrs. Onassis at 1917 Bradford, but it was functional, only three blocks from the ball park and a perfectly tolerable home for myself and my sixteen-year-old daughter Alissa, whom I imported from her mother's home in New Hampshire as a program salesperson (five cents for each one sold) and office assistant (salary uncertain, depending on the mood of Ms. Gerace).

Alissa is redheaded, witty, slim-waisted and significantly anxious to be worldly. In my proprietary paternal view, I believed that Eleanor of Aquitane was worldly at the age of sixteen but Alissa Avril Kahn was not. Liss was questioning the value of an education that summer and I thought exposure to the minors might send her bounding back toward books with enthusiasm. At the same time I worried about her strutting about Murnane Field among all those well-coordinated young ball players—"hunks," as you say at sixteen.

The summerlong interplay between Alissa and the ball players would not follow the cliché of horny animals in baseball suits slouching toward a pretty redheaded teenager in jeans. Rather, the players, and Jim Gattis and Bob Veale, became, variously, older brothers and kindly uncles, and if Alissa fell in love with any of the Blue Sox she kept it to herself until the season was over.

The few days of Blue Sox spring training, really a final weeding of the best available talent, combined verve (Gattis), organization (Moss), and professionalism (Veale). A shy, black-mustached pitcher named John Seitz, who grew up on a farm near Felton, Pennsylvania, showed us a good slider and an outstanding overhand curve. Another right-hander, Mike Zamba, who had majored in communications at a state college in Connecticut, knew how to mix sliders and fast balls. He was not shy. Zamba would gripe about working conditions from time to time, all season long, threatening once in a while to organize a Minor League Players Association. "And I'm going to start it right here in Utica," he said.

"What are you going to demand?" I said. "More meat in the ball park hot dogs? There isn't any money in this franchise, Mike."

"I'm not going to give away my demands just yet." He was about five percent serious. "But when the Zamba Union strikes, you better be ready."

Jimmy Tompkins, the sensitive, soft-voiced native of Austin (with the good fast ball and knuckle curve), drew great satisfaction from buying bubble gum for the neighborhood children who were drawn to our workouts. (I'd sometimes think that Jimmy had come to us not from the Braves organization, which had released him, but from a casting bureau in Hollywood. He was a warm, impassioned, handsome and sometimes angry man.)

Roy Moretti, simply a complete pitcher by New York-Penn League standards, reminded me, as I've remarked, of a small John Wayne. He was good and he knew that he was good. He spoke softly and carried himself very straight, with the slightest suggestion of a swagger. One night, after Gattis had imposed the twelve-thirty curfew, Moretti and I were talking in a bar at twelve-fifteen. "Let's go over to the Ramada Inn for a few more beers," Moretti said.

"Roy," I said, "how would it look for you—and me—if you got caught breaking curfew in the company of the club president?"

"I've been around," Moretti said. "The curfew doesn't apply to me."

I went home and the next day checked out the matter with Gattis, who flared. "The hell it doesn't," the manager said. If Roy suggested John Wayne at the age of twenty-seven, there was also a hint of Early Wynn, that great, glowering Hall of Fame right-hander, who could take a drink, handled what he took, was always ready to pitch and did not like being treated like an irresponsible child. What somebody with Roy's gifts, maturity and confidence was doing in the New York Penn League, abandoned by the big omniscient baseball organizations, mystified Bob Veale and myself. "He could and maybe should be in the major leagues right now," Veale said.

"Then why isn't he?"

"Some of the organizations can't see and some of them won't see," Veale said, "which is the same thing, isn't it? He's been cut a couple of times, so to sign him up now one of these big organizations would have to admit that some other big organizations have made mistakes. So you have to ask yourself are these organizations looking mostly for talent, or maybe looking to protect each other's asses? What do you think?" This was not an entirely impersonal comment. Veale had recently been released, for mysterious reasons, by the Atlanta Braves.

Then there was Willie Finnegan. Willie is tall, broadshouldered, and although he lives in Central Islip, Long Island, his speech is pure concrete Noo Yawk. During our four days of spring training, Finnegan walked to the mound in Cardinal red pants and a white T-shirt and began to throw fast balls to Mark Krynitsky. After he got loose, the workout paused at the sound of Willie's fast balls hitting Krynitsky's glove. Many minor league teams travel with a radar gun that times the speed of pitches. But a radar gun costs $1,000, which the Blue Sox didn't have. That left us armed only with eyes and ears.

"He's over ninety miles an hour easy," Gattis said, with a tiny smile. Had we stumbled upon a find, a potential Gossage, a nascent Koufax?

"But where is he throwing them at ninety?" Veale said. "Mostly high and his curve is in the dirt." Finnegan had been released by the Cardinal organization, which had concluded that, for all of mighty Willie's speed, he would never learn to throw strikes.

"I'll send up some hitters," Gattis said.

Finnegan started pitching to Ed Wolfe, a husky first baseman from Arizona who had played for the Blue Sox in 1982, a solid right-handed hitter with power to right center field. Finnegan threw a few bad pitches. Then, pressing, he took some speed off his fast ball and loosed it at the outside corner of the plate. Wolfe all but jumped out of his spikes and drove a long batting-practice home run high over the wall in right center.

"Next pitcher," Gattis ordered.

Finnegan walked off the mound, sweating in the hot June night. "Don't be concentrating so much on getting the ball to go where you want," Veale said. "When you're getting the feel of the mound, just let it go. And once you do the ball is gonna jump like a March hare, move like the wind. I want you to have control, sure, direction, and we're gonna work on that. I'm gonna make you imagine a box"—Veale outlined a small box with his huge hands—"and you're gonna learn to throw inside that box. We're gonna work on that later. Direction."

"Direction," Finnegan repeated. He seemed annoyed that his sheer velocity had not overwhelmed the staff.

"Sure," Veale said. "It's like racing a Volkswagen

against a Cadillac. You know the Cadillac can run away from the Volks, but it's gotta be going in the right direction on the course.''

"At least I beat that hitter," Finnegan said. "I made him hit to the opposite field." Then Willie ran to the outfield to shag flies.

"He beat the hitter?" Gattis said in wild surprise. "Wolfe *likes* to go to the opposite field. He just went to the opposite field all the way."

"We got to work on Finnegan's thinking," Veale said. "A lot of control is like everything else. Mental."

Willie became a pet project. He would respond slowly—some pitchers don't learn control for five seasons, or ever—and with an ebullient, semiswaggering personality that concealed a lot of sensitivity within. He would also, unasked, compose a Blue Sox team poem, which he recited over beers with burning lyric passion and Hell's Kitchen diction, a combination that would have given Dylan Thomas pause. And might, now that I think of it, have given him pleasure.

Particularly when I recalled the Mets' operation at St. Petersburg, I picked up a distinct sense of disorder in our midst. There was a small, noticeable strain between the front office, exemplified by Joanne Gerace, and the clubhouse: that is, the players, managers and coaches. Veale was having trouble finding an apartment. This was not, as far as I know, because he was black; rather, it was because he and his wife were somewhat particular. One ambient stockholder took to bursting into the office and ranting at Joanne, "Found an apartment for Veale yet? No? Jesus Christ. What the hell do you do in here? *I'll* find Veale an apartment."

Barry Moss was upset at the condition of Murnane Field. ("This is the only ball park I've ever seen," Roy

Moretti said later to Eric Brady of *USA Today,* "where the infielders ought to wear mouthpieces.")

"Why isn't the field ready?" Barry asked me quietly. "Joanne's been here all winter. Is she surprised that the team showed up?" He presented me with a list of complaints to pass on to Joanne and the three-man grounds crew. This ranged from weeds sprouting along the box seats (unaesthetic) to trouble with the fence behind home plate (dangerous). There, curls of metal curved outward. A catcher retrieving a wild pitch during the pressure of a game would get not only the baseball but a six-stitch cut.

Veale didn't like the outfield grass. "You know anything about grass?" Veale said to me. "You're the president. You're supposed to know about grass."

"Sure, I know about grass. You lime it and you fertilize it and you mow it and you water it."

"Well, how you gonna water all that outfield?"

"I've got Joanne negotiating with the fire department. We're going to get a fire hose."

"That may be good," Veale said, "but I got something better." He launched into a description of an interconnected series of three sprinklers, his own design, one sprinkler feeding water both to the grass and to the next sprinkler, and each sprinkler making a different sound. "One goes whoosh," Veale said. "The next one goes whish and the third one goes whash. It's really something."

"And?" I said.

"I just need some money to go to a hardware store and buy the parts. Maybe a hundred dollars at the most."

"I'll check the books," I said.

"Hey, Jay," Veale said to Acton. "I believe our president is suffering from a terminal disease."

"What's that?" Acton said.

"His hand's too short to reach his pockets."

                    *   *   *

In the front office, Joanne, who had seen the team approach bankruptcy in 1982, practiced fiscal conservatism. "You've got to watch the ball players," she said. "I love them, but ball players will take anything that's not nailed down. Baseballs. Caps. T-shirts. Anything. You know one of them last year went to a sporting goods store and bought three sets of spikes and signed for them, Utica Blue Sox. That stuck us for $300. We can't waste money on Veale's thing."

"Veale's Wheels," I said.

"All right. Veale's Wheels. The fire department has agreed to give us a hose, no charge, if we simply put up a deposit."

Just then the large figure of Robert Veale appeared outside a window. He was working a weed trimmer, tidying the lawn and crabgrass that grew around the used trailer. He was a pitching coach, a professional engaged to do professional work, and here he was, working out of a love for gardening and order as a volunteer field hand. Clearly this was beyond the call of even the standard no-rights minor league contract.

"I want to keep the big guy happy," I told Joanne. "Give him his hundred dollars."

"Those hundreds will eat us up," Joanne said.

"It's in the account, Jo. Let's everybody get along with everybody else."

Veale's Wheels never worked to specifications. After he spent our hundred and assembled his machine, he found out that the water pressure at Murnane was not strong enough to drive it. We had to use the fire hose to keep our outfield green. Veale and I needled back and forth all summer, but I never once teased the man about the abject failure of Veale's Wheels. Somehow, that would have been too cruel.

*   *   *

Joanne's parsimony peaked during our home opening game on June 20. That night, in the second inning, I heard Veale call me from the bull pen. "Mr. President," he said in a deep, sarcastic tone.

"What is it?"

"Do you think I could have some baseballs for my pitchers? They're only relief pitchers out here, but they just might have to warm up."

"Didn't Joanne give you baseballs?"

"One," Veale said.

I jogged back to the office. Why hadn't Joanne given Bob Veale baseballs?

"I gave him one," she said.

"Jo," I said, "let me give you a scenario. We want to warm up a right-hander and a left-hander at the same time. And there's only one baseball. What do they do, throw alternately?"

Joanne's right hand went to her face. "Oh, my God. I never thought of *that*. I guess I made a mistake."

I grabbed three new balls and jogged back to the bull pen, president and loping errand boy at the same time.

My working theory was to create for the Blue Sox a kind of extended family. A few players had never been away from home before. Indeed, Ralph Sheffield, our center fielder from California, announced that, as long as he was in Utica, he just might drop in on New York City one day. He seemed dismayed when I told him that New York was not the next town down the canal but a five-hour high-speed drive distant.

Some players were going to have to learn for the first time how to work coin washing machines and stock a refrigerator. All of us would be cooped together on bus rides that would run late into the night and in one instance (coming back from Erie, Pennsylvania) let us limply, blearily greet dawn on the New York State Thruway. Forging the family sense seemed essential. We were all in this New York-Penn League together. Out there, beyond Murnane, eleven other teams were waiting to knock us down. If we bickered and fussed and fought among ourselves, the summer would be that much more difficult for everyone.

But we were a rather curiously assorted group. Gattis' obsession with winning sometimes transported him into a ferocious and solitary world. Joanne saw her position—a mine field of details before it was anything else—as a launching platform to a career as baseball executive. She had worked at lesser jobs in two other minor league cities and had tended bar in Utica at a friendly, rock-loud working people's saloon known as Spilka's. But, having tasted baseball, Joanne did not want to return to bartending. She brought so much passion to her job that she did not complain about fourteen-hour days.

Beyond, but not above, this formidable duo were the ball players. "Never forget," Gattis told me, "that every ball player knows that the fans are paying their money to see him. Not you. Not Joanne. *Him*. They don't talk about it but they know it pretty deep." There were, in short, enough bounding egos in Murnane Field to fill a much larger, better ball park.

As Herbert Marcuse pointed out in *One-Dimensional Man,* it is not happenstance that Americans consume so much time worrying about money. According to Marcuse, the people who—or the systems which—control American society want it that way. An individual who is worried about money can be manipulated by threats of bankruptcy or an impoverished old age. Such threats and all our fears, Marcuse postulates, make modern society conform, and work as well as it does, as surely as in medieval times you either conformed to baronial demands or else you screamed your life away while a stranger manipulated the levers of a rack.

Fear of bankruptcy dominated the Blue Sox front office.

Over several seasons, about $80,000 worth of stock had been sold and that number represented an exceptionally optimistic view of what the franchise was worth. After I paid the power company and a few other bills, we were left with about $3,500 in the bank. We were not General Motors, nor were we even the Seattle Mariners. We were a poor company with a rotten credit record.

The brighter baseball people, Veale and Gattis, understood our situation, but amid the furor of daily games they didn't give it much thought. So Joanne and I became stern parents, or stony bankers, doling out few treasures. We had few to give. The ball players and Gattis, like large, indulged children, tended to ask for more and more: a more expensive bus, a fancier motel. I resisted about as often as I yielded. There was an investment and a franchise to protect.

I got my extended family, all right, but it was a family nagged by bickering and quibbling. Since I worked in the front office and checked the books, I tended to side with parsimony. This was good, in that the Utica Blue Sox did not, in fact, go bankrupt. But in one notable instance my borrowed frugality went too far.

"We have these rules," Joanne said, "and we have to follow them." She listed procedures for providing baseballs and bats.

"What about warmup jackets?" I said. The Columbia Mets had all been issued handsome blue and orange jackets with thick linings. The Blue Sox jackets, pale blue on darker blue, were manufactured in Sri Lanka by people who had no idea that northern New York State experiences chilly summer nights. Our jackets had a lining suitable for afternoon wear, say, in Sri Lanka.

"The players have to buy their warmup jackets," Joanne said. "We only charge them what the jackets cost us. Twenty dollars."

"Oh," I said.

There was not one Blue Sox rule, none, that I lacked the power to change. There was not a player or coach whom I could not have dismissed, including Jim Gattis, without cause or notice, simply by executing a form. A key to running a team, over which you have absolute power, is to refrain from Hitlerian conduct. You want to delegate, work to reach a consensus, reason. So, with equal parts of Marcusian fear of bankruptcy and inertia, I allowed the twenty-dollar-buy-a-jacket rule to stand.

As far as the earliest signs could tell me, the team looked good. In workouts there seemed to be more than decent amounts of speed and power. We played an exhibition against an amateur club from Rome, New York, and won by so many runs that I lost count. But aesthetically the team was looking less than good. More like vagrants rounded up from miscellaneous sandlots. A few players, trying to make ends meet on $500 a month (before withholding), bought our twenty-dollar Sri Lanka Blue Sox jackets. Most did not, preferring to eat.

After the romp over Rome, Gattis gathered the players for a brief review and the players gathered their jackets and put them on. This, then, was the sight: Blue Sox knickers showing under warmup jackets bearing logos from the following teams:

> The Braves
> The Brewers
> The Pirates
> The Cardinals
> The Giants
> Sahuaro (a Mexican team)
> Long Beach State (a college)
> And the Blue Sox.

All the colors clashed in the chaos of Murnane Field.

*   *   *

To get to Watertown (and to get on with the season) we needed a bus and I handed that assignment to Mike Zalewski, a gigantic cherub, curly-haired, narrow-eyed, round-bellied, part Polish, part Italian, whose interests divided equally among baseball, young women and beer. Zalewski was our official scorer, our team statistician and our road secretary, duties he performed proudly and (if directed) ably for the sum of fifteen dollars a game. Michael was a recently divorced man of twenty-eight, who had an idiot savant skill with figures and who could move toward a single woman with such speed that you almost forgot the enormous stomach he had earned by mixing beer and Polish salt potatoes. If his courage was high he would open on the girl with all guns firing. "Hi, I'm Mike Zalewski of the Utica Blue Sox. The *baseball team*. You've had the rest. Now try the best." On at least two occasions during the 1983 season Zalewski's approach worked well enough for him to declare himself hopelessly and permanently in love.

Zalewski first compiled a list of nearby bus companies that would not carry a Blue Sox ball club one block down Genesee Street. These companies had transported previous Utica ball clubs and never been paid. A humanitarian named Tim Birnie, the proprietor of Birnie Bus Lines, said he would take us on a pay-as-you-go basis. That is, he would not move the team on Trip B until Trip A had been paid in full.

"What option do we have?" I asked Zalewski.

"Don't you know somebody at Greyhound?" Zalewski said.

"Joe Black. The old Dodger pitcher. I've talked to him three times and it turns out he can't help us even if we run Joe Black night on July 4. So forget Greyhound. All we can get is their standard rate, which is too high."

"You talk to Birnie," Zalewski pleaded.

I explained that this was not how companies, even the Utica Blue Sox, worked. The road secretary made the arrangements, even if he was earning only fifteen dollars a game. "Then, if you run into trouble, you call me in."

"Who's publishing your book?" Zalewski said, eyeing me carefully, as though, I thought, I were a twenty-year-old blonde.

"Doubleday."

"Isn't that the guy who owns the Mets? Nelson Doubleday?"

"It's a guy, Michael, but it's also a publishing company. Doubleday & Company."

"Well, if I do good, do you think Nelson might get your editor to hire me as their statistician?"

Mike wore sneakers and jeans and an old polo shirt and did not like to shave, unless he either was in love or Barry Moss and I complained about his stubble. I tried without success to picture Mike Zalewski at Shea Stadium.

"I'll do good. I'm a great statistician. Ask anybody. You'll see."

Michael, I thought; poor Michael, young Michael. Doubleday publishing is a corporation and Doubleday baseball is a corporation and the baseball people don't make book contracts and the book people don't hire statisticians. Michael, I thought, poor Michael, the world is more complicated than I can tell you in this little trailer.

"But you know people. You know a lot of people. You know Joe Black."

"Do well, Mike. Watch your grammar. Shave, God damn it. Shave. Now call Tim Birnie and get me the best price you can for a bus."

"School bus or coach?"

"School bus for short hauls. Coach for long."

"How about intermediate trips, between short and long?"

"Go, Mike. Get out of here. Get the best deal you can get and give me the figures."

He was back within the hour, rattling numbers at me until I felt an old trapped sensation, reminiscent of trigonometry class. The buses would cost the Blue Sox $10,250 across the season. As it turned out, that would devour fully a quarter of our net gate receipts.

"It's a good deal," Zalewski said. (It was the only deal in town.) "Will you tell the Mets I made a good deal on the buses?"

"I promise, Michael, that I'll report the Utica Blue Sox bus deal directly to Nelson Doubleday at our next corporate conference."

"Okay," Mike said. "Okay! Listen, I want to take you to the Foxy Lady [a topless bar]. There's a girl there that does bumps you wouldn't believe." He paused.

"Doubleday. Do you think Nelson Doubleday would want to go with us? She's got great boobs."

"He isn't in Utica, Michael," I said.

One of the lessons I learned in talks with Walter O'Malley is that local television is a mixed blessing for a baseball team. It provides supplementary income and de facto free advertising, but it also encourages fans to stay at home. There they watch your team without having to buy a ticket and they drink beer without patronizing your concession stand. O'Malley refused for decades to allow home Dodger games to be televised in Los Angeles.

Radio, on the other hand, is ideal. Hearing a baseball broadcast creates an urge in fans to come to the park, really to see the team and pay cash for your scorecards, beer and popcorn. Vin Scully, who broadcasts Dodger games, has a well-deserved reputation as a good reporter, but he is more than that. He is also an extraordinary ticket salesman, preaching the delights of Dodger Stadium and baseball, in a controlled, seductive, seemingly noncommercial way. "Come on out tomorrow if you can. It'll be the Mets, with a host of young, exciting rookies. I'm looking forward to seeing 'em, and I sure hope you are too."

Television was out for us in Utica, which is home to only two channels. Indeed, television was an enemy of our box office. People with cable hookups saw not the Blue Sox but the Yankees and the Mets in their living rooms. That put our Class A ball club in direct competition with famous major leaguers.

But I talked to several radio station executives. Although I didn't start out by admitting it, I was ready to give away—*free*—say three games a week to broadcasters in exchange for the publicity. Everyone was polite and nobody was interested. The radio directors did not believe that Class A baseball could compete with music: the shrill omni-audible theme from *Flashdance*, and later, to my pleasure and surprise, a revival of Cole Porter's witty "Puttin' on the Ritz." Radio in Utica was a music medium, they told me.

Jay Acton, commuting between New York and Utica, owned a radio station in Brockton, Massachusetts, and was a mine of information about broadcasting.

"But nobody wants us, Jay," I said.

"You must be asking too much," Acton said.

"I'm offering them for nothing."

Acton, an able executive, whom I had installed as the Blue Sox vice-president for business affairs, said the only thing that could be said. "Oh."

If radio would not take us, we could force ourselves on the air by buying time. Joanne contacted WIBX, which broadcast some Yankee games in preference to ours (understandable) and some professional soccer games in preference to ours (outrageous; where were we? Europe?). If we bought the time, WIBX would prepare a commercial and assign Tom Coyne, its crack (and only) sportscaster, to read our blurb.

The station advertising department prepared the copy and on opening day WIBX listeners heard a nondescript, suitably loud fanfare and then the recorded voice of Tom Coyne:

"Go for the All-American Good Times! Utica Blue Sox baseball!! The Utica Blue Sox, the American Dream Team, is getting ready to kick off another season of professional baseball in Central New York!!! With Roy Moretti in relief"—this seemed to assume our starting pitcher was knocked out—"and Barry Moss hitting them out at the plate. Don Jacoby on third. Ed Wolfe at first. Plus promising newcomers to heat up the action. They'll give you a run for your money to be on top this year. You'll like what you see in '83. Utica Blue Sox baseball." (Up music.)

I spent a fair amount of time over the summer explaining to the smirks of visiting friends that no, I did not write the ad copy for the team.

We were to assemble at Murnane at ten o'clock on June 19, first to get the players to sign their contracts and then to leave by a yellow school bus, number 169, for Watertown, the largest city in Jefferson County, New York. The contracts were yellow forms, about four pages long, in which the players promised to give their best efforts and most of their civil rights to the Utica Blue Sox.

The Texas Star Baseball Company would pay us, Utica Baseball, Inc., and we in turn would pay the players through a payroll account run by Joanne Gerace. (Like all our corporate procedures, this was cumbersome.) In exchange, Texas Star would keep the proceeds from the sale of player contracts if anyone wanted our ragtags after the season.

Trying to be a good fellow, and to induce people to work for $500 a month, the man from Texas Star promised most of the players a share of the proceeds from the sale of their contracts, should higher-level teams want them later. But for reasons I never understood, he promised different cuts to different players, as though the players would not talk among themselves.

It was a lovely June morning. Murnane Field still had its basic junkyard look, but it was a green junkyard. And here we were about to start a season—my third, counting the New York Mets and the Columbia Mets—with the old boyhood enthusiasm making bubbles in the blood. "Hiya, guys," I greeted the players. "Come on, guys. We've got a beautiful little bus ride going and then we're gonna be the first team in New York-Penn League history to finish 76 and 0. Nobody beats us. Nobody. That's an order."

"Please," Bob Veale said, "lay off that 76 and 0 stuff. You gonna jinx us and we'll lose our first game."

"We're not going to lose," Gattis said in an aside to me, "but I'm worried about this team. I'm afraid we just won't score many runs."

Dave Chase, who works for Miles Wolff in Durham, had flown in to help with paperwork and David sat at Joanne's desk behind a hill of contracts, waiting for the players to enter one at a time.

Mike ("Minor league ball players ought to have a union") Zamba was first. He looked at his contract and snapped, "I'm not signing."

"Why not?" Chase asked mildly.

Zamba, brown-haired, straight-shouldered, intelligent and quick, stood up. Chase, a rather small, chubby man, peered at him. "Texas Star said I get forty percent. This contract says thirty percent. I'm not signing." And he walked off.

The second player signed. The third, on grounds similar to Zamba's, refused. Chase sighed and said, "You know the rules of baseball."

"I know they can't play without signed contracts."

"What would you do," Chase said, "if I told you it looks as if you don't have a team?"

"I'd call the man from Texas Star."

"I think you better," Chase said, leaning back like an onlooker at an *opéra comique*.

Outside the trailer, on a slope of grass, neatly trimmed

by Bob Veale, the players milled about, looking unhappy. I spotted Gattis. "Bad," he said. "I guarantee you this is bad on opening day."

"Come in the trailer and we'll get Texas Star on the phone."

While Gattis talked urgently to Texas Star, I asked Chase why I was expected to sign contracts I had not negotiated. It was time for further on-the-job training at Utica. The National Association, a sprawling, amorphous confederation that governs the minor leagues, did not formally recognize the Texas Star Baseball Company. So, to stay within baseball's complex and perplexing rules, Texas Star negotiated the contracts but could not sign them. Utica Baseball, Inc., which lacked the money to pay the players, had to be the employer of record. Like it or not, I was in a fiscal marriage with Texas Star.

"All right," Gattis said, looking distraught. "Everybody who's played a full year of pro ball gets forty percent from the sale of his contract. Guys who've played part of a year get twenty-five percent. People who've never signed before get nothing."

"Now you've got to tell that to the players," I said. "Or do you want me to do that?"

"I can handle it," Gattis insisted.

He called a meeting on the grassy knoll and spoke with great assurance, completely masking his own anxiety about the suddenly real possibility of a strike. "I promise you you're not getting screwed," he told the players. "This is my fourth year with this Texas Star situation, and nobody has ever gotten screwed. I guarantee it."

John Seitz, our mustached Pennsylvania farm boy, was scheduled to start our first game. "I don't like getting screwed," Seitz said when Gattis finished. "I haven't read my contract but I know baseball organizations. I know they'll cut your nuts off. Five hundred dollars a month is not enough to live on and pay rent."

Gattis flared. "Listen, if you don't like the contract, I'll tear it up tomorrow. Damn it, Seitz. You worry about getting batters out today. If not, I'm gonna start somebody else."

That broke the strike. Our collective power over the Blue Sox flowed not from legalities and overlapping contracts but from the hearts of the players themselves. Every one of them from Seitz to Zamba to a shy young rookie outfielder named Bob Merenda desperately wanted to play ball.

"Hey," Bob Veale said gently after Gattis' tough talk, "you guys are gonna get paid for very enjoyable work. Where else can you do that besides baseball?" Veale looked toward me. "Am I right?" he said.

"Right," I said in my most presidential morning manner.

We rode bus number 169 through rolling upland meadows, hard Northern farming country, with Adirondack foothills rising to the east. We drove through poor small towns, named Boonville and Lowville, where shoebox houses lined the blacktop road. We were in New York, the Empire State, and as far from Manhattan as Tobacco Road. It surprised all of us, after this pastoral journey, to find, at the Alex Duffy Fairgrounds, a boisterous crowd of 4,500 people waiting to watch our first game.

The players dressed silently. Nerves. An opening day in Watertown and an opening day at Yankee Stadium produce the same emotions in young athletes. Excitement. Tension. Yet unanswered questions. Are we any good? Christ, will we win?

The questions were answered very quickly. With two walks, some sloppy Watertown fielding, and a key single by Barry Moss, we scored four runs in the first inning. Then Moss crashed a double to right center, scoring two more in the second. Seitz, nonstriking John Seitz, overwhelmed the Watertown hitters with his hard slider and his snapping overhand curve. "Lookin' good," said Joanne Gerace.

As a baseball writer, I tended to root for close games. When a team jumped ahead, 6–0, in two innings, I automatically pulled for the team that was behind, hoping for a close score, the better to hold my interest. This reasonable, neutralist tendency died on opening day in Watertown. "A six-run lead is good," I remarked to Joanne, "but a twelve-run lead would be better."

"Really," she said, giggling at the sheer pleasure of being ahead.

I climbed to the roof of the fairgrounds ball park to see a local newspaperman for a brief interview. "What do you think of your team?" he began.

I was still nervous about our lead, but I managed to echo an old cry, raised against super Yankee ball clubs of earlier eras. "Break up the Blue Sox," I said.

He laughed and we talked amiably for ten minutes. I left the press box and headed down a runway atop the roof of Watertown's crowded little park. The sun was bright. Our lead had climbed, 8–0. In our old blue uniforms we were looking as good as the Dodgers.

Abruptly two men stood before me, breathing hard. One was David Israel, a Blue Sox director, whom I had first met long before when he was a promising intern at *Sport* magazine. Israel had since performed well, earning himself a variety of newspaper columns. But once, during an uncertain period, he told me he intended to take some courses in law. That combination—quick journalistic success and a preoccupation with legalisms—can create problems, as it was about to.

Israel's companion, also a trustee, burst forth. "You gotta fire Joanne."

"I don't gotta do anything," I said. "Let's watch the game."

"We both think you have to fire her," Israel said.

"For what reason?"

"Murnane Field is in terrible shape."

"I wish we had $5,000 to hire a crack groundskeeper. We don't."

"She didn't fix the field because she's incompetent," Israel said. He is a tall, potbellied man, who was wearing a soiled Blue Sox jacket and a cap.

"Look," I said. "There was no money in the Blue Sox bank account to hire help until I got there. So let's calm down. Nobody gets fired opening day."

Israel's legal inclinations burst like a grenade. "My friend and I are both directors," he said. "I hereby call a meeting of the board of directors. We have a quorum. All right. The vote is 2–1. Joanne is fired."

I am not sure to this day of the actual legalities of the situation. Even less certain then, I wheeled and walked and found a telephone and called Acton in New York. "It's crazy," he said.

"Right," I said, "but can they actually call a directors' meeting just like that?"

"I know they can't change the directors for a full year," he said. "The Utica club is organized under the laws of North Carolina, which I don't happen to know offhand. But"—he was speaking slowly and thinking quickly— "common practice is that you can't call a directors' meeting without reasonable notice, say at least forty-eight hours. Tell them that if they bother you again. What do they have against Joanne?"

"I'm not sure yet. Maybe her sex."

"What's the score?"

"We're breezing. Our lead is up to 9–0."

In time I would come to know most of Joanne's strengths and weaknesses in her first full season as a general manager. She worked fourteen-hour days without complaint and she was a fierce watchdog, a Cerberus, guarding the

Blue Sox books. She was supremely honest, essential in a minor league general manager, the person who counts each night's gate receipts. All those singles and fives lie in stacks subject to easy skimming. She knew the political ways of Utica better than any of us and her commitment to the welfare of the ball club seemed to be the most important element in her life. On the debit side was her lack of formal training in business administration—the specifics of the various tax laws that applied to us, for example—and a tendency to become overwhelmed by details, particularly when someone snapped at her with demands. When Joanne felt overwhelmed she became disorganized. Once in a while she would weep briefly.

"Please stop crying," I would order. "This is supposed to be a business office. Besides, all those tears remind me of my second wife. She cried at lacrosse games." That usually drew a smile, after which we could go back to work.

In sum, Joanne's virtues outweighed her faults. Once in a while Joanne made a mistake, but at work here was really a power play. Gattis liked to test people, ball players and civilians, to see how far they could be shoved before they shoved back.

"Look," David Israel began with me again.

"No meeting, David," I said, "without at least two days' notice." I was beginning to boil. No point in more of this. Israel would be returning to Los Angeles in two days. I found a seat next to Joanne to watch the last two innings.

"Trouble?" she asked, reading my face.

"Nothing much."

"With Israel?"

"Partly."

"That guy," she said, shaking her head. "He just walked into our office, started going through cabinets and helped himself to three Blue Sox caps. We charge the ball

players for jackets and David just stole three of our caps."
(Israel's version is that Joanne had given him permission
to take the caps. Whatever, neither had asked the keeper of
the exchequer and master of baseball caps, the club president.)

"Easy," I said. "Let's watch Moretti wrap this up."

John Seitz had pitched two-hit ball over seven innings,
but Gattis did not want to tire him. Moretti, an alumnus of
the 1982 Blue Sox, liked frequent work to fine-tune his
control. Roy struggled a bit, walking two men, but preserved our opening day shutout. In all, the Blue Sox lined
out sixteen hits. We won the game by fifteen runs.

The little Watertown clubhouse was as jubilant as the
front office discussions had been strained.

"How about them Sox?" shouted Mike Zamba.

" 'Attaway Sam,' " yelled Mark Krynitsky, our catcher.

"Who's Sam?" Zamba said.

"You're Sam."

"I'm Mike," Zamba said. (Krynitsky had heard others
addressing Zamba as "Zam.") "Get my name right before
you get on me."

Everyone was still getting to know everyone else but the
common bond was joy. "I don't know if I like winning
more than I hate losing," Gattis said to Veale.

"I like watching these kids develop," Veale said. Then
the two began to sing Harry Belafonte's old banana boat
song.

Mike Zalewski bounded in belly first. "Hey, Mike,"
someone shouted. "Get us some hot dogs."

"There aren't any left," Zalewski said.

"That's because you ate them all," Moss said.

"Hey," rang a chorus of young male voices. "How
about them Blue Sox!"

On the bus ride back to Utica the players discussed
which member of the team was "down and dirty ugliest."
No decision, but that led to a major league story.

When Tom Lasorda was coaching third base for the Dodgers, during the reign of the late Walter Alston, engineers from NBC wired him with a small microphone one Saturday before a game with Cincinnati. The idea was to broadcast samples of Lasorda's chatter.

"Hey," Tommy said to Pete Rose, who was playing third, "the Dodgers took a vote on handsomest Red and you finished second."

"That right?" Rose said. "Thanks."

"Yeah," Lasorda said. "The other twenty-four guys finished tied for first."

The next day's New York *Times* ran a pleasant little story about the Blue Sox victory, concluding that if I worked at my typewriter as well as the players had worked on the field we would surely see both a pennant and a best-seller. It was probably the first time the New York-Penn League had made the *Times* in twenty years, which created a nice sense of validation. Somebody beyond Utica was watching us.

I allowed myself to hope that the victory and the newspaper story would calm the contending forces arrayed beneath me, a hope that promptly turned out to be naive. In baseball, a losing streak invariably shortens everybody's temper, but a victory, or even a string of victories, does not necessarily calm anything or anyone. Baseball history is rich in accounts of ball clubs that won pennants among internecine battles. It is said that Joe Tinker and Johnny Evers of the famous double-play combination of Tinker to Evers to Chance did not speak for entire seasons. Babe Ruth and Lou Gehrig did not like each other's styles much when they were playing together at Yankee Stadium. More recently certain Yankee and Oakland teams and the 1982 Philadelphia Phillies won the World Series with a notable absence of camaraderie. Baseball is a high-ego game and victory is a detonator to certain egos. Despite our victory and the blessing of the *Times*, one more wretched confrontation lay in the immediate Utica future.

Dave Chase, the rotund man from Durham, on hand to help install sound business procedures, remarked that I showed symptoms of amateurism as a baseball executive. "You say what the score was first," Chase said. "Then you mention the crowd. A real professional announces the receipts before the score."

Froebel ball games and Dodger days flashed within my mind. To think as Chase suggested would shrink baseball from an American art form to a MasterCard statement. I wanted to retain, thank you, some remnants of amateurism, a term, of course, that derives from the Latin verb for "love."

"Cost controls are essential," Chase continued. "Otherwise—this is pretty much a rule of baseball—the players will steal you blind."

The players, I thought, rode the buses, stood in against ninety-mile-an-hour fast balls, had no days off and earned $500 a month. The players had just won, 15–0. I resisted the idea of the Blue Sox as a gathering of petty thieves.

"For example, bats," Chase said. "Ball players like bats. They like to collect 'em. So they'll come in and say they've broken a bat and need a new one. What you or Joanne has to say is this: 'First, show me the broken bat. Then we'll give you a new one.' "

"I'll say it," Joanne said carelessly. "The players know I care about them."

"You *should* say it," Chase pointed out. "It isn't the club president's role to get into a discussion of Louisville Sluggers."

I liked discussing Louisville Sluggers with professionals, the different models, their weights, their lengths. But I simply nodded.

Somehow the sense of this conversation sped, as if by wire, to Jim Gattis, with an error in transmission or interpretation. Whatever, Gattis concluded that Chase was concerned that he, Jim Gattis, the manager, was in the sly sideline of stealing bats.

I was chatting with Moss outside the trailer—we were deciding that we'd room together on the road—when Gattis and Chase collided a few yards away. "What's this about the bats?" Gattis demanded.

"We want the broken ones returned to the front office before we issue new ones," Chase said.

The veins in Gattis' neck bulged. "Dave," Moss said, "what we've been doing here is keeping the broken bats. Then we tape them as best we can and use the taped bats for batting practice." Moss turned back to me. "If that's all right with you."

"That's fine with me."

Tension between Gattis and Chase went back at least a year. "What do you think?" Gattis shouted. "That Barry and I are going to cheat you on bats? Okay. We'll return the broken bats and use new ones in batting practice. That way we'll break more. God damn. I guarantee that. What's the God damn problem with the God damn front office?"

Moss, recognizing that Gattis was in the grip of self-feeding rage—provoked, to be sure, but also self-feeding—said to me, "See ya. I have to go wash my hands."

Chase said, "The front office isn't the problem here, Jim. The problem is you. Your attitude. It's always been bad. People have done a helluva job in that trailer and you don't appreciate it."

Gattis strode towards Chase, towered over him and put an index finger in front of Chase's nose. "There are gonna be some changes around here," he shouted, "and they're gonna happen this week. This week! If these changes don't happen this week, I'm quitting. I'm going back to Tucson. This whole place is disorganized, a fucking mess, and now you're messing with me. I'm gonna quit!"

Chase stood still, neither giving ground nor retreating.

Gattis continued to rant, ignoring me, waving a finger at Chase's nose until at last he had talked himself out.

Almost forty years earlier, when Walter O'Malley presided as a trustee of Froebel Academy, the Brooklyn Dodgers were the collective ward of an exuberant, hard-drinking man named Larry MacPhail. Sober, MacPhail was volatile. After a few drinks he erupted and when that happened, particularly after a loss, he was inclined to fire his manager, Leo Durocher. Indeed, after one particularly jarring setback, MacPhail announced that Durocher was fired and two drinks later repeated the announcement fortissimo across the bar in the pressroom.

"You already fired him," said Bill Boylan, the bartender at Ebbets Field.

"You're fired too," MacPhail shouted.

Durocher, who played shortstop, cards and power games with a reckless skill, countered these threats with warnings that he was about to quit. Newspapermen rejoiced in the rantings, which fed their columns with unquenchable flames of rancor.

Eventually, MacPhail would sober up, recognize Durocher's gifts, and nobody quit or got himself fired, not even the pressroom bartender. I mention this to illustrate that I did not come to Utica as a stranger to managerial crises. I had read about them in boyhood and anything I forgot was renewed by the subsequent interplay between Billy Martin and George Steinbrenner that stirred the climate at Yankee Stadium with five years of hot and noxious winds.

There was, I thought, returning to my clapboard house on Bradford Avenue, one difference between the Durocher-Martin incidents and Jim Gattis' sudden threat to quit. Even if indirectly, the Gattis threat was directed at me. I was not observing the crisis. I was in it.

I had chosen, for that week's late night reading, a volume which tried to measure and balance the lives of

Count Tolstoy and Mohandas Gandhi, who had been a disciple to the novelist in the first decade of the century. This was no accidental choice. After fourteen hours of tending baseball checkbooks and egos, I didn't much want to turn to the literature of the game. I wanted escape. But on the night of June 19, after our 15–0 victory over the Watertown Pirates, there was no escape. So Tolstoy waged war with his wife for fifty years. So Gandhi's philosophy was altered forever by the trauma of his first sexual experiences. I had something *important* to worry about: my manager's ruffled feathers.

I put down the book and walked upstairs and stole a look at my daughter, who was asleep. She looked tranquil, her head resting on a pillow and outlined with a halo of red hair. Alissa, who was just sixteen, had been going through one of those mid-adolescent stress times which have been sweeping America like a pandemic. She wanted very much to be grown up. She wanted to be done with all the important and trivial business of the teen years; to be, at once and in short, a finished woman. And at the same time she was not yet ready, if anyone ever is ready, to put away childish things. Selling Blue Sox programs and working in the trailer would be her first job, and I wanted most ardently for the summer to go nicely for this lovely, loving child who was now dreaming, I fancied, the secret dreams of girlhood. Let her sleep. A fire was roaring in my head. By tomorrow morning the Blue Sox might not have a manager.

I now abandoned Tolstoy, Gandhi and my daughter to think through contingencies. It was 1:30 A.M. If Gattis were going to threaten to quit all summer (he did not), it might be best simply to release him. I supposed that I could preside over three months of war. But that was hardly why I had come to Utica.

I would have to talk sense to Gattis. Although he had been subdued—or perhaps guarded—in Los Angeles, he was clearly one of that breed of managers who protects territory with bobcat ferocity. You had best not waste time telling that breed whom to pitch or when to bunt, much less how to establish a security system for bats. With Gattis in Utica, or on a vastly different level with Earl Weaver in Baltimore or Whitey Herzog in St. Louis, you either let the man manage or you replace him.

I poured myself a 2 A.M. scotch. Two of the directors wanted to fire the general manager. I was now having to contemplate dismissing the field manager. This on opening day, plus two hours.

I didn't want anybody fired or replaced. Shuffling personnel may be exciting to corporate commanders but here in Utica it suggested only disorder. I could find all the excitement I needed in the ball games and the ball players, the magical mixing of youth and baseball and dreams.

I needed a plan. All right. If Gattis wanted to go home to Tucson, we would survive. Barry Moss could manage the club. If Gattis expected to dictate terms to everybody, I would *send* him home to Tucson. What would be the worst-case consequence of that? Grim. There was no solution to that problem either in the relationship of Tolstoy and Gandhi or in another glass of scotch. I slept briefly and early the next morning called Miles Wolff in Durham.

"Gattis blew up like that?" Wolff said in a tone of controlled annoyance. "I'm glad you're there instead of me."

"And right now," I said, "I'm under threats that he'll quit."

"If Gattis quits we'll simply get another manager," Wolff said. "Have you thought about Barry Moss?"

"Sure. But the other ball players worry me. They seem a little restless anyway and the ones who like Gattis may start taking off."

"The ball players are under contract to Utica Baseball, Inc. That's you. If anybody takes off, you can put him on the restricted list. That means he can't sign with another team for sixty days, which would be August. In August other minor league teams won't be looking for ball players. So anybody who takes off loses this season. And we'll call some farm directors who have some excess talent and get some help.''

The idea of replacing our playing personnel appalled me. Briefly as I knew the athletes, they seemed good and likable and unspoiled. But after Cooperstown and Columbia, I was learning what professional businessmen and generals discover early. If there is any possibility of a disaster, you had better have a disaster plan in place.

I appeared at the trailer at ten-thirty, feeling glum. At eleven I intended to call Barry Moss, at his temporary home in the Econo-Lodge, and suggest that he join me for a conciliatory lunch with Gattis. If Moss declined, I would simply take Gattis to a restaurant and recite the rules of the game, one on one.

Dunkirk, I thought. This thing could turn into a miniature Dunkirk. Well, whatever, I *would* survive to be president for another day.

"How would you compare," a reporter later asked me, "being president of the Blue Sox to being president of the Dodgers?"

"About the way," I said, "I'd compare it to being President of the United States."

I sat in the trailer sipping coffee at ten forty-five, when Gattis and Moss suddenly appeared. "Damn it," Gattis said, "I'm back to smoking. And I'd quit cigarettes for a good while, too. Damn it, that thing last night upset me."

"We have something for you," Moss said.

The two blond six-footers handed me sheets marked "Player Publicity Questionnaire." Moss, who had little running speed, set down his nickname as "Bullet." Over that, on Barry's questionnaire, Gattis had written "Snake!"

Gattis, whose forebears are Dutch and Irish, listed his nationality as Mexican-Arab. After the entry asking if he kept pets, Jim wrote: "About 5' 5", 104 pounds, blue eyes, Norwegian.

I can recognize a peace offering when I see one. "Thanks," I said. "Your reward is going to be lunch and drinks paid for by the ball club." I wanted to say "paid for by the front office," but last night's screaming was still too vividly on my mind. I had better keep the term "front office" out of my vocabulary for a while.

In my time with the Mets at St. Petersburg, I noticed that every minor league manager did what Steve Schryver directed, without argument. That is one nature of organizational life. Obedience. Ambition to advance enforces discipline.

No such factor was at work at Utica. Not I, not Acton nor anyone else, could offer Gattis the carrot of promotion. If he did well, some large organization might notice him. I could help Jim by calling friends in the major leagues. But, for him and for the players, moving up was a chancy thing. That made discipline that much harder to realize.

Besides, Gattis had come to see himself and the Blue Sox as an anti-organizational ball club. We were the misfits, the rejects, the unwanted of the game, and he would work this toward a point of pride. He wanted to establish a sense among the players that it was us against the world. Perhaps Gandhi and certainly Tolstoy sometimes felt the same way.

I had a lot of work to do at lunch. "First," I said to Jim, "I want to know why you call Barry Snake?"

Gattis sipped a beer. Moss, who had to play that night, drank soda pop.

"You don't have to know that," Moss said.

"I only said I *wanted* to know."

"Well," Gattis said, grinning, "when you're at a party with Barry, after a while he makes a sort of hissing sound, like a snake, and suddenly he's gone and so is the prettiest girl in the room."

"Not true," Moss said.

He laughed a bit. Then I could get serious. "When you get as mad as you did last night," I said to Gattis, "you don't do anybody a favor, including yourself. The cords in your neck were as big as hawsers and you looked as if you were going to throw a punch."

"No way," Gattis said. "I was nowhere near punching out Dave Chase."

I looked at Barry, who seemed uncomfortable. "I've seen him throw punches," Barry said.

"Well, look," I said. "Here's a rule. Nobody throws any punches on this club, unless we get into a brawl with somebody else, and if that happens we've got Big Bob Veale."

"What gets me pissed," Gattis said, "is that I work so damn hard and where I have weaknesses I'll admit them. Like I'm not that great at being organized. Barry is. Snake keeps me organized. But you have people in that front office who first of all don't know what they're doing and, second, won't admit what they don't know. We did our job on the field yesterday, didn't we?"

"By 15–0," I said.

"We know about players stealing bats and baseballs. We can put in controls."

"He's managed before," Moss said.

"Like stealing balls," Gattis said. "If they've got to steal balls, if they've got a compulsion, I'm gonna tell them to steal 'em from other teams."

"But Murnane Field is a disgrace," Moss said.

Both grounds keeping and concessions had been assigned to Joanne's brother, Rocco Gerace, who was nine-

teen and did not know much about either soil or grass.
Three teenage assistants worked for him.

"I'm going to change the table of organization," I said
to Gattis. "The three kid grounds keepers now work for
you or Barry or Veale."

"Good," Gattis said. "That will help."

"Anything else?" I said.

"Another beer, maybe," Gattis said. "Damn, I miss
my kid, Luke. He's four and a half."

"Let me tell you how I see my role," I said. "I want to
help make your job easier, Jim. So when something bothers you, come to me, or I'll come to you."

"That's great," Gattis said. "Isn't that just great, Barry?"

"I think this is going to work," Moss said.

You could not have recognized the raging manager of
the night before.

I had heard one commandment from a dozen minor
league owners. If you offer people baseball and only baseball, your grandstands will be empty. To attract customers,
you have to promote.

In my boyhood days promotions came infrequently. The
prevailing outlook within baseball was that the game was a
national institution and that it was a civic duty to buy
tickets. Even in the majors, this approach is as dead as
Charlie Ebbets, for whom a ball park once was named.

Much contemporary hype dismays me. I don't like designated hitters because I've seen games won by pitchers
cracking out one of their three annual base hits. Artificial
surfaces destroy a subtle baseball attraction: surveying neatly
tended grassland amid the asphalt plazas of a city. I don't
like electronic scoreboards, with disembodied hands clap-
ping in spurious transistorized enthusiasm. I don't like
promotions trumpeted over loudspeakers because they break
my concentration on nine innings. ("Good. It's Veterans

of Foreign Wars night. Great. All hail VFW Post 1999. Now can we stop this and get on with the next pitch?'')

But in the minors you confront simple alternatives. Just play the games and draw 500 purists. Or promote, adjust to the hype that marks the times, and triple your crowd.

Stop the game in the fifth inning and invite a few fans to throw a baseball through a hole in a wood slab painted into an advertisement for a local hamburger heaven. Anyone who succeeds wins a dozen cheeseburgers. (Ketchup extra.)

Run ethnic nights. A free beer for anyone who can prove Latvian ancestry. Give the people single-parent nights, American Legion nights, Little League nights, reduced-rate hot-dog nights. Appropriately discounting a number of tickets, you will draw crowds.

Little as I like promotions, we had to run them. One of our staples turned out to be, shades of Herbert Wishengrad, the Commissar of Columbia, a nightly trivia question. The first fan who could tell us, say, how many stitches are required to enclose a baseball in cowhide gets a super sandwich from Utica's famous Frick and Frack's Flying Food Factory. (Baseballs are made in Haiti. It takes a Haitian seamstress 216 stitches to finish a ball.)

I amused myself by getting some scotch into Fred Snyder, the public address announcer, hoping to hear him say, "Flick and Flack's Flying Frood Flactory." He never did.

Alissa had to memorize a spiel of her own for peddling programs.

"Buy a program, mister. Fifty cents. Two for a dollar. [sic]. You may get a lucky number that's good for a prize. And there are other prizes, too. And you get coupons, like take the one for Arby's. Buy one roast beef sandwich and with the coupon the second one is free."

This was rather a long commercial to direct at individuals who were walking down Murnane's grassy knoll in clusters, eyeing the beer bar with excitement. Lissa, now a sixteen-year-old pitch-person, spoke it quickly, with generally beneficent results, until one night she encountered an elderly satyr. Considering Alissa, her Blue Sox T-shirt, her white shorts and trim legs, the satyr said, "Say, I'll buy a scorecard, little lady, if you come with it."

I wanted the bastard barred from the ball park. Joanne suggested that I relax. Alissa said I was acting like a Jewish mother of a father. "I know about people like that," Alissa said. "I can handle them."

"How?"

"If he touches me, I'll whomp him and maybe scream."

"Liss," Joanne said, "don't do that. If someone bothers you, just go to one of the ball park cops."

Remembering Veeck, I sought a good promotion for our home opener, something genial and attractive as spring, that would not interrupt the game. Joanne knew of a parachutist who was willing to land on second base. "Suppose he misses," I said, "and hits a light pole or lands on three small children in the bleachers."

"Insurance covers that," Joanne said. I was relieved when the parachutist turned out to be occupied. He would land to cheers in another county.

First ball, I had been thinking. First ball. We had to do something centered on the ritual of throwing out the first ball. I had been in Chicago one opening day when Bill Veeck issued Styrofoam balls to all his customers so that *everyone* got to throw out a first ball. This created lumpy clouds of Styrofoam. Then the game had to be delayed for twenty minutes while plastic baseballs were removed from the field.

Splashy, but inglorious. Besides, if we got any gate at all we couldn't afford, or even find, a sufficient number of plastic balls in Utica. Joanne then suggested that we run a letter contest. "Why I Should Throw Out the First Ball Opening Night." The author of the best letter would get to tramp Murnane's lumpy soil to the pitcher's mound and toss a baseball to Mark Krynitsky.

Good, I thought. Then, picking up the ball player's patois: That'll do it.

Our contest drew only seven entries, even though the winner would get to keep the baseball. The most appealing note came from one Gene Carney of Ferndale Place, on behalf of his three-and-a-half-year-old daughter, Mary Ellen. "In another fifteen years," Mr. Carney wrote, "the major leagues could be ready to draft the first female player. Mary Ellen, if her career gets this boost, could be ready."

A little investigation showed that Mary Ellen Carney was blond, blue-eyed, thirty-eight pounds and thirty-nine inches tall. The tiniest first-ball thrower ever. She was even smaller than Veeck's pinch-hitting midget. Cuteness and women's liberation on the diamond. I thought that the promotion would make a nice picture story for the Utica *Observer-Dispatch*. I even imagined the right photo being transmitted by the Associated Press and winning the Blue Sox further national attention. (I also hoped, when it came time to throw, that Mary Ellen would actually let go of the ball.)

The moppet proved a trouper. She walked to the mound with assurance and made a nice four-foot throw—longer than her height—to our large, black-mustached catcher. But no photo of the event exists. I had reckoned without the vagaries of small-town newspapers. *Observer-Dispatch* photographers were all busy elsewhere at game time, and none reached Murnane until the fourth inning. By that time Mary Ellen Carney was seated in the stands, her father was guarding the baseball and Watertown was beating the Blue Sox, 2–0.

I wandered about the sidelines and the bleachers, determined to see that everybody had a good time. I felt responsible for that, as if I were the host at a party.

"Dave," I told Chase, "you walk around too, but stay away from Gattis. Take notes and we'll meet after the game to review everything you think ought to be improved."

Some of the fans recognized me from press pictures and shouted pleasantries. "Hey. Are we gonna win the pennant?"

"Yes," I would answer. "You bet."

"Then how come we're losing?"

"We're keeping it interestng."

Watertown had us, 6–2, in the last of the ninth inning, but the Blue Sox began to come back. Larry Lee, our switch-hitting second baseman from Pepperdine, singled. Brian Robinson, an interesting prospect who had been overlooked in the draft, walked. So did Mark Krynitsky. We had the bases full with no one out and our lead-off hitter Ralph Sheffield, all flash and speed, came to bat. At least, I thought, we were not vulnerable to a double play. Sheffield could scoot down the line like a sprinter. Ralph then hit a medium-speed hopper close to second base. The Pirate shortstop, Dan Smith, grabbed it, stepped on second and threw to first. Double play. The unlikely double play. The rally died. The Pirates beat the Blue Sox, 6–3.

The players, particularly the rookies, lost hard. I climbed to our dressing room in the brick blockhouse and patted a few backs, but the atmosphere was heavy. The players simply dropped on the benches in front of their orange lockers and sat silent.

"Hey," said Mike Zamba, who had been up as high as Double A. "You guys are going to see more like that. Don't take it so hard."

Daryl Pitts and Sheffield both threw their jerseys angrily into the dirty-linen basket. At length Roy Moretti, who had shut down the Pirates for the last two innings, walked in. His hair was wet with sweat and his spikes clicked on the cement floor. "Why is everybody so damn quiet?" he shouted. "There's a lot more to come. We got seventy-four fucking more to go."

Rocky Coyle, a short stocky outfielder, entered, carrying his year-old son Joshua. Sheffield, disturbed by the double play, now brightened and lifted Joshua from his father's arms. Then he began to babble at the baby.

"Sheffield," Bob Veale said, "you got a lotta things to learn, but one of the first of them is this. Ain' no use talking baby talk to a baby. Babies don't understand baby talk."

That drew a smile and the team mood lightened, although Gattis sequestered himself in his office. Our upstate Achilles had found a tent.

"You don't want to lose too hard, specially this early," Veale said. "That Gattis loses so hard, I got to worry about his coronary artery. But, you know, I been up there with big guys. Clemente. Willie Stargell. I played with them. Big as they were, big as I am, we all got beat some nights. You got to take your licking like a man and move away." Veale winked at me. "A little Remy Martin to ease the pain?"

I said I had to go back to the trailer.

"You *better* get outa here," Veale said. "You jinxed us. You cost us this one with your talk that we'd go 76–0."

"Maybe I lost it, Veale, but don't underestimate your president. Without me, you'd still be warming up two pitchers with one baseball."

"Shee-yit," Big Bob said in peroration.

Our crowd, 1,387, had been loud, blue-collar, baseball wise. Someone had rigged an old ah-oooga auto horn system to a battery, which he sounded when we put men on base. Beneath the press box a grizzled group cracked into song in the seventh inning when Saul Lopez, the

Pirates' starter, seemed to be tiring. Their lyrics ran to a singsong melody:

> "Take me out,
> My arm is sore.
> I don't wanna
> Pitch no more.
> I don't wanna pitch
> No more.
> Take me out,
> My arm is sore."

Not Coleridge, nor Shelley, nor even Marianne Moore, but nice in a bowling-alley sense. The fans directed their voices toward me as I wandered before them and one of the singers sprang down from the bleachers and said, "How do you like it? We can sing like that for you every night."

He was a youngish man, perhaps thirty, who managed to look at the same time youthful and lined.

"Fine. Keep it up. Keep singing every game."

"You know about the Bleacher Bums in Chicago. Over at Wrigley Field, they got these guys who make a lot of noise. I hear the Cubs' management ropes off a special section for them. The Bleacher Bums section. Well, we're the Utica Bleacher Bums. Can you rope off a special section for us?"

"Maybe," I said. "We've got a lot of things to go over. We'll see." I was annoyed that we had lost to Watertown. I was annoyed that I would have to hold a staff meeting after this disappointing game. I was annoyed that our hitters had not destroyed the mediocre right-hander called Saul Lopez.

"You gotta be nice to your fans," said the young, lined man, "if you expect the fans to be nice to you." Every fan, I thought, knows how to run a ball club. Only a few sing on key.

* * *

I told Gattis, "Tough loss," and he grunted and said that we couldn't afford to blow games against a weak club like Watertown. Then I returned to the trailer for a general meeting of the front office staff.

We numbered four on the night of June 20. Joanne Gerace, still embarrassed by the bull-pen-baseball episode, didn't look as though she could withstand much more in the way of criticism. Penny Lacey, short, dark-haired, wanted to work and she wanted to learn. Then there was chubby Dave Chase, the professional front office man from North Carolina.

"Have you critiqued tonight's operation?" I asked.

"I have," Chase said, and handed me two pages of notes.

I thanked him and suggested that he continue to stay out of Gattis' line of sight. "It's nothing personal. Just a bull and red flag situation."

"I'll be back in Durham in two days," Chase said. "Frankly, I wish I could leave tonight."

"Morale," I said. "Morale. I want everybody concerning himself with everybody else's morale."

Then I began to read Chase's memo aloud.

"These are notes on making our operation better. I'll now list Dave's points: The trailer office should be cleaner and neater."

"We're trying," Joanne said. "There's just so much to do."

"Let's go over all Dave's points," I said, "before we comment on any. People—fans—entering the trailer should not have to wait to buy tickets. A cash box and tickets should be placed at the front counter, ready for our customers.

"No beer drinking at the front gate. Security"—the three Utica policemen we hired every night—"can see to this. And no beer drinking by our ticket takers in the sentry box.

"Baseball knowledge is necessary for the person who types the insert." The insert was a group of Xeroxed pages that Alissa folded into the programs. They provided current batting and pitching statistics for each player.

"Better staff communication with RK [me] on negative matters. Tell RK about problems as well as about good things. He does not bite.

"There's too much traffic in the trailer. Only people with legitimate business should be admitted.

"The concession people got tired in the eighth inning tonight and closed down. A concession stand *never* closes until the game is over. Every hot dog we sell we *need* to sell.

"The popcorn boxes are too large. We're giving too much away. There's not enough ice in the soda cups. Remember, ice is cheaper than soda.

"Cups. There are always plastic cups in this office, with some coffee, beer or soda in them, that somebody hasn't finished. Half-empty cups are *always* spilled. I am a nut on the subject of cups. When you're through with your cup, throw it out.

"Further comment on the popcorn situation. We run a risk at Murnane of electric overload if we pop corn during the game, when the field lights are on. Pop a sufficient number of boxes before the gates open. Cold popcorn is better than a blackout.

"Go nowhere in Utica without pocket schedules. The Blue Sox schedule is everybody's business card.

"Distribute our large glossy schedules to all stores that will take them. Hotel lobbies. Barbershops. Bars. Et cetera. We want everyone to know when the Blue Sox play at home.

"Paint and repair outfield-fence distance markers.

"Post a price list at the souvenir stand"—for Blue Sox caps, bumper stickers and such.

Now came four tough ones.

"No TV watching in the office. This creates a bad, nonbusinesslike impression.

"More general baseball knowledge on front office staff. RK will help. The rest of you will have to be willing to learn.

"Better individual organization. Many times long hours mean a lack of organization. Plan ahead. Make lists. Delegate.

"No socializing with players."

I had been reading in a careful monotone, noticing that Joanne and Penny each wanted to spring to her own defense at almost every point. By the time I finished, Joanne was blinking away tears.

"What do you mean, no socializing?" she snapped. "I *like* the players."

"We need to keep a certain distance," I said.

"What are you suggesting?" Joanne said. Ultimately—and everybody in the room knew this—I was suggesting through Chase that I didn't want love affairs to blossom—no, explode—between athletes and staff. At the least, they could expose the front office to charges of preferential treatment. At worst, the gossip mill that was the ball club would grind out trouble in larger chunks than I could handle.

"What the hell!" Joanne said, taking Holy Roman offense. She and Penny exchanged long looks.

"There's nothing wrong with being friendly with the ball players," I said, "but we have to set limits." I wondered how to make an important point without further angering the women. Where was Masters? Where was Johnson? I only had Dave Chase. Then, looking at the women, I realized that the point had been made.

"At the same time," Chase said smoothly, "we don't want the front office and the other personnel isolated from the ball players, so I have an idea I'd like you to try. After the games are over and all the fans have left the park, reopen the beer bar. Then serve employees and ball players up to two beers for free. That way everybody can get to know everybody else in a controlled situation."

"Fine, Dave," I said. "We can start that tonight. Then we'll curfew the free bar, say an hour and a half after the game. We can all have some nice talk there. Baseball talk."

Black-haired Penny Lacey bobbed her head. "You remind me of my father," she told me.

"Anything else?" asked Chase. I adjourned the meeting.

Joanne lingered in my office, looking ravished. "What kind of a woman do you think I am?"

"A good, hardworking woman."

"So why did we have to go through that business about my not getting laid? All spring, damn it, in the cold, I've been alone in here, with one lousy black and white TV to keep me company. Is there anything wrong with that? Is there something wrong with the way I've run this operation, when I was alone, when Miles Wolff was in Durham, when you weren't even here? Is there? Do you want to fire me too?"

Tears spilled out of this pretty woman's eyes as she stood feeling hurt and unappreciated.

I gave her a hug, which surely violated the new nonsocializing rule, and said, come on, we were all going to have a wonderful summer. She brightened slowly and, at length, said she did not mean to be a pain in the neck. A few glasses of red wine would get her back together, she insisted.

Alone, stacking papers, like one of those television news people who has finished his evening's public reading, I mused about egos. Mighty as they were around the clubhouse, they were just about as formidable in the front office. Everybody wanted to be a star, which is why people work in Hollywood, or in baseball.

The telephone rang, startling me. It was a journalist in

New York, lost in the wilderness of an uncompleted book, wanting to hear another human voice. "Say," he began with a dogged cheer that belied the hour, "I'll admit I envy you. You're having fun."

"Actually," I said, "I've been working. I've been working a fifteen-hour day."

"Come on," the man said, still oppressively cheerful. "You're not going to tell me that running a baseball team is work."

Then he asked if he could play left field some night when we were ten runs ahead. He seemed offended when I told him he wasn't good enough.

Those writers, I thought, who choose to write about themselves—a goodly number—often cite loneliness as the dominant element in their lives. A book is best written by sitting alone in a room with the door closed, the world shut out and your joys and cares focused on a blank piece of paper, preferably numbered. That is how most writers function, not because they are necessarily antisocial but because practically there is no other way to do the job.

Running the Blue Sox was forcing a diametric change in the circumstances of my life. All summer I would have to meet dozens of people every day. To keep our little ball club pointed toward a pennant, I would have to concern myself with fans, the press, the front office, the manager, the coaches, the ball players and a wide variety of minor characters including umpires. ("Be nice to the umpire," Barry Moss had remarked archly. "The umpire is your friend. Be nice to the umpire. Otherwise he'll take the close ones away.")

I noted in my desk diary that the first day had brought a tantrum from the manager and the second day had drawn tears from the general manager. As much as possible, within the intensity of a season, I wanted such febrile passions cooled. I would have to abandon my private writer's ways, I knew, and work in a group situation. I would have to help everyone find a balance between spirited behavior and hysteria.

This night, anyway, Gattis turned out to be calm, if grumpy, in defeat, and Joanne's tears probably were drying as she sipped Lambrusco in Spilka's bar among old friends.

The team had played very well and then played listlessly. Although I would tell reporters that I had seen enough to be certain that we had a contending ball club—contending clubs sell tickets—I really didn't know. There were twelve teams in the league. I had seen two.

I walked out to our new free beer bar and told our trim, black-haired shortstop, Brian Robinson, that on a particular play he had made one hell of a throw.

"I have a fine arm," Robinson said.

A few minutes later Brian appeared before me again. "I didn't mean for that to sound boastful, sir," he said. "It's just that a lot of coaches have told me I have a good arm. I mean, I should have thanked you. So, thanks."

On the following night the Blue Sox began to play a kind of baseball that seemed too good for the New York-Penn League. We swept everything before us with fierce and brilliant play and by July 21 we held a seven-game lead over the Little Falls Mets. Our record, the best in organized baseball, reached 26 and 6.

I actually became concerned that we would win the Eastern Division championship so easily that our fans, with their ah-ooo-ga horns and doggerel songs, might well lose interest. It would not work out that way but our month as invincible Olympians was a merry and wildly exciting time.

4

The Utica Olympians

A baseball team, like any other group pressed into daily intimacy, develops a collective personality as it coalesces. This is, to be sure, the sum of the individual ball players, the solid citizens, the drinkers, the chasers, the loud and the silent, but it is more than that as well. The character of a team also proceeds from interaction among the various athletes and the cliques that inevitably form. Finally, the personality is shaped by the manager and the coaches, and the response of ball players to authority.

There is generally no simple satisfactory answer to the fan who asks, in ingenuous curiosity, what a certain team is *really* like. (Fans employ the word "really" as regularly as lawyers use "whereas.") A team is happy and sad, bristling and fearful, open and secretive. In short, a baseball team is various, affected by victories and losses, wives and girl friends, hangovers, the schedule, the press, the management and the weather.

During my early years of traveling with a major league team—one of nine reporters from New York's then frenetically competitive newspaper business—I noticed first a certain bridge that separated the ball players from the civilians. With few exceptions, the ball players tailored their conduct to the fact that I was a reporter. Although it was a point of macho honor for the athletes to insist that they didn't worry about what they called their "ink," they generally *did* worry about what they might read about themselves next day, next week, next month. True and relaxed friendships between myself and ball players developed memorably, but not all that frequently. Do starlets sleep with critics? Seldom, according to critics I have heard complain.

The exceptions fill a rich garner of recollection: Willie Mays philosophizing solemnly on love, marriage and money at the age of twenty-six; Mickey Mantle describing the strange terrors of retirement one cold spring night in Dallas; Jackie Robinson sharing the pain imposed by racial vitriol hurled at him in St. Louis; Early Wynn any time the bowl of life sat full before us.

But a major league season runs across a long span. Company manners have a way of breaking down. Reality has a way of breaking through.

The old Brooklyn Dodgers were loud and exciting, compulsively anxious to share each day's experience with anyone, particularly when they felt wronged by fate or an umpire. The later Los Angeles Dodgers—the Garvey-Cey teams—moved about with a hint of corporate bankers, all employed by the same firm, mouthing a company line but not at length very fond of one another. The old New York Yankees were close-mouthed and tempered steel. When a new pitcher beat them they had no praise for his performance. Gene Woodling or Hank Bauer would simply snap: "He'd damn better wear an iron jockstrap next time he goes against us. That's how hard we're going to hit him." The new Yankees have descended into a cloying, sad-faced clownishness.

I once even wandered about with the late Washington Senators. People were still trying to get laughs by saying, "Washington is first in war, first in peace and last in the

American League.'' That ball club was alternately bland and silly, in defense against the chronic condition of being beaten. If the Senators admitted to anyone, mostly to themselves, that losing five games a week was a clear comment on their professional skills, they would have been worse than silly.

Depressed.

As the Utica Blue Sox hurried up the mountain to first place and their 26 and 6 record, individual characters and the character of the team came into gradual delineation. Gattis had an obsessive need to control. He demonstrated this by holding meetings every day, which became occasions for assertive speeches. He seemed partial to a patterned kind of meeting in which he first praised the players for winning and then, anger growing, picked apart flaws in the previous night's effort. As Gattis complained, the players sat on the wooden benches below the orange lockers and looked at their spikes.

This bothered him. "I wish there was somebody who'd lash back," Gattis told me. "I worry about this team. We've got too many easygoing guys."

"You can't expect them to be angry when they're playing .800 ball," I said.

"Maybe," Gattis said, "and maybe not. But what's their character going to be when they lose a few? I wonder how this team will react the first time they lose three in a row."

I thought we had enough good pitching to make extended losing streaks unlikely, but Gattis' question was a good one and it stayed with him. He never became manic during the winning spurt because he could not stop worrying about how everyone would behave when times grew tougher, which, he assured me, they definitely would.

"I'll tell you the truth," he said as we ate a late breakfast at Peter's Parkway Diner. "I was kind of thinking I wanted the team to play .500 ball for the first twenty or thirty games. That would be when we were all working out the kinks, moving the players around. After that we'd begin our charge for the pennant.

"As a manager, you're in a .500 ball situation a hell of a lot of the time. This team has been winning in a lot of different ways. That good starting pitching, Seitz and Zamba. Moretti coming up strong in relief. Barry and a couple others making hits. The defense, except for maybe Don Jacoby at third, giving us big plays. Maybe you get tired of hearing my speeches. Maybe they get tired of them. I don't care. You're my boss and I appreciate that you got a lot to do but I see a big part of my job as making sure we play with a surplus of intensity. I want them ready to play, not thinking about some movie or some girl, when it comes game time, and you don't have to tell me that it's hard to come up with maximum effort, game after game, night after night, when there's no day off, because I know that. Maximum effort. Intensity."

Gattis was burning with intensity himself.

"It's easy for a manager to get lax, particularly with these players. Texas Star and I found them, but the reason you could sign them is that they're *unwanted*. If any of the organizations wanted them, they wouldn't be here. So I could be lax and say I'm gonna do what I can with what I have, which isn't much, but no way. I'll never manage like that.

"Right now, even though they don't lash back at me, they're feeling a little cocky. They're winning and everybody likes to win. But when I get on some of them, for a dumb pitch or a missed sign, it isn't just to keep intensity high. You see, some nights when they win, they forget *why* they're winning. The reason is that they play hard and intelligent baseball, harder than the other team, like Tom Lasorda told us we ought to do. But it's too easy, dangerous really, to sort of slip into success without recognizing cause and effect. The effect is that we win. The cause is that we have played intelligently and we've played so hard that it sometimes looks like our lives depend on it. And that's the only way to play professional ball. Do you want more coffee?''

"No. I'm fine.''

"I like to teach,'' Gattis said, "get people to think, to understand themselves. I'll bet you I'd make a hell of a teacher in a ghetto.''

Bob Veale was more aloof and more contained. He indulged in a little basso chuckle after victories and a small scowl following defeats, but in the manner of a former major leaguer and a man who was within a few months of his fiftieth birthday, he knew how to drop his intensity when he left the ball park. "This game can give you a heart attack,'' he said, "and a heart attack is not what I'm looking to get. I can relax. That's how it is when you're black. Most black people are *born* relaxed.''

Barry Moss found himself in a perplexing role. Gattis wanted to show the other players that he indulged no favorites. Even though Moss had grown up with him and even though Moss was his confidant and coach, Moss, the player, was a favorite target. Sometimes, in one of Gattis' daily sermons, he paused and turned to Moss and said, "Barry, in the fourth inning you looked real horseshit chasing that low inside pitch.'' Pause. Inhale. *"Real* horseshit.''

Barry batted .400 for the first month, so he did not look bad often at the plate. "Jim gets me a little confused,'' Moss said. "I know what he's trying to do. He likes pressure within the team, so that the players keep driving one another. He tries to get that by setting up different groups. Sort of the hard workers and the fuck-ups. The names change. You can move from one group to the other. But right now I'm having a hard time deciding whether I'm one of the coaches or one of the fuck-ups.''

"And if you had to make the choice?" I said.

"Oh, no contest," Barry said. "I'd be one of the fuck-ups. I may go on and coach or manage for years. But this can be my last season as a player. I want to remember it that way, as a ball player."

"The fuck-up .400 hitter," I said.

Moss laughed. He was pleased to be playing well.

The other athletes emerged a little more slowly, but not, given time, any less vividly. Mark Krynitsky, our best catcher, had a Slavic face that I associate with actors who played American coal miners, fighting to organize a union, in long-ago movies that were heavy with social significance and now appear on television in stark black and white in the hour just before dawn. Mark asked from time to time about the book I intended to write, but not with the suspicion of a contemporary major leaguer, who may be wondering, in the middle of an interview, why you, not he, is being paid the publisher's advance. Mark was just curious and when I told him I couldn't define the book very clearly since it was based on events that had not happened yet—the rest of the season—he understood at once.

"I don't know if there's something wrong with me," Krit said, "but I don't read books. I never have, except when they made me at school."

"It may be a question of habit, Mark. I started reading when I was a kid, and so did Gattis. And we still read."

"But you're a writer," Krit said with a tone of respect that warmed me. I have heard major leaguers, who would not know Turgenev from a *National Enquirer* reporter, describe writers as a devious, treacherous breed, the best and the worst, equally contemptible, in the blur of their Neanderthal thought.

Krynitsky, who was trying to complete work toward a college degree, came from Fairfax, Virginia. His family had labored in coal mines to the north during rugged times, he said. He was a slab-muscled two-hundred-pounder, recessive off the field but a driving leader during games.

Gattis had developed a voice code to order certain pitches from the bench. When he wanted a slider, he shouted, "Come on, little fella." For a curve it was, "Come on, big fella." (A curve, of course, breaks in a bigger arc than does a slider.) But you can't use a voice code often without the cryptographers on the other side deciphering it. Most of the time Gattis let Krynitsky select the pitches.

Mark called infield plays in a strong sergeant major's voice and he even roared out calls on fly balls to the outfield. He was not the best catching prospect in the league, but he was sound defensively and his bellows created a sense of enthusiastic professionalism.

"That voice," I said. "You carry to downtown Albany."

Krit grinned and suddenly did not look tough at all. "You got to do something," he said, "when those outside breaking balls keep getting you out."

Ed Wolfe, our first baseman, a strong, quiet twenty-three-year-old from Arizona, was deeply, profoundly, endlessly committed to rock music. He traveled nowhere without his glove and his ghetto blaster. The harsh sounds of rock worked as a tranquilizer. "It's tough," he told me one day, "being in a pennant race, and Gattis doesn't make it any easier."

We were canoeing on Lake Hinckley, fifteen miles north of Murnane Field, after a noontime softball game against learning-disabled children at Camp Northwood. (The Blue Sox managed to lose to the children by one run in the ninth; I cannot imagine a more admirable performance.)

It was a gloriously warm July afternoon. At the edges of the lake you could see cedar and maple and white birch, and wildflowers proclaiming Adirondack summer.

"You know I played for Gattis last year," Wolfe said. "I've played for a lot of managers and coaches, ever since

Little League. But I never met anyone who liked to rip like Gattis.''

I wanted to let Wolfe speak his piece, since he spoke seldom and I could hear him now. The ghetto blaster lay on shore. But I did not want to encourage ball players to complain to me about the manager, unless they presented a specific problem I could remedy, or a serious crisis arose.

''Jim does a lot of things well,'' I said. ''If you think he rips, you ought to hear Billy Martin.''

''Look,'' Wolfe said, ''Gattis is the best technical batting coach I've ever known. Get into a little slump and he's right there. But the ripping every day. I mean, it's like he's good at baseball but he isn't any good at people.''

''I go to the meetings. I haven't heard him rip you yet this year.'' Wolfe was working hard at first and batting .330.

''But last season,'' he said, ''I used to catch it. Now in the meetings I just turn myself off, just in case he starts again.''

We let the canoe drift. ''I appreciate how well you play, Ed, and so do the fans.'' He nodded. The only sound came from the little boat as it skimmed cedar-dark waters. He felt he had said enough. But the season would be more fun, Wolfe believed, if he were praised regularly by the manager, or even loved. Meanwhile, anxious lest Gattis attack his play, Wolfe was performing like a star.

I was left puzzled. It was possible that the diet of approbation Wolfe craved might have produced a smiling, relaxed first baseman, and might have snapped his addiction to hard rock. *That* first baseman, however, might have gone cheerfully about his summer trade hitting .200.

''It's not a gentle game, Eddie,'' I told him, ''when you're a pro.''

Don Jacoby, another mustache, our high-energy, hard-hitting third baseman, became the subject of ethnic incidents that amused me. Sandy Schlesinger, the New York lawyer who had bought stock in our team, called one day to announce that he was voyaging from Madison Avenue to Utica and that he looked forward to watching our fine Jewish third baseman.

"He's not Jewish, Sandy," I said.

"What? That's ridiculous. How can you not be Jewish if your name's Jacoby?"

"If your name was originally something else."

I wanted a Jewish ball player as badly as I wanted a Utica local to make the team. The better the mix, the better the gate. But neither want worked out. I had to tell Schlesinger that the closest we came to a Jewish ball player in Utica was Sandy Koufax, whose likeness was displayed at the Hall of Fame in Cooperstown, ninety minutes away.

Then an American Jewish sports encyclopedia asked for Jacoby's biography. "You want to be in there?" I said to Donny.

"Nah. I think I'll stay Eye-talian, like I been."

Jacoby came from northern New Jersey where an Italian family named Giacobetti had settled two generations earlier. Then, to feel and appear more native in the new land, they revised the spelling of their name. Somehow—we never did get it all straight—the older Giacobettis had been led to believe that Jacoby had a fine Revolutionary War ring to it, like Hancock or Trelawney. They never suspected they were moving their identification from Naples to Tel Aviv.

Although some of his teammates called him "Jake," Jacoby preferred a nickname he had created out of the rear end of his name. "I like to be called 'Cobra,' " he said. He was a patient batter—which is to say he waited well, taking strikes that caught the black rims of home plate, hoping to see a better pitch to hit. His swing was compact and smooth, and that combination, the patience and the swing, made him one of the best hitters in the league.

His natural defensive position was second base but we had two second basemen who surpassed him. This led Gattis to position Jacoby at third. There Don suffered and did not improve. Since Gattis had been a third baseman himself, he brought personal passion into Jacoby's daily instructions.

They began easily enough. "Now, Donny, third base is basically a reflex position. You've got to react on reflex because there's no time to do anything else. It isn't like second. Are you with me?"

"Yeah, Skip," Jacoby said.

"But you have to think. The hitter. The pitch. The game situation. You should be moving, away from the line or toward it, and getting set, even before the batter swings.

Jacoby nodded vaguely.

"I was a good third baseman," Gattis said, "and I'm slow, probably because I've got a big ass."

"You sure do," said the Cobra. "You got a *huge* ass."

The men were standing on the grassy knoll outside the clubhouse, where groupies were beginning to gather after our games. "Whore Hill," some of the ball players called the knoll.

"Getting ready, reflex, not speed, is the important thing. Would you believe me if I told you some games when I played third, I'd get exhausted without a single ball ever being hit to me? That's how hard I worked at moving and getting set."

"I'd believe you, Skip," Jacoby said. He had a way, pleasant enough, of providing answers to rhetorical questions.

But in the Murnane infield, with its rippling base paths, things were not pleasant for the Cobra. Third base—and Gattis had studied the position as hard as anyone I've met—requires before anything else a kamikaze mentality.

Strong right-handed hitters whack hundred-mile-an-hour smashes at you from a distance as short as ninety feet. Line drives hammered at a third baseman look routine on television, which, aside from its miscellaneous faults and merits, compresses the game, dissolves dimension and slows the speed at which a baseball appears to move.

A line smash at third is not routine on a ball field, where only a quick glove stands between the fielder and an encounter with agony. Line drives hook and sink and sail in ominous and unpredictable ways. I once asked Billy Cox, the great Brooklyn infielder, if a line drive had ever hit him in the face. "No," Cox said, giving me a little smile, "but one skipped off my glove and caught my nuts."

Hard ground balls are even more trying. There is a droll baseball line about a third baseman who went down for a three-hopper and found himself stopping the baseball with his jaw. As he was carried off, someone remarked, "He played every bounce right except the last one."

The Murnane Field ground ball was a particularly dangerous breed. With our rippling infield and patchy grass, hops were as hard to predict as honest dice. Al Rosen, the fine old Cleveland Indian third baseman, who now runs the Houston Astros, visited us in June. After watching for a while he asked if Jacoby had a nickname.

"Cobra."

"Why is that?" Rosen said.

I was watching the game and made a mindless answer. "A cobra is a snake found in India, Al. More dangerous than a rattler."

Rosen patronized me with a look. "Well, that clears that up," he said. "But if your third baseman's nickname is Cobra, then you ought to nickname the baseball 'Mongoose.' "

                    *   *   *

Gattis would make Jacoby a third baseman. He *insisted* that he would, as surely as he insisted that he would have been a great ghetto teacher. Afternoons, at two o'clock, Gattis took a batting-practice bat, a taped-together batting-practice bat, and skimmed hard ground balls toward Jacoby. Then he shouted, "Down. Keep your head down. Keep your God damned head down. Oh, Christ, Jacoby, will you look that fucking ball into your glove."

Jacoby tried. He'd had to work as a short-order cook the previous winter and his batting skill encouraged him to think that he might make the major leagues. (Others there would have to short-order cook for *him.*)

But Donny could not do what Cox and Brooks Robinson and Graig Nettles did every afternoon of summer. He could not keep his head down and look the hopping baseball into his glove.

Gattis became frustrated and angry. One afternoon, while hitting grounders, he shouted at Jacoby, "Coward."

Absurdly harsh, I thought. Abuse is not a teaching tool. After a bit Gattis and I sat in the dugout.

"The lights are not great in the New York-Penn League, Jim, right?"

Gattis became watchful. "What are you getting at?"

"You've got a ball player, Jacoby, who stands in against ninety-mile-an-hour fast balls in bad light. He's hitting .397. When pitchers throw at his chin, he won't back off an inch. The guy can't make it at third base. So you shout at this ball player, who'll hit the roughest fast balls, you shout, 'Coward.' And maybe ten of his teammates hear what you shout."

"It's a complex fucking game," Gattis said. "You can be brave in one area and afraid somewhere else. You remind me of my brothers. They think they know the game. *I* know the game. That's why I'm managing. And I say Jacoby is a coward at third."

"So switch him and Eddie Wolfe," I said. "Wolfe

plays better third than Jacoby and Donny's okay at first base.''

"No," Gattis said. "I'm gonna make Jacoby a third baseman.''

Then he stood up. In a minute he was hitting more ground balls to third and repeating the word "coward" in a low angry way, hissing in his own cold version of Barry Moss as snake.

I'm gonna make Jacoby a third baseman.

My ball players were in Class A because they had not developed major league skills. In time they might. They had not yet.

Neither, I suppose, had my manager.

For a time our starting shortstop was a solemn stringy young Californian named Shawn Barton, who talked to himself in intricate ways. Waiting on deck to hit, Barton muttered, "You're gonna get your pitch. Nah, that curve was nowhere. Your pitch is coming. Here it comes. Give it a ride.'' He'd be kneeling as he spoke, very softly, so that from a distance you saw his lips move but heard no sound. Shawn sprinted on and off the field and, between innings, fielded imaginary grounders to his right or left. He was solitary, courteous, and a curiosity to the other ball players. They were sufficiently puzzled by his behavior to spare him needling for a while.

"This is how I always play," Barton told me. "I keep myself, you know, pumped up.'' He did not look you in the eyes when he spoke. "Little things, you know, and I don't bother anybody with what I do. Like after an inning, I run in hard because I like to be the first player to get to the dugout.'' It was a race he ran with swift determination against no rivals.

Gattis and I puzzled over Barton without solving him, this being Class A baseball first and group analysis only coincidentally. "But you got to wonder," Gattis said.

"All that funny muttering. Do you think, maybe, if it wasn't for baseball, Shawnie might be holding up banks?"

Whatever, Barton was a loner who never seemed lonely. He always had himself to talk to.

Larry Lee, the second baseman, was nicknamed "Francis" because of his vague resemblance to an erratic character in the Bill Murray movie *Stripes*. (Murray was the most famous of the minority shareholders in the Blue Sox, and the ball players wondered whether he would travel from Hollywood to observe them and review his modest investment. He never did.)

Actually Lee was the quiet, occasionally droll son of a college teacher in San Luis Obispo, California. Larry wore his black hair in the manner of Prince Valiant and had a look suggesting both intelligence and softness. Curiously, he made a few mental errors at unfortunate times, but when Gattis berated him, he showed no softness whatsoever. Attacked, our resident pageboy struck back like a dead-end kid.

Brian Robinson, the third of the Blue Sox good defensive infielders, grew up in Chicago where one of his brothers, Dewey Robinson, had played for the White Sox. Brian could perform well at second, third or shortstop, yet he had been overlooked in the annual major league draft of prospects despite a fine record at a small college in Louisiana, where he played ball and majored in computer sciences.

He batted from an extreme crouch and had trouble with strong right-handed pitching, but his over-all skills were promising, and he was young.

"Do I want to make the majors?" Brian remarked to me one night at the free beer bar. "Sure. Am I gonna? Well, I know a little bit about computers and possibilities and probabilities and if nobody drafted me my possibilities aren't all that great. Are they?"

"Work on your hitting," I said. "Work with Gattis. I

see you practicing in the field for hours, but you already have your skills there. The best way to practice is to work on weaker areas. I know it's fun to work on your strengths, but that's not a great use of your time.''

He listened and nodded and said no one had told him that before.

"If you work intelligently, you'll be a major league prospect.'' From time to time after that, I called him "Prospect'' Robinson.

Our starting outfield, one of our starting outfields, was the shortest you could find anywhere in professional baseball. Daryl Pitts, Ralph Sheffield and Rocky Coyle each claimed to stand five foot seven. The real height was closer to five foot five. They were all good ball players, but one reason we had them proceeded from an obvious rule of major league scouting. Scouts look for size.

Pitts, who had run into trouble recognizing Gattis' signs, was the one Blue Sox who was always broke. "That alimony, man, it eats you up,'' he said one day after borrowing lunch money from me in the men's room of a dreary roadside diner.

"How much alimony are you paying, Daryl?'' I said.

"Eighteen hundred a month.''

"I've paid alimony, Daryl. Gattis has paid alimony. How the hell can you pay $1,800 a month alimony when your salary is $500 a month?''

"You beginning to see the problem, man,'' Pitts said. "Got stuck big when I had a job as a truck loader. I was making more. We got a team lawyer can maybe go to the judge for me and explain?''

"Where's the judge?''

"Los Angeles.''

"Our team lawyer is in New York.''

"You see,'' Pitts said. "Everything's a problem.''

Sheffield was a smiling, stylish center fielder who had

minored in drama at Pepperdine and promised that he would give the team "my famous Richard Pryor imitation," when enough players pleaded to hear it. Sheffield worked that particular game—*I really want to be wanted*—so hard that when he finally began a Pryor act on a bus the other players shouted him down.

Sheff had small even features, a glistening style and, as Barry Moss reported to me after a long conversation, a sense that he was the second coming of Willie Mays. He was always running out from under his cap and snaring line drives with graceful dives. At this early-season point, at least, he was a pearl of undiluted charm.

On our first trip to Elmira, on June 26, we had a Sunday game, which we won 9–5, and then a Monday night game at what the Elmira Chamber of Commerce calls "Beautiful Dunn Field." That meant lodging for a night at the Howard Johnson Motel in an Elmira suburb called Horseheads.

After the day game, Sheffield sought me out in a group of ball players and said, "Hey, Prez. Can I borrow your Mercedes? I got to get me to a movie."

"Watch out for the hubcaps," said Robin Dreizler, a backup catcher.

I knew Sheffield didn't drink. It is an old Mercedes but a good one, and meaning to say "No!" I heard myself assenting with a low-voiced "I guess so."

"Oh, I can see it now," Dreizler said. "A cop pulls up and figures, Little Black Man, that's too much car for you. Then he says, 'Let me see your license and your registration.' Good-bye Ralph. Hello, slammer."

Sheff simply laughed and I gave him my keys.

"Did you want to do that?" Moss said.

"No," I said. "I want morale high, but there are limitations."

"I'll carry that message," Moss said. "I lent my Datsun

to somebody last year and he totaled it.'' Whatever Moss told the players, no one tried to borrow my car again.

We had promised the Howard Johnson Motel that next day we would be out of our rooms by 3 P.M. It was a cloudy, muggy, sleepy Monday in Horseheads, New York. No hordes milled in the motel lobby demanding beds. The 3 P.M. checkout time seemed academic, a formality that might well be observed in the breach.

Gattis' son Luke had arrived two days before and the manager took the four-year-old to see *Return of the Jedi*. "I think it's Luke's sixth time for that picture," he said. When Gattis and son had not returned by three, the motel manager let himself into Gattis' room and moved partially packed luggage onto the sidewalk.

Veale's wife Deane, a teacher from Birmingham, Alabama, was traveling with him. Bob felt, hell, what was there to do for the hours from 3 P.M. to 5 P.M.—between checkout and the start of practice. There was nothing to do, that was what. So the Veales chose to remain in their room. But I dutifully drove off at three, to sightsee Elmira. I had to be filled in afterward on everything that happened.

Jim Tompkins, the smooth and handsome right-handed pitcher from Austin, Texas, stepped out of his bathroom wearing only a jockstrap at five minutes after three and found a chambermaid gathering his belongings for an eviction. The woman did not seem displeased to have come upon a nearly naked young man. She gazed at Jimmy without comment.

"I'll be out in a minute," Tompkins said. "Stop moving my things. Don't touch my cowboy boots."

The woman said, "You're supposed to be out now." She threw Tompkins' boots toward the door.

Jim held up a can of underarm deodorant and aimed it at the chambermaid as though it were Mace. The woman fled. The hotel manager called the chief of police in Horseheads.

Another chambermaid told Mike Zamba, our combative union organizer, to get the hell out of his room. "I don't like rudeness," Zamba said, "and, ma'am, you're being rude."

The hotel manager himself, an officious bantam rooster with a tiny black mustache, let himself into the Veales' room and ordered them out.

Bob stood up. He denies that he acted in a threatening way, but sometimes, just standing made Big Bob seem threatening. Little blond Luke Gattis, going out of control, sprinted through the open door into the Veales' room.

"You see that little kid?" Veale asked the manager. "Well, he's my son, and I don't like you being rude to my wife and son."

The team had taken a stand. Hotel managers, the Elmira baseball team, nothing frightened us in those early season days when we outplayed every club we met. But by the time a Horseheads policeman arrived, everybody was packed and ready to leave.

"I don't see a police problem here," the cop told the motel manager.

"There isn't any," Gattis said. "We're the Utica Blue Sox, the best-behaved ball club in the New York-Penn League."

"Well, you better tell somebody else that," the motel manager said. "I'm never booking the Blue Sox into my motel again."

The cop said people might be getting mangled on the highways even as we bickered. He left. The team left. We reassembled in the third base grandstands at Beautiful Dunn Field, watching a storm collect its strength in the summer sky.

"You missed it," Gattis said, "You missed the fun. How can you put it in the book if you weren't there?"

"I guess you guys will have to tell me just what happened."

"We were evicted. No big deal, maybe, but we got evicted."

"Like in Stalingrad," Bob Veale said.

"Yeah," Gattis said. "That motel manager. We got evicted by the Hitler Youth." (I believe it was the Red Army, not *Hitler Jugend*, that did the evicting at Stalingrad. No matter. We were winners. Winners always get to rewrite history.)

Rocky Coyle, the third of our short, gifted outfielders, sprang up and began to run an imitation meeting of a football team at half time. He was also imitating a standard Jim Gattis motivational talk, but football offered a decent disguise. Rocky—that was his baptismal name—wanted to parody the manager without a confrontation.

"Now listen up," Coyle said. He started pacing in an aisle, both hands behind his back. The team, in full uniform, sat and slouched in the big empty ball park. "We're going to get them," Coyle barked. "We're going to go hard and we're gonna hit 'em high and we're not gonna be afraid to hit 'em low.

"Jacoby," Coyle shouted. The Cobra grinned and chewed tobacco and spat. "In the first half, man, you were a pussy out there. What are you anyway? A coward? You're twice as big as those guys and you won't suck it up and get 'em."

"Hendershot." Bob Hendershot, a quiet, powerful outfielder from Auburn, New York, had been another target of Gattis' anger. "You call yourself a quarterback. My Mom throws better than you. And she looks better than you do, too.

"You understand what I'm saying. You're not that great. You got to play with more intensity. You all go out there and bust your butts in the second half."

Coyle, a thick-armed, blond-mustached man, had been nicknamed "Mister Magoo," out of a supposed resemblance to the cartoon character. Here was Magoo, our road company Rockne, doing a creditable imitation of Gattis. I began to laugh.

"And Kahn," he shouted. "You call yourself an owner. Trouble at the motel and you're sightseeing Elmira. You call yourself an owner? I don't believe it."

"You better believe it, Rock," I said.

"Why?"

"Because otherwise I fine you fifty dollars."

The storm burst out of the sky and the Blue Sox headed back toward Utica.

Rocky Coyle was an Arizona native who suffered from (or thrived on) extremely intense religiosity. He was married and a father and somehow had found the means to bring his wife Debbie and his son Joshua to Utica. Although Coyle could call Jacoby "a pussy," he could not say "God damn." Coyle traveled with a Bible. I had a faint concern that he might reveal, with preaching, lamentation and exhortation, that he was an evangelical zealot. He was not. Rocky read Matthew and Mark and the Psalms without enlisting the rest of us to do the same.

But Gattis said excessively religious ball players bothered him. "I'll put it to you brief," he said. "They lose. Then they say, 'God meant for this to be.'"

Joanne looked refreshed in the trailer office next morning. With the team away, she had found time to have her dark blond hair coiffed and get her clothing back in order. She was an attractive young lady. I know worse ways to begin a day than to share coffee with Joanne.

"What did you *do* in Elmira?" Joanne said. "What did the team do? What did you *let* them do?"

"Nothing. We won one. The other was rained out."

"I got a call late last night and another call this morning from the man who manages the Howard Johnson Motel down there. He says some big black dude threatened him and shoved a finger in his face.''

"Well, let's see, JoJo. That might have been Bob Veale.''

"Figures.''

"Or it could have been Daryl Pitts, if he was standing on Ralph Sheffield's shoulders.''

Sheffield threw his batting helmet during the day game in Elmira. He threw it because he struck out, swinging too hard at a pitch below the knees. The helmet bounced in the dugout and struck Bob Veale on a hip. Veale flared—he wore eyeglasses and said he was damned if he was going to be blinded by a midget who couldn't tell a ball from a strike. Then he calmed and seemed annoyed with himself for having let so much emotion show.

The rain that began in Elmira continued the next day in Utica and the club—7 and 2 at this point—took on the bedraggled look of ball players in the rain.

"I don't want it to rain when we're winning,'' Gattis said. "You only want rain when you're going bad or you're out of pitchers.''

The players had gathered in the clubhouse and put on uniforms—they all enjoyed the act of getting into uniform—and sat around in small groups, gabbing and asking everyone if there was a report on when the rain might stop. I had Joanne call Griffiss Air Force Base, which regularly flew B-52s over Murnane Field. Each aircraft was armed with six nuclear-tipped cruise missiles. The planes were flying toward distant rendezvous points assigned them by the Strategic Air Command, somewhere between Utica and the Soviet Union. I resented the big bombers, which looked black against an early evening sky. At our little ball park, we wanted to win at baseball, and drink beer afterward and let the summer sing a song of peace. The planes were ominous. Intruders. Death machines.

Griffiss, near Rome, New York, fifteen miles west, stayed

in a continuous state of World War III alert. I never saw a
B-52 without thinking that Alissa, and the young ball
players as well, had a right to grow up, wander the world
and die, at a great age, in a comfortable bed. Still, Griffiss
had good weather information.

"What's the nuclear report?" I asked Joanne.

"A lot more rain," she said.

Back in the locker room, I relayed our news from the
Strategic Air Command. The players moved restlessly.
Abruptly Veale decided that it was time to make a speech.

I noticed that Jimmy Tompkins had draped a towel over
his head, under his Blue Sox cap, managing to look like a
ball player from Oman. Jacoby, Moss, Rocky Coyle and
all the others squirmed on the benches, rained into inactivity.

"You know you maybe think I was a pitcher and that's
all I know," Veale said, beginning so softly he was hard
to hear. "But I could swing a bat in my day and, besides,
I made a study of the game.

"That helmet shit, Sheffield. You strike out, the helmet
didn't do it. You did it. You got that anger, don't take it
out on a piece of equipment, and listen, midget, because
I'm gonna tell you something worth hearing, if you got
your ears open.

"You was goin' bad in Elmira. I guess you was maybe
0 for 4. But it ain't hard going up to the plate 0 for 4. You
already done your worst. You can only get better. Hard is
going up to the plate 3 for 4. You got something goin' you
want to sustain. You understand? Don't interrupt me, but
you can ask me questions later on.

"Remember this, Sheffield. You bust your helmet throwing it, it's the only one you got, with that funny head of
yours. Next time, you got to hit wearing a busted helmet.
You got no protection. Don't look to Doc [the trainer,
Danny Gazzilli]. He's only got aspirins. They ain't protection."

A few players laughed.

"That's the truth," Veale said. "We live on a damn shoestring budget and you got to remember that, before you throw a helmet or a bat. I mean, don't worry about that helmet getting busted when you're up hitting. Don't worry about cracking that bat when you swing. But we're on this damn shoestring budget, and we're all a team, so we all got to worry about not busting things too damn dumb.

"So we got this shoestring budget and nobody likes it, not even our president, so here is what I tell you. Change that shoe around. Put it on the other foot. Then make your mark."

The collected sayings of Chairman Veale, I thought. He had his personal syntax and his personal eloquence.

"You batters. You got to harness that energy. Just try to get one hit. First time you're up there, don't go thinking 4 for 4. Just think, Damn, man, I don't want to be 0 for 1. You do that every time you come to bat because every time is different from the one before. Goals. You guys are always talking about goals. Set yourself for each game to get yourself one hit and one walk. I guarantee, you're gonna hit .300.

"The name of the game ain't baseball. The name is winning. I don't care how you win and Jim don't care how and Roger don't care how. You pitchers, you want to go into the bathroom and come out and throw a shitball? That's okay, long as you can get away with it. Hell, Gaylord Perry, for years, he's been putting Vaseline and K-Y jelly [a vaginal lubricant] on the ball and making it dip and dance like crazy. No one cares, long as you win.

"And you will not always win, but at least you'll know that you been fighting. If you want to fight a big guy like me with your fists, you might not win. Hell, Willie Stargell will tell you I can uproot a tree with my bare hands. But if you fight me there's a couple of lessons in it. Like you'll learn never to fight nobody strong as me and I'll learn you're a competitor. I'm talkin' baseball to ya and I'm talkin' life.

"Another thing. You know I got this little black dog, Smokey, and Smokey, he just loves to run. If you guys can get yourselves to enjoy the running part of practice, like my dog Smokey does, you'll be a lot of damn fast sons of bitches.

"Remember, sayin', *'I can't,'* sayin', *'I tried,'* the two of them ain't worth shit. You got to *do* it. You got to get it done."

The players had left their benches to hear the major leaguer talk. Veale stooped a bit as he spoke into a semicircle, mostly looking beyond the Blue Sox, suggesting, perhaps, that his words were aimed beyond Class Single A baseball.

"I'll tell you pitchers something. You got a 5–1 lead and a big man comes to the plate. Don't be afraid to knock him on his ass. Hell, he's trying to rack your ass against the left-field wall.

"You want to throw hard on the outside part of the plate. That makes him foul them off. But then you got to come up and in with a pitch, when he starts leaning.

"There's one thing man don't like and that's called fear. You got to make that work for you. God gave every man, big as me, little as Sheffield, the same instinct and we call it fear.

"Outsmart 'em with a shitball and remind them of their fear. That's all I got to tell you guys in this fucking rain."

After I had performed some chores, I found Veale next in the trailer, talking to Alissa, who was assigned to answer the telephones that afternoon.

Gently and softly, this gigantic man was saying, "Liss, you've got to get yourself out of the ninth grade."

"I'm trying," Alissa said.

"Not good enough," Veale said. "Young lady, you're

intelligent and pretty, but if you don't get out of the ninth grade, all the rest of your life, the whole thing, is gonna be spent working in a Burger King, serving sandwiches. Life is a wheel. Did you ever hear that before?''

Alissa looked up, small pine to towering oak, and said in a tiny voice, ''Yes.''

''But it's a funny kind of wheel, Alissa. It only goes round once. In life you only get one turn. Get an education.''

''Yes, Bob.''

''Without an education it's Burger King.''

''Yes, Bob.''

''Now, young lady, I've got a question for you. Are we still friends?''

''Yes, Bob,'' Alissa said, still nodding. Then, her lesson done, she asked, ''Is it true you were Willie Stargell's best friend?''

Veale noticed me and grew embarrassed. He had been caught showing tenderness and concern. To cover himself, he offered a fast wink. He had his persona, his baseball toughness, to maintain.

''I pitched on the team that Willie played for,'' he told Alissa, ''along with a feller named Lamb and another feller named Bob Moose. Ask your Dad. He can tell you it's true. Veale and Lamb and Moose. The Pittsburgh Pirates. Strictly kosher meat.''

Baseball is a game of talk and meetings. Managers meet with teams. Catchers meet with pitchers. Pitchers meet with coaches. And then, completing the cycle, the manager meets with the team.

There is less idle chatter than people imagine, fewer surveys of pretty short-skirted blondes high in the grandstands. Particularly under a manager as serious as Jim Gattis, 1983, the meetings are business, like base hits.

What, for example, does the manager say to the relief pitcher during their conference on the mound when the reliever enters the game? I tried this question on two experienced sportswriters. Both fumbled and offered inanities. Neither knew.

The manager runs through a checklist. He asks the reliever what the count is. How many out? Are there base runners, and if so where are they located? First and second, or second and third?

Doesn't the professional relief pitcher know these things? Not always. He's been working in the bull pen, out of the game, trying to get more snap into his slider. Now he walks into a crisis and a good manager, like Gattis, makes certain that the pitcher knows just what he has walked into.

The sportswriters told me that the manager says, "Go get 'em." He well may. But first the manager makes sure, in the argot, that the pitcher's head, as well as the pitcher's arm, is in the game.

Baseball is nine men playing individually at the same time as they are playing as a team. It is not like football where two offensive linemen can determine whether a running back has a good day. It is not like basketball and hockey where most of the time everybody has to pass to everybody else. In those team sports, interdependence equates with survival, which is built into the rules of each game.

In baseball, the interdependence of players is less constant, more subtle, not ultimately revealed until we see the final score and analyze what happened. Of course, good fielders help a pitcher, and great pitching dominates a night. But an outfielder can enjoy a perfectly splendid game while a shortstop goes hitless and misses three ground balls. The shortstop may not immediately affect the outfielder's offshoot, victory or defeat, as the member of a team. Touching this point, repeating this point—team!—is one reason baseball managers talk as much as they do. That the job of managing seems to attract compulsive talkers is not notably relevant.

*   *   *

Pee Wee Reese, the Hall of Fame shortstop and chronic Brooklyn Dodger captain, once remarked that stories about "team spirit" struck him as naive. "The writers seem to like them. They *write* them often enough. But that isn't what really goes on."

"What does?" I said. I was twenty-three that afternoon, a good age for a Blue Sox player a generation later.

"We all want to make enough money," Reese said. Major league salaries then began at $7,500 a season. "We all know that the better we play the more money we can ask. And we all know that if we get into the World Series we're gonna get an extra check. That's what holds us together. 'Money spirit.' "

I blinked in surprise. Reese was described in the press as a model team player.

"You don't think that everybody on this ball club likes everybody else, do you?" Reese said. "Write this sometime. 'Money spirit' makes the Dodgers win."

A similar force played on the Utica Blue Sox. The athletes who drove themselves to fine individual seasons could double or triple their baseball salary for the following season. The better a Blue Sox hit in 1983, the more money he could expect (or hope) to make in 1984.

But though the force was similar, it was not identical. Reese's Dodgers were accomplished, veteran professionals with firmly established careers. The Sox, well as they were playing, remained mostly novices in professional baseball. The bulk of their experience had come in amateur ball, high school and college, where coaches preach team spirit as a first commandment. Fewer than five percent of school and college ball players will ever be offered pro contracts. *Win this one for Siwash, guys (and get yourself a good education).*

The Sox showed outstanding skills as they rolled over major league farm teams from upstate New York villages:

the Auburn Astros, the Batavia Trojans, the Geneva Cubs. But they were still very young men, a decade away from the suave, direct professionalism I found in Pee Wee Reese. Our daily meetings were aimed at molding them, toughening them, teaching them; in short, creating Reese's money spirit without drowning out the fervor that high school coaches had drummed into them. On one occasion we found unexpected help.

I was reviewing promotion ideas with Joanne in the trailer when Penny Lacey answered my telephone and said, "Are you in to a Mr. Al Rosen?"

I stopped the meeting and heard the president of the Houston Astros say, "I'm calling to ask if you want to swap jobs."

I knew Al first when he was a rugged third baseman for the Cleveland Indians in the early 1950s, a fierce competitive batter who one season knocked home 145 runs. He was not immensely gifted at third, but he taught himself and drove himself to excellence in the field. His life had led him down many windings—he bore the bleak ones bravely—and he had now emerged as a substantial and respected major league executive.

"What's the salary at Houston?" I said. (I suppose I was still thinking of Reese's money spirit.)

"Seriously," Al Rosen said, "I thought I might drop in on your little ball park."

The Auburn ball club was a Houston farm and Rosen wanted mostly to see his youngest prospects. But he also looked forward, as I did, to renewing a friendship of three decades.

"If you come to our ball park," I said, "you can throw out the first ball and we'll run a promotion called Al Rosen night."

"That will put three extra people in your grandstand," Rosen said.

"There is no grandstand at Murnane Field, Al. Only

bleachers. But I'll order some vodka and, listen, would you mind making a talk to our ball players?''

"I've quit drinking," Rosen said. "Haven't you noticed the drop in vodka company stock prices? I quit after I had a coronary bypass—*and* after I stopped working for George Steinbrenner.''

"Should I know who Al Rosen is?" asked black-haired earnest Penny Lacey.

I explained that he had been president of the New York Yankees four years earlier and, yes, it was a good idea for a young minor league official to know who has been running various major league clubs.

"I knew who he was," Joanne said. The women began to discuss a suitable promotion and settled for a baseball card idea. Anyone presenting an Al Rosen card at the gate would be admitted to Murnane Field for a dollar.

"I'll work up a promotional flier," Penny said. "Meet-greet Al Rosen in person." (Al was wrong. Five, not three, Rosen baseball cards turned up in Utica.)

He made our pregame meeting remarkable. I introduced him as a man who had played with great intensity, who battled hardest when it mattered most and who, incidentally, hit thirty-seven home runs as a rookie in the season of 1950, three years before the oldest Blue Sox regular was born.

Rosen wore jeans and a polo shirt. At the age of sixty he had regained his playing weight, a hundred and eighty pounds. He has a strong-featured, handsome face and executive-gray hair. The players sat on their benches and Al began to speak.

"I know some of you fellers think forty is old and fifty is positively ancient. But let me tell you this. The world is full of people forty, fifty, even sixty, who go around saying, '*If only* I'd given more to baseball I might have made the major leagues.'

"There's nothing sad about having white hair like me,

but what is sad is to become an *if only* person. Don't do it. Don't let that happen to you.

"Why am I telling you this? Because I know from personal experience that it's a hard life in the minors. You play every day and there never seems to be enough money to pay your bills. Listen. Long before I made the majors I lived in the minors.

"You fellers, every one of you, are doing the right thing. You're giving baseball a shot. You're young—that only happens once—and you're trying to see how far you can go in a wonderful, difficult profession.

"And what happens—you don't have to tell me—is that you have a bad day, a bad week, and you get discouraged.

"Let me tell you this. You want to fight through that discouragement. The first time I went to a tryout camp the manager told me, 'Son'—or did he say son of a bitch? —'you just better forget baseball. You're not good enough.'

"And I walked away feeling like I'd been stabbed. But I heard about another tryout camp, four hundred miles away. And I took what money I had and bought a bus ticket. I was a reject, but they signed me. That's why I was able to do the good things in the majors that you've heard about.

"So I'm gray and Roger's getting gray, so he's old enough to remember, but I'm not a gray *if only* person. When I started out, they paid me ninety dollars a month, but I went as hard as I knew how to go and it worked out and, gray-haired as I am, I'm proud of the major league years. Real proud. I'm just as proud of my minor league years as well.

"So forget *if only*. You're ball players. Professional ball players. Get out there on the field and do your best. Personally, I'm looking forward to watching you."

Utter silence preceded applause. It was the silence of awe.

We played the kind of game young people now call "hyper." Three of our pitchers had off nights. Gattis called more pitches than usual, flashed a blur of signs and charged at umpires.

"You better tell your manager," Rosen said, "that this is one ball game out of many, and he's going to get himself sick. Look at the cords sticking out on his neck." We sat watching in the Blue Sox presidential box, two folding chairs placed behind the home plate backstop.

Auburn jumped ahead by a run. We caught them. Auburn came back with two more. The game was rocking back and forth, out of control. We grabbed what looked like a safe lead in the seventh when Bob Hendershot and Barry Moss lined long home runs to right. But Auburn scored six runs in the bottom of the inning, pounding Roy Moretti and tying the score at 11–11.

In the eighth, Rocky Coyle was safe when Auburn's shortstop misplayed a grounder. With two out, Coyle stole second. Two men walked, loading the bases. Then Gattis signaled Coyle to steal home. Rocky made the dash. He was out by at least two yards.

"Give your skipper a big thanks from me," Rosen said. "I like to see overmanaging like that, as long as it's on the other side."

"It wasn't all that bad a play, Al. Besides, Gattis knows you're watching and he's trying to look like a genius."

"Your problem," Rosen said, looking smug.

Moretti moved easily through the Astros in the ninth.

Our turn. Larry Lee singled to right with one out. Sheffield forced him. Then Hendershot hit another long home run, over Murnane's beckoning right-field fence. Final score: Utica, 13; Auburn, 11.

"Damn," Rosen said, still and always the competitor. "Where the hell is our hospitality?"

"Hospitality has limits, Al," I said.

He nodded. "You know," he said, "except for tonight's score, I can enjoy this more than major league ball. The way the kids are so young and fresh. The way you get

so close to the game and to the fans.'' Rosen made his
way toward the Auburn bus, offering me a wave, a man
who lived each day fully and well and who would have to
say "if only" fewer times than almost anyone I knew.

A less formal meeting site than our stout brick clubhouse was the free beer bar we opened when the last fans
had trailed away into the Utica night. There were always
several kegs of Matts, a pleasant local beer, brewed in
handsome old red brick buildings on the west side of town.
And there were always willing hands to pull a spigot.

Gattis rationed his appearances. He would be close to
the players, he said, but not too close. The atmosphere at
our bar was relaxed and the cast typically mixed ball
players with boys from the grounds crew and people who
worked in the concession stands.

Moretti drank his beer quietly and usually waited for
people to come to him. He had even features, an assured
deep voice and large shoulders which he held straight
enough to please a marine colonel. He was good and he
knew that he was good. The star—and Roy was a star—
learns that he does not have to seek out others. Others will
seek him out. So Moretti drank quietly and if he had
pitched a good inning or two in relief he accepted congratulations with pleasing grace. Roy admitted to the age of
twenty-seven. He had been good in many minor leagues
for a long time.

John Seitz, our best starting pitcher, looked older than
his twenty-three years, probably because of his black mustache, but except for that he reminded one of the basic
good kid, raised on a farm, whom we have all seen in a
hundred potboiling movies. He'd come from a tidy farm-
house in Pennsylvania where his mother presided and painted
pictures.

"What kind of pictures?" Barry Moss asked, bringing
his California sophistication into play.

"Norman Rockwell kind," Seitz said. Then, defensively, "Is there something wrong with that?"

Barry extended strong hands. "No. Nothing at all. I was just asking, John."

"Well, they're pretty durn good," Seitz said.

When Seitz was ragged, the way all earnest people seem to be ragged in baseball, he sometimes could rag back, but every so often he would get so impatient that he lost the power of speech. "You'll never win the national fast talkers contest, John," Moss said with avuncular affection.

Little Falls, the Mets' farm team thirty miles east on the Barge Canal, was developing into our strongest rival for the championship of the Eastern Division of the twelve-team league. Gattis sent Seitz against them one early July night, and John breezed for four innings with his fine overhand curve. Then in the fifth Chris Maloney, the Mets' first baseman, singled and Corky Swindell lined a sharp single to left. One out later, Seitz, trying to keep Swindell close to the bag, carefully stepped off the pitching rubber and faked a throw to first base.

"Balk," bawled the umpire, Jake Falvey.

It was not a balk. Once a pitcher steps off the white rubber slab he can make just about any move he wants, so long as it is not obscene.

Gattis sprang from the dugout to protest. Seitz joined him. The call was not reversed. I have never seen a balk call reversed anywhere from Little Leagues to the majors.

Seitz kept his poise and we won, 5–3. Afterward a reporter from the Utica *Observer-Dispatch* asked Seitz about the balk.

"I stepped off," John said. "No professional pitcher would fake a throw to first if he had not taken his foot off the rubber."

This appeared in print as "No professional pitcher would *not* fake a throw to first if he had not taken his foot off the rubber."

"Look," Seitz said, at the bar, "that quote makes me sound ridiculous. I'm trying to keep a scrapbook on this year and now I'm stuck with a balk I didn't make and a quote that makes no sense. How could the reporter do that to me?"

"He didn't do anything to you. Or he didn't mean to. He put in an extra 'not.' It's an honest mistake."

"What's my mom going to think when she sees a quote like that?"

"I'll talk to the reporter, John, but sometimes, you know, newspapers have a hard time admitting mistakes."

"You don't have to tell me," Seitz said.

I sought out the writer and after a brief caucus on grammar he not only admitted he had erred, he ran a correction. Although I've been mildly misquoted in more famous newspapers, I've never gained for myself what I won for John: a correction on the grounds of clarity, accuracy and accepted English usage.

Probably the most assertive character around the free beer bar was Willie Finnegan, the fastest, wildest pitcher on the club. In our early rush, Seitz, Mike Zamba and a rather solemn right-hander from Tucson named Dan Roma established themselves as reliable starting pitchers. Jim Tompkins was a gritty middle relief man. Moretti was supreme at the end game. We had other pitchers, of course, and Wild Willie Finnegan ranked near the bottom. Veale, who had been wild in his own youth, viewed Willie as a reclamation project. I recalled pitchers who had spent a decade mastering control. And while we marveled at his speed, we didn't pitch him.

Since he wasn't allowed to pitch, Finnegan had to find a compensatory factor. It was his tongue.

"When I get in there," Willie would say over a Matts, "anybody leans in on me, you better keep those doctors ready at Faxton Hospital. I'll break his jaw."

Or "I got a heater [fast ball] and, under these lights, they ain't gonna see it. They'll be lucky if they hear it."

His voice remained pure New York, or that part of New York that used to be called Hell's Kitchen. He enjoyed talking tough and his take-no-prisoners chatter, night after night, might have unnerved Muammar el-Qaddafi. As the season developed, you could recognize it for what it was: bravado. The tougher he talked, Finnegan reasoned, the more likely he was to be told to start a game.

We relaxed together across a number of nights. He loved New York City, he said. His father, a retired vice-president of a large brewery, knew a great restaurant, Gallagher's, where you could find a few green grandstand seats preserved from the old Polo Grounds. We ought to go there, some night, Willie said, he, his Dad and I, and suck up a few brews and maybe even get hammered.

But as the free beer bar was a recreation area, the diamond at Murnane Field could be a rack. It was for Finny.

We were tied for first place with Little Falls on July 2, when Veale and Gattis, in cabal, decided to start Finnegan against the Mets at Murnane Field.

"You pick the pitchers," I said to the manager, "but if I were doing it, I'd use somebody else. Save Finny for a weaker team. Watertown."

Gattis looked distressed. "This can work," he said. "Anyway, Veale thinks it's a good idea."

Finnegan stood six foot two and weighed about one eighty-five, but three hours before game time the toughness slipped away. He began to smoke Marlboros at an emphysematous pace. "Days like this make it all worthwhile," he announced. He walked to his locker and placed his neatly folded uniform on the bench. "Never wash your socks or your stirrups before you pitch," he shouted. "Lets go, freakin' seven-thirty."

Barry Moss said, "Finny's worrying me a little. A pitcher shouldn't go out on the mound as if he were a boxer going into the ring. Control. Calm."

At seven-fifteen Finnegan began to warm up with one of our reserve catchers, Steve Sproesser. He threw harder and harder and the ball popped so loudly into Sproesser's mitt that fans wandered toward the bull-pen railing to see the fast balls.

Exertion reddened Finnegan's Irish face. "Hold it," Bob Veale said in his drill-instructor tone.

"Just two more pitches," Finnegan said.

"Hold it," Veale said, half an octave deeper.

"Okay." Finnegan put on his jacket and started toward the dugout. The beer bar jawbreaker was now going to have to dance a two-step with real life.

He walked the first batter, Stanley Jefferson, a prime Mets prospect. Jefferson stole second base. Finnegan filled the empty space by walking the second batter. By the time the half inning ended we were two runs behind.

Another walk in the second. A single. Jefferson hit a long home run to center field. We were down five. The Mets would win it, 8—2.

Gone by the third inning, Willie marched to the clubhouse and his cigarettes. "Friggin' Gattis," he said. "He made me throw pitchouts. I got trouble with control and he's making me pitch out." (It was, of course, Friggin' Gattis who had given him his start.)

"And my girl friend. She came up. She's a great girl and all, but that pisses me off. When I'm in the heat of battle, stay away."

He continued to mutter and rant. "I just wanted to beat those suckers for first place, but until I throw my breaking stuff for strikes, they're going to do what they did tonight.

"Damn. I stunk out the yard." He took his uniform off slowly, so slowly that he was able to finish two more Marlboros while he undressed. At the end of the game he reappeared at the beer bar. "He won't start again," Gattis was saying.

"If you don't start Finny again," Jimmy Tompkins said, "you're messing with his *life*. I'm glad I don't have to make that decision."

"We can spot him somewhere," Bob Veale said.

The losing pitcher sipped beside his girl, and beer restored bravado. I heard him tell her, "Nobody can stop the Finny Express."

But, to be sure, tomorrow morning would come and with it a slight headache for the Finny Express. Thinking of Willie, who was young but not so young as he had been before this failure, I mused that baseball in Utica, summer of '83, had found a way to pose a frightening question. How can you get older without getting more scared?

If I enjoyed my time at the Blue Sox free beer bar, and I almost always did, Alissa was enthralled. Baseball's hold on American males has been traced by many (including myself) to the relationship of fathers and sons. When you play catch with your father and perform reasonably well, you are striding away from the gardens of childhood and toward the world of men. Liss at sixteen, slim, intense, perceptive and pretty, underwent a kind of parallel experience in the sheer companionship of baseball.

Suddenly (to me) or at last (to her) she was away from schoolbooks, quixotic maternal dictates and other instances of what she perceived as childish drivel. She was *staff*, Blue Sox staff, and (almost) grown up. She felt compelled, in the manner of adolescence, to display maturity, which she did by smoking cigarettes, sipping at beer and trying as hard as she could to hold her poise.

Unlike the cliché athletes who tramp through the jumble of baseball exposés, bawling expletives that bloody the air and pawing waitresses, the Sox were, with one exception, mannerly, if sometimes teasing, with Alissa. More than that, they were protective. She was one of them.

One night one of the ground crew boys said "fuck."

"Watch it," Jimmy Tompkins ordered.

"What the fuck should I watch?"

Tompkins nodded toward Alissa, who was standing nearby, and said sternly, "Watch your language."

On another evening Gattis, seated on some wooden slats, invited Alissa to try his lap. She did, as decorously as she knew how.

"Better cut down on the hot dogs," Gattis said.

"What? I don't know what you mean, Jim."

"You feel a little heavy, Liss."

"I do? Oh, my God. I will cut down."

She complained quietly to John Seitz that there were twenty-five players on the team and no one had asked her for a date. "Will you go out with me?" Seitz said.

"Do you have a girl friend?"

"Back home. Yes, I do."

"Then I won't go out with you."

"All right," Seitz said, "but now you can't say you haven't been asked."

She worked hard selling programs, for the commission fixed by Joanne at five cents each. She was dismayed to discover that making significant money at this rate scale was impossible. And that dismay led her back to Bob Veale's persistent urging: "Alissa, you got to get yourself an education."

Roy Moretti, with whom I sometimes discussed the stresses of career and marriage, softly counseled her to limit her enthusiasm. "If you give your body to a ball player," Roy said, "you'll be in love and the ball player will be gone."

Such a comment from me, if I'd thought of it, might have triggered hot words. Alissa felt surfeited with fatherly counsel. But the remark coming from cool, handsome Roy

Moretti, the best pitcher in the New York-Penn League, so impressed Alissa that she repeated it to me many times. As well she might. It was, I thought, a wise and caring observation that did not wither in its repetition.

Our third meeting site, which we kept strictly stag, was the team bus.

We began with a school bus for short trips and a coach only for overnights, until we started to win. Then Tim Birnie relented and said we could always ride a coach when he had one available for the same price as a school bus. (Victory hath its privileges.) The difference was that the coach offered reclining seats, air conditioning and a toilet, the last a significant amenity when the team played particularly well and I bought the ball players a few cases of beer. We rolled back and forth to Auburn, site of that gray-walled maximum security prison, and Geneva, which offered Hobart College. Since we were defeating everybody, the rides were pleasant and, once we left the drab ribbon that is the thruway, reasonably scenic. Rolling country. Small farms. Metal-topped silos. Red barns.

Rocky Coyle, the outfielder nicknamed Mister Magoo, took to calling out the stars of each game and demanding applause. Rocky would order a golf clap (quiet), a tennis clap (louder) or a concert clap (rhythmic, in the manner of European audiences urging an encore). Eventually, someone ordered a Magoo clap for Rocky. To execute a Magoo clap, the hands come close together but miss. The applause is silent.

Gattis had a parlor trick that he played on many bus-ride nights. Place six beer cups on the floor. The manager had to look away during this process. Invert them and conceal a coin under one. Gattis would then turn, kneel, work his right hand back and forth over the inverted cups and invariably select the one hiding the coin. We suspected

Moss, or Joe Picchioni, our first-base coach, of flashing a signal.

"Naw," Gattis said. "It's a kind of magnetism from the coin toward my brain. You know I've got this metal plate in my skull. Metal seeks out metal."

Perfectly absurd. But we never caught a signal. And Gattis never missed.

Moss organized the most elaborate bus-ride merriment. Following Finnegan's Wake on July 2, the Sox worked their way back into first place and made the first extended trip, to Jamestown and Batavia in the western part of the state. When we swept Jamestown, a Montreal farm, we moved a game ahead of Little Falls. The bus trip to Batavia next day turned into a kangaroo court.

Moss structured the proceedings in his thorough way. Somewhere he found a black cape, which he gave to Dan Gazzilli, who was to preside as judge. He prepared a written list of charges. He appointed Robin Dreizler, our backup catcher, as clerk. Moss himself would run the prosecutions. Defense attorneys could be selected by defendants from the balance of the team. Or one could elect to defend himself.

Bailiff Rocky Coyle stood up as the bus rode north on Route 60, past summer-green farms and hills, and spoke into the driver's microphone.

"The Utica Blue Sox first kangaroo court"—there never was another—"will come to order. No talking. Judge Daniel Gazzilli presiding. All rise, please."

Everybody stood, and then sat down.

"The prosecuting attorney will now read the cases. Anyone accused must stand trial. He will be granted five minutes for himself or his defense counsel."

Moss rose. The bus rolled smoothly. It was not hard to keep your footing. He spoke in carefully austere tones.

"Case Number One. The Blue Sox vs. Shawn Barton

for wearing his stirrups as high as his knees and for continually talking to himself in a psychopathic manner.''

Laughter. Barton grinned and blushed.

''Case Number Two. The Blue Sox vs. Daryl Pitts and Larry Lee for wearing knee pads at their ankles during batting practice.

''Case Number Three. The Blue Sox vs. Ralph Sheffield for continually throwing equipment, notably after striking out, and for swearing at children alongside the first-base dugout.

''Case Number Four. The Blue Sox vs. the pitchers for not carrying the trainer's gear.

''Case Number Five will be the Blue Sox vs. Alissa Kahn, in absentia, a minor who must be represented by her father, for sipping beer and smoking a carton of cigarettes a day.

''Case Number Six is the Blue Sox vs. Michael Zalewski for not abiding by his contract with the court. The court has determined that, to be employed as traveling secretary and statistician, your physical body must be maintained within twenty years of your chronological age. The prosecution further charges, Mike, that your body is that of a sixty-five-year-old woman. It is also alleged that your body is hazardous to your health.''

''Wait a minute,'' Zalewski screamed.

''Silence,'' ordered Judge Gazzilli.

Unruffled and unsmiling, Moss proceeded. ''We cite a case from 1982, when Zulu, convicted on various charges, failed to complete his sentence of brushing his teeth for seven consecutive days. He brushed them once, that being after french-kissing his dog during a wet dream.'' Our prosecutor-designated-hitter sat down with just the smallest suggestion of a smile.

Shawn Barton engaged Wild Willie Finnegan as his mouthpiece. ''My client,'' Finnegan began, ''wears his stirrups high to show our fans that his sanis [white undersocks] are clean. I say that's good for the ball club. As for talking to himself, he's in better company than he would be talkin' to some other members of this club who I won't mention. The defense rests.''

Debate. Vote. Barton was acquitted. This prompted Pitts and Lee, next on the docket, to reengage Finnegan as counsel. Willie simply pointed out that knee pads at the ankle might not look tidy but they were protection against foul balls hit straight down. "There's no way," he said, "a fair-minded club like the Blue Sox can convict two good ball players for protecting themselves. What are you gonna do next, take away their cups?'' Another acquittal.

Sheffield insisted on defending himself. "I can either do that," he said, "or give you guys my famous Richard Pryor imitation.''

The Blue Sox hooted. Someone called, "Fuck Richard Pryor. You gonna set yourself on fire, Sheff?''

Ralph made a mistake. He grew contentious. "Now *you're* cursing," he said. "I didn't swear at little children. I was swearing at myself for striking out.''

"Little children heard your swear words," Moss said.

"They ought to be watching the game," Sheffield said. He was convicted quickly and sentenced to help the pitchers carry gear.

"You want a hundred-and-fifty-pound man to carry out two hundred pounds of bats?'' Sheffield said.

"Quiet," Gazzilli ordered, "or I'll cite you for contempt.''

Outside a tractor-trailer swept past us. Inside the bus everyone—except Joe Braun, the driver—had been transported to a fairy-tale kangaroo world.

Jimmy Tompkins, wearing mirrored sunglasses, strolled to the front of the bus and made an elaborate defense on behalf of the pitchers. "Every day," he said, "we have a starter and possibly four or five relievers. Now anyone who knows basic kinesiology recognizes that it can hurt an arm to extend it and carry heavy equipment. We have men here like Mike Zamba, John Seitz, Roy Moretti, who continually go out and pitch well. For our defense, then, we state: if we're carrying the team, why should we carry the equipment too?''

Ten pitchers stood up and applauded. All the position players jeered. Moss called on Joe Picchioni, who quickly penciled a pseudomedical sketch to show how lifting gear builds the triceps and the pectorals. ''Carrying equipment can increase fastball velocity five to maybe ten miles an hour,'' he concluded.

''Now,'' Moss said, ''on the issue of carrying the club, will Don Jacoby please rise? Ah, thank you, sir. How many hits did you get last night [in a 7-1 victory over Jamestown]?''

''Five,'' Jacoby said.

''In how many at bats, sir?''

''Five.''

''That's 5 for 5, Mr. Jacoby. Would you feel you carried the club?''

''I ain't gonna say that,'' Jacoby snapped. ''In your face, Moss.''

''I believe the answer to my question should have been yes and I ask the court to so record it. Jacoby carried the club last night. Others have on other nights.''

A long deliberation followed. Moss announced the decision. ''The pitchers are found guilty and hereby sentenced to carry all the equipment, and carry Ralph Sheffield, for the remainder of the trip.''

Moss cleared his throat and proceeded. ''We come now to the Blue Sox vs. Alissa Kahn, represented by her father, for sipping beer and smoking a carton of cigarettes a day. Will you kindly stand, Mr. Kahn?''

I stood.

''Remove your Blue Sox cap,'' Moss said. ''You are in court. You may proceed.''

I took the microphone. "I don't think any of you men has a daughter yet, but believe me, when you do she'll be a light of your life. When I first thought of bringing Alissa here, I was not concerned with smoking and drinking. I just knew she'd be around twenty-five horny bastards."

The players loosed a cresting wave of laughter.

"As a father I concentrated on the area of chastity. Now we have, at the mercy of the court, a redheaded sixteen-year-old girl."

"Sixteen?" shouted Brian Robinson. "She told me she was eighteen."

That broke up the bus (and the club president). When I recovered, I said, "I'm not going to burden you with denials. But think of her youth and remember these lines from the Bard: 'The quality of mercy is not strained/It droppeth as the gentle rain from heaven.' Not only myself but Shakespeare speaks for Alissa. If you can sentence her despite that, you have hearts of stone."

"Through?" Moss said.

"Yep."

Barry took the microphone and said, "William Shakespeare is not on trial here. Alissa Kahn is on trial." She was convicted and sentenced to go out with a young, ungainly batboy, a sentence she later reversed when she appealed and cut down her smoking.

The Zalewski case was resolved quickly. He was sentenced to sleep with Bob Veale's little black dog, Smokey, but not to molest the animal sexually.

Finnegan came forward. "Last night our manager, Jim Gattis, walked into the motel restaurant with his uniform on. At the beginning of the year he ordered all of us not to hang around the concession stands in uniform.

"What's good for the players is also good for the manager. I say we give Jimmy a stiff punishment."

The deliberations came alive with pleasure. The players could get back at their stern and volatile manager. Rocky

Coyle announced the sentence. "From now on Gattis cannot mention that game in Auburn [of June 24] which we lost 6-5, which we admit we should have won. He can't bring that ball game up for the balance of the season."

The bus pressed northward toward Batavia, site of a factory which manufactured a cloth guaranteed to clean your automobile as thoroughly as a car wash. Advertisements for this product began: "Does your car get *shameful* dirty?" That would be Batavia (and two more early victories) but, amid the laughter and the fellowship, we might as well have been rolling east toward Eden.

We did not lose many games we should have won. During that first month we didn't lose many games at all. Gattis continued to lecture on intensity each day. Considered in retrospect, his talks seem repetitious, but repetition is an accepted teaching tool. And he was teaching.

His forte was the art of batting and he worked constantly on weight shift, hand position and all the other technical details that comprise a successful swing. By mid-July eight Blue Sox were batting .300 or better. Don Jacoby was hitting .463.

Still Gattis was not satisfied. "Too many of our guys go up there," he said, "without looking for a specific pitch to hit. They hit, or not, but they don't learn. You ought to learn something each time you come to bat."

We then prepared forms for everyone to fill out after every game. You listed the pitcher's name for all your turns at the plate. Then you made written answers to written questions. Did you hit the ball hard? What was the count? What pitch were you looking for? What was the sequence of pitches leading up to the one you hit (or missed)? Some players grumbled that this was too much like school.

"This is Class A, damn it," Gattis said, "and they're *supposed* to be learning."

We won three of our first four, all against Watertown. We took two out of three from Auburn. We swept Elmira, swept everything but the Howard Johnson Motel. We swept the Geneva Cubs and the Batavia Trojans. I heard rumbles from general managers around the league. The Blue Sox, derided as castoffs as recently as opening day, were called a bunch of dangerous ringers. Older players. Overly experienced players. "You are disrupting the balance of the league." This came from an assistant general manager, young enough to be direct and indiscreet.

"Right," I told him. "We're nothing *but* ringers. And by the way, isn't this professional baseball?"

Seitz, who had been cut loose by the Atlanta Braves organization, won his first five starts. So did Mike Zamba, who had been released by a Pittsburgh affiliate. Moretti had played in three different farm systems and been released three times.

It was the resolute position of men employed by the big organizations that these athletes had been released because they were not major league prospects. The general managers and farm directors in the major leagues insist that the minors are "a developmental area." You don't play the best *athletes* you can find. You play the best *prospects*. You don't want first to win. You want first to develop talent. The Blue Sox, playing the best ball players we could sign and trying ferociously to win, were charged with disrupting the grand design of baseball. We were suspect—"fraudulent" in one major league official's term. We were out to win the pennant at all costs (just like the Dodgers).

It pleased me to refute these allegations. Actually, only a very small percentage of Class A baseball players ever reaches the major leagues. There is an occasional super prospect—Dwight Gooden at Little Falls in 1982—but a large number of New York-Penn League players were no more prospects than I. What were they, then? The baseball term is "roster-fillers."

Second—I grew to love these debates—some of the Blue Sox *were* real prospects. In releasing them the big organizations had made mistakes. Now their spokesmen could either whimper that we were playing ringers, or they could admit that mistakes had been made. I have yet to work with a big organization in which a front office man advances his career by admitting mistakes.

Finally, I would point out, if we kept playing as we had, wait for the rush after the season. Then the big organizations from Baltimore to Seattle would bump into one another attempting to buy the contracts of our best kids.

One day, when we were pummeling Watertown, I sat beside Pittsburgh's farm director, Branch Rickey III. "I'd like to talk to you for a book I'm going to write," I said.

"I'll be glad to talk to you," Rickey said, "but only with the understanding that you don't quote me in your book."

A high whirring sound assaulted my ears. Somewhere in the Midwest Rickey's grandfather, the first Branch Rickey, the *great* Branch Rickey, was spinning at high velocity in his coffin. For the old man's answer would have been somewhat different. "I'll talk to you, but only if you *promise* to quote me in your book."

We broke open games with Bob Hendershot, that quiet, bespectacled native of Auburn, New York. Bobby hit eight home runs in our first seventeen games. Fred Snyder, our public address announcer, celebrated each one at Murnane Field by announcing portentously: "That's a Hen-der-SHOT." We broke games open with line drives, pounded off the bats of Coyle and Moss and Jacoby. We played good defense, except for Jacoby's agonies at third. Ralph Sheffield, in center field, had perfected his gift for diving catches. ("Of course, he sometimes holds back a little,"

Moss reminded me, "to make sure he *has* to dive to catch it.") Whatever, Ralph looked like a stumpy version of Willie Mays.

Gattis worried that we were playing over our heads. I worried about Jacoby. "The trouble with putting a man at a position he doesn't field well, Jim, is that eventually, and you can bet me it'll be in a big game, he makes a bad play and it will cost us."

"You don't have to tell me," Gattis said. "I call that the ugly finder. The ball will always find the ugly fielder."

We won because the team and the manager were tuned always to stay on red alert. Caught in the sixth inning of a 2–2 tie game against Batavia late in June, we began to nibble at their starter, Steve Abrogast. Sheffield smacked a single to center. Hendershot walked. Moss cracked a single to right, scoring Sheffield and sending Hendershot to third. Rocky Coyle hit a short fly to left. Hendershot tagged and beat the throw home on a close and exciting play, banging hard into the catcher, Vince Martelli. Moss took second base on the throw home.

Pitching to Ed Wolfe, Abrogast concentrated on his waning fast ball and Moss stole third. Gattis, in the coaching box, told Barry, *sotto voce,* "Home is yours if you can get it."

On the next pitch Barry wandered down the line. Both Abrogast and Martelli ignored him.

"Either steal it or get picked off third," Gattis ordered. (He could talk quietly to Moss because the third baseman was playing Ed Wolfe very deep.) The failed steal of home had looked amateurish before the eyes of Al Rosen, but now Moss ran a textbook play. He began by walking toward home plate. Then, as Abrogast went into his windup, Barry, not the fastest of the Blue Sox, sprinted. He beat the pitch by two strides. He had stolen home.

Moss trotted into the dugout, fighting back a grin. Rocky

Coyle cried, "I'll never call you slow again." Then Coyle threw his arms in the air and bowed to Moss.

On July 20, at Veterans' Park in Little Falls, John Seitz pitched a powerful game, and homers by Moss and Jacoby had us tied 2–2 going into the ninth inning. Then a single by Moss, a walk to Coyle and Jacoby's looping single to center put us ahead by one run.

Seitz got two out. A Met outfielder named Jeff Dinkel grounded a single to center field. Gattis lifted Seitz for Moretti. The Mets batter was a lanky Canadian black named Andy Lawrence, who had played for me at Columbia, South Carolina. I used to ask him if he'd remembered to bring his ice skates.

Now, switched to Little Falls, Andy was the enemy. Intelligent. Fine athlete. Limited baseball experience. Good power. Gattis and I were afraid of a home run.

Moretti got the feel of the mound and Lawrence bounced a slow ground ball to Don Jacoby. *The ugly finder*. No. Not yet. The Cobra threw out Lawrence. Seitz's record was now 6 and 0. Our first-place lead had reached six games.

Veterans' Park at Little Falls, a mill town populated by the descendants of German and Dutch immigrants, was the acknowledged emerald of New York-Penn League ball fields. "If I ever saw a jewel, it's Little Falls," Vince McNamara, the league president, liked to say.

The entry walks were paths among rosebushes, tended by the older people of the village. The infield dirt, so-called New Jersey clay, was a reddish earth that blended beautifully with grass. And the grass itself was manicured like a historic lawn in Devonshire. There was neither a barren patch nor any sign of wear. Before batting practice could begin at Veterans' Park, the grounds keeper set down a large triangle of mesh in front of home plate. Sharp grounders would leave no mark with their first hop.

From the grandstand you saw an enormous green expanse, articulated with soft red earth and dabs of white—the foul lines and home plate. Beyond that, trees in leaf rose on a faraway ridge. "Believe me," said Tommy Holmes, a former National League batting champion who works for the New York Mets, "this playing surface is superior to the ones at Yankee Stadium and Shea. It's the best playing surface in New York State."

The next night, July 21, we started Zamba. Mike's arm was not as "live" as some. He attributed that to overwork imposed on him by a college coach but said he was getting stronger with each professional season. His forte was intelligent pitching. He knew how to move the ball from spot to spot, how to change speeds, how to keep a hitter from swinging in a groove and how to disrupt the hitter's timing. If Mike possessed Wild Willie Finnegan's fast ball, he would be working the major leagues today.

We scored a run first. Eddie Williams, an eighteen-year-old third baseman, who is a solid Mets prospect, tied the game with a home run in the second inning, polewhacked long and deep to left center field. It was a grinding kind of game, close and tense most of the way. Williams slammed out two more hits. Larry Lee homered for us in the seventh, hitting as long a drive as he would hit all season. Daryl Pitts, alimony slave and left fielder, homered for two runs in the top of the ninth.

When Zamba tired, we went to Moretti in the last half of the eighth inning. Roy got the last four outs in overpowering fashion. A pop fly. A tap to the mound. Two swinging strike-outs, including the formidable Ed Williams.

Both teams had played splendid baseball; there was a major league feel to this particular game. When the Blue Sox won it, 7–4, our lead over Little Falls reached an even seven games. Our winning percentage, .813, was the highest to be found anywhere in organized baseball.

As we rode back in a school bus and Rocky Coyle

called for various shadings of applause, we drank beer, joked and smirked. Jim Tompkins broke out his guitar and began to sing a country song. The scene about me was young, beautiful, alive. Hearts and voices moved to the joyous, tuneful singing.

Whatever Thomas Wolfe declaimed—and Dylan Thomas set down in his glorious tale of a Swansea park—I *was* going home again, to my own boyhood. In the dark bus happiness filled my eyes with unseen tears.

The cowboy pitcher crooned the words:

> "Goin' home,
> Goin' home
> To the place where I was born."

But time, which takes survey of all the world, can never stop.

The next day we collided with reality.

5

Dog-Day Nights

No one can really explain what happened next, but, quite simply, fortune turned. We had been both good and lucky in playing .800 baseball and now the team lost some of its competitive edge and some of its good luck all at once.

In a style of writing that was popular fifty years ago, one blamed such change of circumstance on angered gods. The hyperbole proceeds tortuously from Homer. Old newspaper morgues are full of musings about an angry Zeus hurling stout thunderbolts at the heads of athletes who have lost his lordly favor. Although Utica, to be sure, existed in a prior incarnation, I have difficulty with the interplay of ancient gods and modern baseball, largely because of some good early training imposed on me at the New York *Herald Tribune*.

An enthusiastic sports editor once asked me if I wanted to cover college football. "You have a chance," said Robert B. Cooke, who had learned his classics at Yale, "unless you call a football game a Battle of the Titans."

"What I really want to write is baseball," I said.

"You have to be careful there too," Cooke said. "I sent one reporter up to the Polo Grounds and it rained. The first two words of his story were 'Jupiter Pluvius.' He actually wrote that Jupiter made it rain on the Giants. After that I limited him to other sports. For example, interscholastic soccer.''

Such instructive encounters linger with a man, like school-boy baseball at Froebel Academy. Whatever the metaphysics of the Blue Sox situation, I can only report that a skilled and rugged Class A ball club, out front by seven games, subsequently proceeded to unravel.

Casey Stengel offered a characteristically cogent description of a slump. ''It's when the hitters ain't hittin','' he said, ''and the pitchers ain't pitchin' and the fielders ain't catchin' the ball.'' Always self-protective, Stengel did not add, ''And when the manager ain't managin' great, neither.''

We did not collapse like a game animal felled by an elephant gun, but little things and then larger things began to go wrong. Larry Lee neglected to dive for a grounder back of second base. The ball carried through and cost us an important run. Gattis tried Moss at first base and Barry made two errors in one game. Moretti, racked between a troubled marriage and baseball, went home to British Columbia for a critical spell. Jimmy Tompkins temporarily lost mastery of his best pitch, the knuckle curve. The knuckle curve drops sharply and has to be thrown low. High, it becomes a long home run.

Our hitters cooled in clutch situations. The horrible hops of Murnane Field began to bounce against us. Frustration gripped Gattis and after a while frustration gave way to simmering anger. Each loss seemed to make his personality more contentious, and we would lose a lot of games.

One night, after a bad one, he actually suffered chest pains on the team bus. Our regular trainer, Dan Gazzilli, was spending that week away from the Blue Sox, picking up extra money by working in a basketball camp. Gattis refused my offer to escort him to Faxton Hospital for a cardiogram but did bow to my demand that he let the assistant trainer take his blood pressure. The assistant reported 120 over 72, which sounded fine, although I was not certain whether the assistant had ever before taken a blood pressure reading.

We had to play a number of games in light rainfall and half the players started to cough and sneeze. We were losing and our collective health was questionable. "They need shots of vitamin B12," Gattis told me. "You have to authorize it."

"B12 doesn't help with colds," I said. "You're talking about vitamin C."

Gattis was too agitated to pay attention. "I've been in the game for years," he said. "B12 is what ball players have to have. And me too."

I told Gazzilli to find the neediest physician in Utica and to negotiate for a group rate. Danny came back with a price quote of $2.17 a shot. The physician administered the injections. I paid him. Everyone continued to cough and sneeze.

As I remarked to James Kunen, a writer who visited the ball club on assignment from *People* magazine, the playing field is baseball's equivalent of a stage and the Blue Sox, moving from town to town by bus, struck me as a contemporary equivalent of an Elizabethan band of roving players. A difference, of course, is that our athletes had to work each night without a script.

Kunen, who wrote a fine book about student protests in the 1960s called *The Strawberry Statement*, was honing in on me with questions about my wife, from whom I was legally and affectionately separated. There was nothing at all to say about this, except what we chose to say to one another, and I used the Elizabethan gambit, not only because I believed it. The comments also seemed like a good diversionary action, away from questions that would make

one aspect of my private life more public than I cared to
have it.

Whatever, the stage that is the ball field, a domain that
the Blue Sox had ruled, now became a chancy place. This
affected everyone. The field is only one aspect of the
baseball scene, but it is the aspect under glaring lights, the
arena that gives everything else a sense of meaning. Take
away the games and, clearly, there would be no point to
clubhouse meetings, no fans to lure with special promotions, nor would there be that wonderful, barbed interplay
among the personalities that make up the team.

By all the history and logic of baseball we were too hot
not to cool down. Teams simply do not play .800 ball
across a season. The 1927 Yankees, with Gehrig and Ruth
in their primes, played at a .714 pace. The 1953 Dodgers,
who had a pennant secured by Labor Day, played .639.
The 1954 Cleveland Indians, who won 111 games, played
.721. Nobody maintains .800. But we were an emotional
bunch in Utica and neither history nor logic tranquilized us
when we were beaten.

What made our descent to normality even more taxing
for Gattis and the players was that when we were going
well our on-field skills and fortune fused into a giddy
dream of glory. We had at least three more remarkable and
(to us) hilarious nights of triumph before the bad times
gripped us with a cold hand.

On July 14, when patriots paraded in the villages of
France, the Erie Cardinals rode into Utica. Their president
and general manager, Paul Mangiardi, suggested that we
meet for a kind of executive drink. He was a stocky,
black-haired, blustery man who had been an army sergeant
for twenty years. He had put his life savings into the Erie
franchise, he said, and then asked abruptly if I put up with
"crappola" from my manager.

"Sometimes, Paul."

"Take nothing," Mangiardi said. "We've got to keep reminding these God damned managers that they work for us, not the other way."

Actually, the Erie manager, Joe Rigoli, worked for the St. Louis Cardinals organization. I let that go. "The managers have to run the games, Paul, every day or every night. It's steady pressure. You've got to grant them a little artistic temperament."

"I give 'em God damned nothing. He's always bucking me for better hotels, like I was as rich as you. . . ."

"I'm not rich. Nobody's rich in Single A."

"So I tell him, 'You better ease off, Rigoli, or you know that order for four dozen new bats? I'm gonna delay my payment and you can send 'em up to hit with toothpicks.' "

The bar I had picked was called The Fingerbullet, named for a local drink I never dared sample. Two women in jeans were playing pool. Mangiardi checked blue flanks as one of the women leaned forward to make a shot.

"Welcome to Utica," I said.

"You let a manager push you around," Mangiardi said, returning to baseball, "and you're dead."

At length I seated him in the Al Rosen box, the folding chair next to mine behind home plate. We moved ahead by two runs in the first inning. The second inning was as exciting to me as it was painful to my new Pennsylvania friend and colleague, Paul Mangiardi.

With one out, Mark Krynitsky singled through the left side. John Costello, Erie's starter, threw a high fast ball to Sheffield, who lined it hard into left center field. Both left fielder Tom Rossi and center fielder Mike Robinson had a chance to catch the ball, but they bumped into one another and dropped in pain. Sheffield kept running. Robinson finally got up and retrieved the baseball and the relay home made for a close play. Sheffield, small, but muscular and combative, dove into the Erie catcher. After a jarring collision, the umpire called him safe. The score was 4–0, on our first inside-the-park home run.

"Shit," Mangiardi said. I spotted Rocco Gerace and had him bring Mangiardi a free beer.

Daryl (Alimony) Pitts cracked a curve ball at Costello, who caught the ball defensively on one hop and threw out Pitts at first. Then Costello threw a fast ball that crashed against Barry Moss's batting helmet.

Barry dropped, face down, and lay still for perhaps five seconds. Then he puffed air through his cheeks, shook his head, rose and trotted to first base.

"'Attaway," Mangiardi shouted, waving his beer. "'Attaway to play the game."

Baseball contains elements of intimidation, but it is also a sport with traditions and acceptable limits. When a pitcher is getting pounded as hard as the Blue Sox were hitting Costello, he can traditionally (and within a loose interpretation of the rules) throw a brush-back pitch. That is, a fast ball literally hurled at the batter's face. Unless the batter freezes, no damage is done. The hitter ducks, avoiding the baseball, but he gets to hear its nasty, buzzing whine as it blurs past him at ninety miles an hour.

But Costello, in his frustration, had exceeded the accepted limit. He threw the baseball behind Moss's neck. That is a classic beanball and truly dangerous. By reflex, the batter ducks down and backward—into the path of a pitch that is thrown behind him.

I didn't think this was any way to play the game and, when Coyle walloped Costello's next pitch over the right-field wall, I stood up and cheered. Mangiardi cursed again and threw his half-full beer cup over his right shoulder.

One of our stockholders appeared behind me and asked for "a few words in private." We walked away from the Rosen box. "You ought to bar that son of a bitch, Mangiardi, from the park," the man said. "He deliberately threw beer at our fans. Call a cop and kick him out."

"Come on," I said. "We're taking Erie apart. And actually he threw the beer at a patch of grass."

"Bar him. He definitely ought to be barred."

"I'm not about to start barring the presidents of visiting teams," I said, "particularly when we're winning."

The man shook his head in impatience and walked away. We scored nine runs before the inning ended. We won the game, 22–7. By not expelling Mangiardi, I avoided an incident that might have carried into the league office and I got to watch him suffer through our entire 24-hit attack. Just punishment, I thought, for tossing a beer and cheering a beanball thrown into the helmet of my rugged, upper-middle-class road roommate, Barry Moss.

Even my own mistakes were going unpunished. On July 19, Ed Wolfe's twenty-third birthday, I remembered a ball park birthday celebration decades earlier and tried to duplicate it at Murnane Field. New electrical technology almost did me in.

When Pee Wee Reese's thirty-sixth birthday fell during a Dodger home stand in 1954, an energetic promotion man named Irving Rudd arranged for a pause in a game that sentimental Brooklynites still remember. The lights at Ebbets Field were turned off. The public address man asked every fan to light a match. Then, in flickering darkness, the crowd sang "Happy Birthday' to the shortstop. It was a warm and pleasant summer interlude.

What worked in Ebbets Field, I reasoned, ought to work on a smaller scale at Murnane. I brought up the idea to Joanne, Penny Lacey and Rocco Gerace and everyone agreed that the scheme I had purloined from Irving Rudd was a good one.

The game against Auburn that night went well. Rocky Coyle hit two home runs. Don Jacoby hit another. When Rocco Gerace turned out the lights before the home half of the seventh inning, we were leading, 7–2.

The crowd sat quietly in a faint moonglow. Fred Snyder, the public address man, recited the drill. The fans lit matches and sang "Happy Birthday" to Ed Wolfe in a variety of keys. I was sitting back feeling pleased when Rocco, whose title was director of stadium operations, rushed toward me in the dark. "The lights won't come back on," he said.

"Throw the switch."

"It's not that," Rocco said. He was breathless with alarm. "These aren't like lights at home. They're not bulbs. They're vapor lamps. They won't come back on until they've cooled down"

"How long will that take?"

Rocco didn't know.

Jake Falvey, the plate umpire, started toward our dugout. I could see him because a few old-fashioned incandescent bulbs remained among the newer vapor lights. These went back on immediately, like the old lights at Ebbets Field. It was bright enough for me to see that the umpire looked angry, but not nearly bright enough to resume the game.

I hurried toward the dugout. Gattis shot me a glance of equal parts pain and fury. "This," announced umpire Jake Falvey, "is horseshit."

"You may not direct obscenity," I said to umpire Jake, "at the president of a ball club in this league."

"It's still horseshit," Falvey said, shaking a finger at my chest.

Actually "horseshit" is a rather mild term by ball field standards. It didn't bother me. What bothered me was that I had made a mistake and what bothered me more was the possibility that Falvey might award the game to Auburn on a forfeit. There was no specific league rule to cover the situation, since no home club before had ever deliberately darkened its own field. But the discretionary powers of an

umpire are enormous. Forfeit was a clear and present
danger.

Bob Hartsfield, a big-bellied Georgia redneck who managed Auburn, joined our contesting group, standing in
half-light near the Blue Sox dugout. "This is fucking
bush-league," Hartsfield began. "This birthday shit doesn't
belong in a fucking game."

I told him he was right and that I was wrong. Where
were Reese and Irving Rudd? I wondered wildly. Why was
I at Murnane, not Ebbets Field? The crowd was beginning
to make mutinous noises. I had Snyder announce that the
price of a beer was being reduced by one third, to fifty
cents, until the lights came back on, "a matter of moments."

We milled and gabbed. Fans charged the beer stand. A
ball park cop told me that it would be hard to control
1,500 drunks in semidarkness. I knew that, but I could
only focus on one nightmare at a time. The forfeit dominated my thoughts.

After seventeen wretchedly long, paranoiac minutes, the
vapor lights glowed back to brightness. As soon as the
Auburn starter, Chuck Mathews, threw his next pitch, I
hurried to my office and poured a scotch. Under New
York-Penn League rules, a protest must be announced
immediately after the incident at issue and before another
pitch is thrown. I was safe from forfeit, if not from
embarrassment. Jacoby hit another home run and we won
the ball game, 9–2.

I celebrated with a staff meeting, during which I spoke
to Joanne, Rocco and Penny about knowing every aspect
of Murnane Field and keeping me informed of potential
problems. I used stronger language than Falvey had used
to me.

Then I trudged to Gattis' office in the clubhouse. Some
of the players sent me sideways, questioning looks. "Damn
it, Jim," I said, "I'm sorry."

He put a broad hand on my shoulder. "Hey," he said.

"You weren't trying to mess up. It happens. You see me manage. You know I mess up some games myself."

The response touched me. "If there's anything I can do to make your job easier," I said, "then let me know."

"Okay," Gattis said. "Get me a car."

On our good days, mistakes went unpunished and free automobiles fell, so to speak, like golden apples from the sun. Someone talked to Carbone Pontiac-Honda and within three days a little blue Japanese car appeared for Gattis, with Utica Blue Sox stenciled on one side. All we had to offer Carbone was a free fence sign advertising his dealership. Since we had more fence space than signs, it was a good deal for both sides. The car delighted Gattis, although before the season ended its encounter with a telephone pole on Genesee Street would provide some stress and merriment during one of our immoderate nights.

On July 20, with Ed Wolfe now twenty-three and our lead holding at six games, we went to play at Little Falls. Like so many of our duels with the Mets' farm club, this one developed into a contest with major league style. John Seitz, who started for us, handled the Mets well until Chris Maloney came up to hit with two out in the fourth inning.

Veterans' Park, Vince McNamara's jewel, was ringed with a low outfield fence, over which a variety of signs was draped. Beyond the fence, in left center—a good ten feet past the fence—rose a tan and yellow sign advertising Little Falls' Best Western Motel. Maloney cracked a long high drive that carried over the outfield fence and smacked resoundingly against the motel sign. Home run.

The ball was hit so hard that it caromed off the sign and bounced back into the playing area. Our man Moss, assigned to left, did not hesitate. He threw the ball in to third base. Maloney, who had hit a home run, stopped at second.

The umpires, Mike Niemiec behind the plate and Jake

Falvey on the bases, conferred. On a bases-empty home run, the plate umpire is to determine whether the ball has cleared the fence, while his partner watches the batter to make sure he touches every base. It was a clear evening, no fog, good visibility. Incredibly they agreed that Maloney had to stay at second.

In the box next to me a Little Falls stockholder, a genial man who wore checked shirts and looked like a farmer, began jumping up and down. "Robbers," he shouted. "What are you? Blind?"

Mike Cubbage, the Little Falls manager, charged the umpires. They let him bellow and turned away.

"Robbers," shouted the farmer. "Blind, dumb robbers."

I fought back a grin. So did our ball players. The next Met batter lined out to Daryl Pitts in center.

That was the bottom of the fourth. In the top of the fifth Don Jacoby led off by duplicating Chris Maloney's smash. He hit a high drive against the Best Western sign, a good 390 feet from home. But Cobra did not hit the ball quite as hard. His carom dropped outside the left-field fence. Home run. Jacoby trotted around the bases, *all* the bases.

The crowd, 701, mostly Little Falls enthusiasts, went apoplectic. People cursed the umpires. Someone screamed at Gattis, coaching third, that he was the luckiest son of a bitch in the whole damn Mohawk Valley. Usually Jim wore a chilly, angry visage during games. Now he turned around and grinned at the furious faces. "Hey," he shouted, "I don't make the calls. I just manage." He held the grin, further enraging the spectators.

The final score was Utica, 3; Little Falls, 2. Had the umpire called Maloney's home run correctly, the teams might have played for twenty innings.

The odds on professional umpires ruling that a home run is a double are reasonably long. The odds on two out of three batters hitting the same sign 390 feet from home plate are somewhat longer. The odds on the umpires call-

ing one drive a double and the other a home run exceed
what I know how to calculate.

If it hadn't been for all that intense *Herald Tribune*
training, I would have told myself that Jupiter smiled on
the Blue Sox.

A portent that things would turn against us appeared on
July 22 in the Utica *Observer-Dispatch* in the form of a
critical editorial. We had good coverage—we *earned* good
coverage—on the sports page and sometimes the front page,
which seemed reasonable. We were giving Utica its only
first-place ball club in a generation. But editorial writers
appear to be a carping breed, at least in Utica.

"At the baseball game the other night," the editorial
began, "a stunt which backfired left the field dark for
fifteen minutes. The Utica Blue Sox moved to placate the
fans by announcing that beer would be sold at reduced
prices.

"As some fans rushed for the beer truck, one woman,
sitting in the dark, asked her neighbor, 'When are they
going to do something for the soda drinkers?' "

The piece continued in its grumbling way. "It's not a
wise policy to reward fans who like intoxicating drink
while neglecting those who prefer a soda with their hot
dog. A Coke or Pepsi promotion would probably cost less
because the cups are two-thirds ice anyway."

Cheap beer attracts people to a ball park. Cheap Coke
and cut-rate chocolate milk do not. If the *Observer-Dispatch*
was going to run any editorial, I thought, it should have
included paragraphs of praise. Our players had run Little
League clinics without charge. We regularly admitted hand-
icapped and retarded people free. And when the editorial
writers finally notice us, what do they decree? Cut your
prices for soda.

"We don't want to confuse the papers," I told Joanne

in early afternoon. "I'm running the ball club. They're not. No cheap soda night under any circumstances."

"You're too late," Joanne said. "I scheduled a cheap soda night as soon as I saw the editorial. We've called the papers with the announcement."

If we let the papers dictate to us on one point, they might proceed to dictate to us on a dozen more. Editorial writers are marvelous at lecturing others on the virtues of self-improvement. "It's like church and state, Joanne," I said. "You have to keep the newspaper and the ball club separate."

Joanne nodded glumly. She had only been trying to please.

My mood was somewhat down because I had been pressed into releasing a sensitive young left-hander named Dominic Perrino. Gattis was worried about our pitching—no team ever has enough good pitching—and Perrino, likable and artistic, wasn't winning. (Eventually we would replace him with a right-hander named James Wright, who had been dropped by the Phillies organization. Wright would play an important last-act role with Utica.)

Gattis insisted that I execute Perrino's release form. I suggested that in view of our over-all record we might stay with him a little longer. Gattis turned away shaking his head. Perrino had to go. His earned run average was 9.17.

I later found Perrino leaning on the popcorn stand after the manager had brought him the heavy news. "It's all right," he said in a wan voice. "There's other stuff in life besides baseball. I sorta figured this was coming anyway."

Alissa, who was popping corn, made her debut as a baseball authority. "It's not fair," she said, "just because you had a slow start, Dom. You deserve a few more chances."

Perrino thanked her. He took pen and pad and sketched a cartoon of a cow whose udder had become impaled on a barbed wire fence that the cow was trying to cross. Perrino's caption read: "So you think you've got troubles." He gave the sketch to Alissa as a keepsake.

That night we made six errors, including two by Moss and two by Shawn Barton at shortstop, and handed a ball game to Oneonta's shaky Yankees, 6–1. Gattis railed at the players. "When you come to Murnane you have a job to do. Ask yourselves what kind of a job you did tonight. There're thousands of pretty good ball players who'd like to be where you guys are and you know—one of the players found this out today—the ticket that got you here also works the other way. You've got to avoid these bad games or there're going to be more changes."

The players sat silent until he was finished. Perrino's release had left them sorry, angry and threatened. When one ball player is released, a bell tolls for everyone on the team.

The next night Oneonta defeated us, 8–2, and Gattis showed signs of real alarm. Oneonta was a paradoxical sort of club, all those Yankee-style uniforms suggesting DiMaggio and Mantle and the team's usual inept play suggesting high school baseball. "This is horrendous," Gattis told me afterward, "losing two games to a team as bad as that. Our lead was seven. Now it's five. Little Falls, on sheer talent, is better than us, with all those bonus kids that the Mets are signing. We got the lead on our intensity and then a lousy team like Oneonta comes and we're asleep and lose two and Oneonta is gone. That's it. They're gone. We can never get those two back. I'm worried and, if you're not worried, you oughta be." Then Gattis repeated a refrain: "When this team loses three in a row, we'll find out whether or not they have character."

I was more annoyed than concerned after the two losses and somewhat surprised by Gattis' hard-eyed reaction. Generally a manager can respond in one of three ways when a team slumps, or, as in our case, shows signs of entering a slump. He can take a laissez-faire approach and assume that his players are professionals and read the box scores. They know they are beginning to lose. Hope that the team leaders—Moretti, Coyle, Krynitsky—will talk with other players and arrange a players-only meeting to work through what's been going wrong. This requires either a manager who feels great confidence in himself and in the maturity of his athletes or a manager who is lazy. Jim Gattis was insecure and a workaholic.

Alternatively, the manager can help a team relax. In St. Louis long ago the late Charlie Dressen, stymied by a Dodger slump, ordered cases of whiskey delivered to his team's clubhouse. "When I keep a curfew on you guys, you don't win," he said. "When I keep you off the booze, you just screw up. So here it is. There's plenty for everybody to drink. Tie one on tonight and beat the Cardinals' brains out tomorrow." This worked halfway. A number of Dodgers followed Dressen's direction and got themselves drunk. But the next day they lost to the Cardinals again. Wet or dry, the team stayed slumping for a week.

Finally, the manager can try to lash his team back to form with angry speeches questioning their sense of purpose, their courage and their manhood. This was the style of Leo Durocher, Billy Martin and Jim Gattis.

Carl Lundquist, a former newspaperman and minor league executive, had sent me a green-bound pamphlet called *Seventy Nights in a Ball Park*, "An All-New Promotion Guide for Baseball." In Lundquist's work you find detailed specific accounts of how to run Barbershop Quartet Night, Antique Car Night, Nationality Night (special prices for fans of Hungarian extraction), Service Station Night, Dry Cleaner Night and sixty-four other special events. I was, so to speak, keeping one eye on the field and the other on our gate receipts. We were drawing roughly 1,100 a game, which was disappointing for a first-place team in a city as large at Utica. We would have to promote and promote as, before Oneonta, we had won and won. Two of Lundquist's hustling schemes caught my attention.

On Player Talent Night the ball players are invited to sing, do rope tricks, show off whatever skills they have. Fans judge their efforts by applause. The winning ball player gets a prize of fifty dollars. Then there was Pick-a-Queen Night. Round up a collection of pretty girls and let the players vote. The girl with the most votes and most alluring bottom would be crowned Miss Utica Blue Sox. (After we announced the promotions, Bob Hartsfield, the redneck manager of Auburn, said, "You gonna have a beauty contest in Utica? Then I can tell you this. Nobody's gonna win.")

Talent Night was scheduled after the Oneonta debacle and just before a game with Jamestown. Five players and Bob Veale had entered. "Damn," Gattis said, "I wish you'd call the thing off. Now you'll have them thinking about their talents, whatever they are, and I want them thinking about baseball." He was so tense anything could have set him off, and he called a team meeting in the red brick clubhouse.

"I don't want any talent contest getting in the way of our game," he informed the players. "Some of you guys have been practicing your acts. Forget it. Get ready to play ball.

"Now listen up. I don't want to be associated with a team that doesn't put out any more effort than you guys did against Oneonta. Am I being clear? If you guys don't put out, you're gonna get those tickets home and we'll get another group in here that *wants* to play baseball every day.

"Anybody want to say anything? Is anybody feeling anything I ought to know about?

"No? Well, listen good. The heat is on you guys and they're saying Oneonta, lousy Oneonta, just kicked Utica's

ass two games in a row. You're gonna fall apart. That's
what the whole league is saying.

"All right. Go out there and show 'em that what they're
saying is total bullshit."

The first result of this meeting was that Ralph Sheffield,
who was continually promising to perform a Richard Pryor
imitation, withdrew from the talent contest. "Bullshit?"
Sheffield said. "Total bullshit is a meeting like that. We
lose a couple and he rags us. We win five and he rags us.
I'm not doing Richard Pryor for him."

Even Barry Moss was upset. "For God's sakes," he
said, "we just lost a couple of games. That's all that's
happened. We weren't going to play .800 ball all year. We
had bad games. I had a terrible game. But there's the
human factor in all of this and Jim . . . hell, I'm talking
too much." Barry forced a smile. "I'm a coach and Jim is
just the way Jim is. But sometimes he wants to win so
much he hurts himself."

I walked outside. It had begun to drizzle. I found Gattis
sitting by himself in the dugout. "Let me try something on
you," I said.

"You're gonna tell me the players are sore at me," he
said. "I know that. I don't care about that, long as they
win."

"You just threatened to move everybody out. Sure they're
sore. But that's not the point I want to make. You ought to
get more player participation in the meetings."

"Damn right," Gattis said. "What wouldn't I give for
that? But this bunch, even when I ask questions, they just
sit and shuffle their spikes." He brightened. "But, hey, I
got an idea to *make* them participate. I'm gonna ask 'em all
to vote on which ball players bring the most intensity to
the games. Written ballot. Secret ballot. And then I'll
announce the results. How's that?"

"Good idea."

"It's a lot better than your damn talent contest," Gattis

said and marched away, accompanied by his own free-floating anger.

The anger was wasted that evening, for the drizzle turned to rain and the talent contest, like the game with Jamestown, had to be postponed.

The pressure Gattis felt was increasing the way the pain of a toothache increases, simply by persisting day after day. The amiable character, Gentleman Jim, whom I had introduced to Tom Lasorda in Los Angeles faded in the summer heat. The June drinking companion who fantasized about playing piano in a bar and singing show tunes in his pleasant tenor voice was disappearing. Now the season without a day off gripped him and the games night after night scraped his nerve ends raw.

After the two annoying losses to Oneonta, we fell into a .500 pattern, mixing defeats and victories about equally. For most of us, a sense of fun persisted, even though we were losing the sort of games we earlier had rallied to win. We still had the lead. It was up to Little Falls to catch us. But our bad games tore at Gattis and our good games never seemed quite good enough. He ripped the players night after night, creating a jagged breach between the team and the manager. A few devised a nickname for him. It was one word, derisively spoken: "Dad."

It became more and more difficult for me to reach "Dad" Gattis. He saw himself as the captain of a dissolute crew and he didn't want any coaching from the commodore. It was *his* crew. He would bend them to *his* will. He would do things *his* way—he would live or he would die—without outside help.

I could understand this conduct in late August, when the pennant race became excruciating, but Gattis' mid-season approach seemed obsessive and excessive. He himself could shed no light on it during a calm conversation after the season. He didn't remember all the things he had said and done, he claimed. He only remembered that he had wanted to win more than he ever had before in a lifetime spent wanting to win. Whether his raging July approach helped the team or hurt it was something we all wondered about— but could not satisfactorily decide—when the summer and the season were history.

Now the nature of my conversations with him altered. They became rather like Gattis lectures instead of discussions. This man who had told me in Malibu that baseball was a game of second guess now sought praise rather than the cut and thrust of dialogue. It troubled me that I could not reach out and lift some pressure from his shoulders. But only one man can manage and Gattis had asked for the job.

Curiously, this was the season when George Bamberger resigned as manager of the last-place New York Mets, telling reporters, "I can't stand the suffering any more."

Someone in Utica sked me if I thought the comment, coming from a professional baseball person, was unmanly. I didn't. I thought that it was frank. Each day I watched our manager, who had a good grip on first place, suffer intensely. I imagine he dreamed of horrifying abysses into which he saw the Blue Sox falling, dragging him into purgatory with them.

On July 25, Jamestown knocked out John Seitz and won the first game of a doubleheader, 8–3. There it was. We had lost three games in a row, a critical point in Gattis' concept. But it did not remain critical for long. We won the second game, 18–5, driving out twenty-three base hits. End of losing streak. *Fin*.

"It looks as though the team has character," I said to Gattis.

He refused to be placated. "Let's see what happens after we lose *four* straight. And, by the way, we played a lousy opener."

In the middle of the second game Rocco Gerace hurried toward my seat, repeating one word: "Trouble." A teenager had thrown a rock through the rear windshield of Barry Moss's red sports car. A policeman collared the rock thrower but was insisting that he would let him go unless "the owner of the vehicle comes forward and presses charges." The owner of the vehicle was coming forward elsewhere as a designated hitter.

By the time I reached the lot a police sergeant had arrived. I told him: "This is Moss's car. We're in the fifth inning, with a man on second, and Moss is due up soon. Your patrolman wants him pulled out of the game to make a complaint."

"Moss?" the sergeant said. "*Barry* Moss? He's a good hitter."

"That's why we need him in the game."

"Hold that damn kid," the sergeant ordered. "Afterward we can see about booking him." There are fringe benefits to hitting a baseball well, even in the minor leagues. Barry singled home the run and later homered.

In the clubhouse afterward he cursed briefly at the bad news. "I don't need this during the season. During the season I need to worry about my hitting."

"I'll handle it," I said, "but the cops are going to ask if you want to prosecute."

"Is he a mugger? Some dangerous little bastard?"

"The cops say no, he's just a punk."

"Then all I want is my car fixed," Barry said.

The next day we had to mount the bus for Erie and a 284-mile ride. I went to the trailer early to make sure that Joanne had prepared meal-money envelopes for our *vagrantes*. A heavyset man, who identified himself as Inspector Danker, was waiting. "What do you want to do about the Moss case?" Inspector Danker said.

"Get his rear windshield fixed and paid for."

"I've watched Moss play," Inspector Danker said. "He looks like a hitter. What kind of a person is he?"

"Fine," I said. "Fine hitter. Fine person. I just have to check these envelopes, Inspector."

"The young man who did the damage is a sort of ward of a monsignor here. He's been in trouble before. The monsignor is trying to help him."

Envelope for Coyle. Envelope for Jacoby. Envelope for Merenda.

"A criminal prosecution could be kind of nasty, with the monsignor involved, if you get my drift."

Envelope for Lee. Envelope for Krynitsky. Envelope for Robinson.

"If you don't prosecute, I'll put a probation officer from youth court on the case. He can talk to the father about paying damages."

"I can talk to the father. Moss can talk to the father."

"That's not a good idea," Inspector Danker said. "I've seen these cases before. You might get angry and do more harm than good. Let the probation officer handle it."

We did and it turned out that the vandal's father was not a wealthy man. He had to pay Barry in installments. I like to think justice was served, within the home, each time the father had to write another check, payable to our designated hitter.

After a long flat ride to Erie we played a dull flat game and were beaten by the Cardinals, 5-1, on July 26. Our lead over Little Falls fell to four games, causing Gattis to point out in anxiety that our seven-game lead had shrunk almost in half within a week. "We *got* to play harder," he said, mostly to himself, then turned for comfort to his towheaded son Luke.

He made a furious fight speech the next day and our outing proved neither dull nor flat. It was rather closer to hysterical.

According to a headline in the Erie *Times*.

Fists Fly as Cards
Drop Tilt to Utica

According to the Erie reporter, Al DeSantis, "The Blue Sox apparently make their own rules and get away with it most of the time." To this questionable statement, DeSantis added, "The instigator of all the trouble was Utica manager Jim Gattis, who has been around long enough to know better."

Jim had his moments of instigating, some deliberate and some not, but in this instance he didn't start trouble. Once trouble appeared, he responded with decided eagerness, but he didn't start anything. Not this night. The true instigator was a hot-weather drink I had not encountered before: iced tea brightened with a hefty shot of vodka.

On the afternoon of the twenty-seventh, I accepted an invitation from Paul Mangiardi, the old beer-throwing army sergeant, to join him for drinks at a working-class bar called Bell's. Paul, a likable kind of roughneck, boasted a bit about his operation and then, as the drinks began to reach him, complained about debts the previous owner had left unpaid. The theme runs through all of minor league baseball. "I pay my bills, but that bastard who sold me the club . . ." (Indeed, at Utica, I had to make an out-of-court settlement with a fence-sign painter, who should have been paid by other Blue Sox management three seasons before.)

I listened, simultaneously glad for the companionship and anxious for the game to start. Erie in July is not a spot that seduces you, like Nice or Cannes. After a while I left for the ball park. Mangiardi was ordering another tea and vodka.

Ainsworth Field in Erie is a relic of the 1930s. A high screen protects a short right field. Beyond it stands an elderly red brick school building. A low fence rims center field and left. There are covered grandstands, but Ainsworth is about as pleasing to the eye as an aging trailer camp.

Joe Braun, our driver, had parked behind the center-field fence and as the game began a slight sun glint reflected off the silver top of our rented bus. We went scoreless in the first inning. Then Joe Rigoli, the Erie manager, marched out to the plate umpire, Ben Byrum, and demanded that Utica move its bus. The sun glint would bother is hitters, Rigoli said.

Byrum agreed and shouted toward our dugout that we had to move the bus. Gattis ran to home plate. The faint reflection hadn't bothered our hitters, he said. Rigoli was just stalling and we had a helluva long ride home after the game.

"Move your bus," Byrum said.

"All right," Gattis said. "We'll move. But lighting conditions here are generally lousy. I want the ball park lights turned on."

As voices grew louder and bellows issued from Gattis, Rigoli and the umpire, Paul Mangiardi tramped onto the field. Considering all the spiked teas, his walk was steady. "I pay the electric bills here," Mangiardi said to Gattis, "and the lights don't go on until I say so." (Wrong. Umpires are the gods of light.)

"What the hell do I care about your electric bills?" Gattis said.

"You don't care about anybody but yourself," Mangiardi shouted, "and that bunch of fucking rejects that you manage."

Gattis squirted tobacco juice into Mangiardi's face.

One New York-Penn League rule is clearer than twilight. Except for press photographers, no one out of uniform is permitted on the field during a game. Mangiardi was a trespasser at his own ball park.

He wiped his face. Rigoli moved toward Gattis. The two managers wrestled each other to the ground. Both benches emptied in what DeSantis described as "a brawl that added nothing to the national pastime."

It was more than a debate but less than a brawl. There was some shoving and some scratching. Nobody was so much as bruised.

I remembered another league rule from our Murnane blackout night. In order to protest a game, you had to announce your protest before the next pitch was thrown. Mangiardi, out of uniform and out of place, was ragging my manager on the field, a clear violation of the rules. But Gattis seemed excited enough to have forgotten the protest procedure.

I walked onto the field, past a number of agitated ball players, to the center of the storm. Gattis. Rigoli. The umpires. Mangiardi. Bob Veale.

The combatants had regained their feet. Umpires were standing between them. Everyone seemed to be yelling at everybody else. I shouted, "Jim, Jim. You've got to protest before the next pitch."

He didn't hear me.

"Before the next pitch, damn it."

"Hey, *I* remember the rule," Bob Veale said in a cool, professional tone. "I'm gonna tell Jim when he calms down. But you shouldn't be on the field yourself. How we gonna protest one owner's on the field, when the other owner comes on the field too?"

"Because I wasn't on the field first."

Veale looked upward toward the early evening sky.

I retreated. Gattis cursed enough to get himself ejected. Veale lodged the protest and took over managing when the game resumed eighteen minutes later.

After the ejection I found Gattis in the dressing room sitting beside Luke. "Did you win the fight, Daddy?" Luke asked.

"Nobody won the fight. It wasn't a fight, really. I never threw a punch."

"Did he [Mangiardi] push you first?"

"Yes, but I spit tobacco juice at him."

"Are you stronger than him, Daddy?"

"I'll put his lights out."

"Are you stronger than Barry Moss?"

"Yes. No. We're both the same."

"How about Big Bob Veale, Daddy?"

"He'd put my lights out, Luke," Jim Gattis said.

Luke's visitation with his father, the manager, would end with the end of July. "Damn," Moss said to me. "Now Jim's going to be lonelier than ever."

"Damn," I said to Barry, "just when the kid was becoming a first-rate research assistant."

Back on the field, John Seitz kept his curve ball low and we went into the seventh inning of a heated, but scoreless, ball game. Then we put together seven singles for five runs. In the eighth Ed Wolfe hit a home run over the screen in right and into the red brick wall of the old school. Two more. Moretti relieved in the ninth and we won the game, 7–0.

The ride to Utica dragged on all night long. Along with a few others, who were solemn and silent in their sleeplessness, I watched dawn break over the New York State Thruway into a sky full of smog. When we arrived back at Murnane it was 6:23 A.M. "How do you feel?" Moretti asked me as we stepped onto the asphalt parking lot under a gray dawn glare.

"Ragged, Roy. How about you?"

"I couldn't sleep," he said, "but, hell, we won the game. I feel like I've been to a New Year's Eve party, except nobody got drunk."

Nobody on our side, that is.

We had, however, lost four games out of six, and I hoped that the rescheduled player talent contest would lift

spirits and generally lighten the atmosphere around a suddenly tense ball club. Gattis was locked into his siege
mentality, but the others were entitled to have as much fun
as they could. Playing baseball hard, which we were, does
not necessarily mean that you have to play joylessly.
"Jollity" was the word that came to mind. "The jollity of
aged men," Hawthorne has written, "has much in common with the mirth of children." At Murnane you could
find old men and children caught up in the jollity of
baseball.

I picked July 28, before a game with the redneck Auburn Astros, as the new time for the player talent contest.
Gattis repeated his complaints. The contest would distract
the players and lead them to play listlessly. "And whenever we play listless we get beat.

"And another thing," Gattis added. "I like the players
hanging out at the clubhouse, thinking baseball all the
time, talking baseball. But have you noticed how hot it
gets in the clubhouse? I want the club to buy us four fans.
If the club is broke, you can take what they cost out of my
next paycheck. The fans will make the clubhouse bearable.
The way it is; the players start sweating again as soon as
they step out of the shower and they can't wait to take off.
So they're not talking baseball as much as they should.
Are you sure you *got* to have that talent contest? I'm
worried about this team."

Yes, we had to have the contest. Yes, I would assign
Joanne to purchase four fans. No, I would not deduct the
cost from Gattis' check. The Blue Sox were poor but
proud. We would not accept welfare, even from our
manager.

The talent entries made for an eclectic program. Sheffield promised again to do his Richard Pryor imitation and
then backed out once more, this time for a good reason.
"Words," Sheff said. "I gotta use a lot of words that
might not sound right here."

"Such as, Ralph?" I said.

"Such as motherfucker," Sheffield said. "Without that word I can't be Richard Pryor."

I hated to lose Ralph, but I had to agree. The word "motherfucker," blared over a loudspeaker in a residential neighborhood, would not be notably appropriate for a summer entertainment in Utica, New York.

Veale agreed to sing "Bye, Bye, Blackbird," but told me he was not to be included in the judging. "I'm a coach," Big Bob said, "and I know it ain't right for a coach to be judged against some of the players he's supposed to be coaching." Very well. Veale could sing as a special, noncontesting added attraction.

John Seitz said that he did turkey calls, including one with an erotic tinge. It was the sound a turkey hen makes, Seitz reported, when she wants to let gobblers know that she is, as it were, in the mood for love. Without telling Seitz, I assigned someone to seek out a live male turkey so that when John mouthed his avian passion we could loose an aroused and lusty gobbler on him. Good idea. Rotten execution. We could not find a live turkey of either sex between Syracuse and Albany.

Jimmy Tompkins was a strong favorite to win the fifty-dollar first prize. He could sing and he could strum like a professional. We sent word of our contest to the newspapers and the radio and television stations. "Come to Murnane! See and hear the Blue Sox entertain you. Songs! Comic Routines! Fun! The Blue Sox stars will be out early tonight!"

To my delight, a large, enthusiastic crowd, almost 2,500 people, jammed the little ball park for the show and for the game. Parents brought children. Young men arrived with dates. The crowd was gabby and alive, and drab old Murnane Field acquired a carnival mood.

Seitz led off with four bird calls. My knowledge of turkeys is limited to frozen butterballs, but the calls sounded authentic enough. They were particularly funny, these high, squeaking sounds, coming from such a serious and earnest fellow. Seitz drew a few outbursts of laughter and sustained applause.

Tompkins sang next, a song called "L. A. Freeway." But the public address system distorted his voice and the notes he struck nimbly on his guitar. A victim of mediocre electronics, Jimmy attracted only moderate applause. He did better on the team bus. He needed a smaller room than Murnane Field.

Rocky Coyle followed, walking out with a shabby brown coat over his Blue Sox uniform. With great energy, he impersonated a comedian named Johnson, whose only act, as far as I know, is to play a semimoron at a bar. It was a good duplication of a mediocre routine. Light applause.

Bryan Oatman, a compact young left-handed pitcher, appeared with a black and white soccer ball that he would bounce on his head as many times as he could. Led by Fred Snyder, the fans counted along with each bounce. Oatman reached twenty-four bounces before the soccer ball got away. The crowd regarded this as good, but not great. Another round of moderate applause.

Veale sang and then Robin Dreizler, our number three catcher, made his way to the pitcher's mound carrying a hefty ten-speed bicycle. Dreizler had taped the front wheel into a secure vertical position. With neither haste nor nervousness, he hoisted the bike and placed the rear wheel beneath his lower lip. He took a few steps for balance and dropped his hands. There he stood, at the center of the diamond, balancing a ten-speed bicycle on his chin. The fans, the Auburn players, the Blue Sox, even Gattis, burst into cheering. We were the Ringling Brothers, Barnum and Bailey Blue Sox. Dreizler won the fifty dollars by roaring acclamation. Seitz finished second. Jimmy Tompkins placed third.

Thus distracted, we cracked out twenty-one hits and defeated Auburn, 11–4. But even on this festive night my manager remained determined to embrace unhappiness. Joanne had failed to purchase the fans for the clubhouse. After a hot July, she said, every store she called had been sold out.

Gattis conceded at the free beer bar that the talent contest had been a good idea after all. He even congratulated Robin Dreizler. But as I told him he had managed a fine game, Jim shifted his weight from side to side, impatient to complain. "Now," he said, "I promised all the players fans that would cool the clubhouse by tonight. This makes me out a liar to the team. If Joanne told me she was too busy to buy the fans, I could accept that. But I'm not ignorant. You can't expect me to believe that in the city of Utica, with 80,000 people, you can't find four fans. I can handle it if Joanne says to me, 'Screw you. I've decided not to get the fans.' But if you expect me to believe that there aren't four fans in Utica, that's like expecting me to believe this town doesn't have a gas station."

Good-bye jollity. Hello, Jungle Jim. I told him to find the fans himself and that I'd give him a ball club check to cover the cost. (At length, he found only two.) Then I said, "I make some notes in my desk diary every night, and over the last week, I can't find an entry that doesn't include at least one complaint from you. I call it 'Gattis' Bitch of the Day.'"

The strong jaw jutted forward. "I may demand a lot," he said, "but I give a hell of a lot more." And he turned away.

Down the bar Moss, relaxed and cheerful, was making small talk with Alissa. Small talk for Barry. Big talk for Alissa. "I sold more than a hundred programs tonight," she said.

Moss spotted me. "Does your Dad give you a bonus for that," he said, "or is he tight with money?"

"Tight," Alissa answered with what seemed undue haste.

"We have a chain of command here," I told Moss. "Liss doesn't work for me. She works for Joanne."

"Tight," Moss repeated, as though I had not spoken. "Well, I've had experience with parents and you have to keep working on them. I'll bet he's never sold a hundred programs in a night."

"Have you?" Alissa said. They didn't let up until I slipped Alissa a five-dollar bill for general merit and for selling programs, in Blue Sox jargon, "with intensity."

Alissa moved off to commend Seitz on his turkey calls. I told Barry about Gattis' complaint and said that his angry mood, whether we won or lost, was becoming a cause for concern.

"Jim needs to control situations," Barry said. "He didn't have a real boss until you got here. He's letting you know in his way that he still wants to be the controlling guy."

"Well, he can control the team. He has to do that. But what worries me is this: if he's as touchy as he is right now, how is he going to be if the pennant race gets really tight?"

"I don't think you have to worry about that," Moss said. "Underneath everything, Jim is a professional baseball man. Don't underestimate him. He'll make the important decisions very rationally. He'll be all right."

If I can get our trainer to stock Valium, I thought.

At the end of July we went on the road for a week, including four consecutive nights that we would have to spend in motels. Years before I had heard from an old baseball writer named Dan M. Daniel that "the road will make a bum of the best of them. And," Dan added in his gravelly, sardonic voice, "kid, you ain't the best."

His reference was to the women who materialize around traveling major league ball clubs, drawn by the glamour, the uniforms, the famous, handsome young men, and motivated by a spirit of adventure and, sometimes, by lust.

They were called camp followers in Daniel's time, groupies today. Dan was a puritanical sort who did not like his baseball mixed with sex, even in conversation. A New York *Times* reporter told him that sex was popular everywhere and mentioned on a sidewalk in Cleveland that a Hollywood entertainer had seduced a member of Britain's royal family "backstage in his dressing room at the Palladium in London." Dan grunted and made a gesture of disgust.

"What's that supposed to mean?" the *Times* reporter asked.

"If you think it, don't say it," Daniel said, "and you shouldn't even think it. Talk baseball."

In the mundane world of the Blue Sox, the road was hardly a nonstop bacchanal. Michael Zalewski, the statistician, was forever flirting with usherettes and forever being turned down. But the players traveled under Gattis' tight discipline. We all stayed in the same motels, so bed check, when Gattis wanted to make one, was accomplished merely by knocking on and opening ten or fifteen doors. I know that goes against the usual randy impression of baseball life, but Gattis, Veale, Moss and I did not have to break up a single orgy all season.

"I like the road," Gattis told me as the bus began a three-hour trip to Elmira, where earlier we had been run out of a motel. "The team is closer together. I'm away from the front office. I sometimes wish we could spend the whole season on the road. You get a little peace and clean sheets every night."

The clean sheets came through, but our stay in Elmira was no more peaceful than brawl day in Erie, even though we swept the series. Texas Star Baseball had heard about a right-handed pitcher named Mark Smith who had good credentials, and we flew Smith into Elmira for a look.

Each day on every team pitchers are required to run. Almost all of them despise running—Don Sutton was an exception—but, with a little grumbling and much panting, the pitchers sprint. Pitching power begins with the legs and if you study a good pitcher's motion you'll discover that a good fast ball, like a good left hook, comes up from the ankles.

Our pitchers were running in right field at Elmira's Beautiful Dunn Field, beside the winding Chemung River and underneath the nearby Jerusalem Hills. Veale had organized the running into a variation of football pass patterns to keep the pitchers interested. They sprinted and Veale threw high lobs over their heads, which they caught imitating the style of wide receivers. Any system that works, that keeps the pitchers running, is a good one.

Mark Smith, a tall, open-faced young man, described as "a rich kid, but good," watched all this sprinting in the heat from a safe distance. He leaned against the left-field fence, two hundred feet away from the activity.

Moss approached him. "You ought to be over there, Mark, working with the other pitchers."

"I don't run," Mark Smith announced.

"You better tell that to Bob Veale, our pitching coach."

"I'm telling that to you," Mark Smith said.

Moss reported the problem to Gattis, who bore down on Smith.

"I told them and I'll tell you," Smith said. "I don't run."

Gattis was speechless. Recovering, as we walked away, he said, "I'd like to see the son of a bitch throw before I come down on him." We then gathered in an empty dugout for a small council of war. We had to do something. We could not very well demand that ten pitchers run, while the new man lounged against a fence, brooding and occasionally watching.

We discussed a number of approaches to Mark Smith. Since I had not signed him to a contract, we couldn't fine him. Gattis could, however, turn on his anger spigot.

Veale could tell Smith how the Pirates had made him run in his own major league days, then switch to his drill sergeant manner. We were still discussing options the next day when Smith solved the problem for us. He called for a taxi and caught the next plane home.

"It really bothers me that I couldn't connect with that guy," Gattis said.

"With his attitude, he would have been a liability anyway," I said. " Forget it."

"Except he might have been a helluva pitcher," Gattis said.

"Hey, Skip," said Mark Krynitsky, our sturdy and uncomplaining catcher. "I want to be like Mark Smith myself. From now on, when we play doubleheaders, I'm only catching one of the games."

That night Ralph Sheffield suffered what sportswriters call a mental lapse and shoved Smith from everybody's thoughts. A walk and Sheffield's single put runners on first and third with two out in the second inning. Moss hit a pop fly back of second and Rocky Coyle ran home. But Sheffield, forgetting the number of outs, went only a third of the way to second base. Joe Picchioni, coaching first, shouted, "Run, Sheff. Two away. Two away."

Sheffield remained frozen. The Elmira second baseman dropped Moss's pop fly, recovered it on two bounces and forced Sheffield at second base. End of inning. We had lost a run.

Gattis yanked Sheffield from the game and Ralph wandered from the dugout to the clubhouse. There he changed from spikes to sneakers. Then he walked back to the motel, a distance of eight miles. This was arrant flouting of a ball player's code of conduct. Whether he is pulled from a game or not, a player is expected to stay with the team, unless the manager excuses him.

When Moss and I returned to our room at the Colonial

Motel, the phone rang. It was Sheffield, asking for Gattis' room number. What he probably meant was, "Talk to me, please."

"Some of the players were worried about you, Sheff," I said. "They thought you might have gotten killed walking along a state highway in the dark."

"I'm all right. Is Gattis mad?"

"And some of the players were saying that, if you walked away like that, you ought to keep walking until you got home to Los Angeles."

"I don't need this shit. I just might do that. I just might go home."

"If you jump the club and your contract, Ralph, your baseball career will end very quickly. Say tomorrow."

"Yeah. Maybe. But there are other things I can do with my life."

"Talk to the manager, Ralph. If you square things with him, you and I can talk some more. But you left the club. Gattis didn't. So you ought to begin by apologizing. And you can get Gattis' room number the same way you got mine. From the front desk."

Moss, my good roomie, surmised who was on the other end of the line. "Are you aware," he said, "that Sheffield thinks he's as good as Willie Mays?"

I was not. Ralph limited his posturing in my presence. "The young Willie was an absolute wonder," I told Moss, "with speed, a great arm, terrific power and the most bubbling enthusiasm for the game. That isn't Ralph. Do you think he's a major league prospect?"

Barry thought not. Sheffield threw well enough in the New York-Penn League, where the ball parks were relatively small. His arm was inadequate for the larger stadia in the big leagues. Besides, he swung too hard, leading to excessive strikeouts by a man who should have been punching out singles and doubles. Further, he could not bunt very well. "His scouting report," Moss said, "would read like this: 'Power below average. Arm below average. Good speed.' " As things stood, Ralph would not score well on attitude, either.

In the privacy of Gattis' room, the manager and the stray center fielder met for more than an hour. According to Gattis, Sheffield did apologize, then began to cry. "But he's still talking about goin' home," Jim said. "What could I tell him? That this could be his only shot at a baseball year in his whole life? He's kind of arrogant and he's pretty now with those small features. But later on, when he's not so pretty anymore, he'll be sore at himself forever if he walks away now. Damn, that meeting upset me."

We were sitting on green lawn chairs in the inner court-yard of the Colonial, a drab little motel. After the eviction incident at Howard Johnson's, however, and certain bills other Blue Sox owners had left unpaid at other front desks, the Colonial was the only motel in the Elmira area that would accept us.

"I got upset and I'm still real upset about Sheffield," Gattis said. "I didn't sleep all night and I can prove it. I can tell you what movies were on the cable. Two-thirty: *The Curse of the Living Corpse*, three forty-five: *Lola in Lipstick*, five forty-five: *Mark of the Vampire*. I saw them all."

"I'm not challenging you, Jim. I think I'll work with the kid a little bit myself."

Mike Zamba approached and addressed the two of us. "You know Sheffield was saying something when he walked away. He was saying he didn't give a damn for all the rest of us. He didn't give a damn for the whole team. I say to hell with him."

"Yeah," Gattis said in a gruff, noncommittal tone. In management, you don't discuss the problems of one player with the other players. You retain distance on matters of policy, matters of the psyche, even from intelligent athletes like Zamba.

"God damn," the pitcher said, swinging his arms in agitation. "I work, whether I agree with you guys or not. I work when my arm hurts. What's so special about Sheffield?"

"Maybe nothing, Mike," I said. "Maybe he's just a kid who lost his head."

"Well, that's not going to help us win the pennant," Zamba said. He was still swinging his arms when he walked away.

A bus ride from Elmira to Geneva took us through soft green counties rich in rolling vineyards. It was a lovely sun-splashed summer day—August had come—and Joe Braun took the microphone and offered us a travelogue he had learned while driving tourists on this same hilly road. "Lake Seneca, over there on the right, is the deepest of all New York State's Finger Lakes, running down to 168 feet at certain points. During World War II (which you guys are too young to remember) the navy put a submarine training base in at Seneca. Those grapevines on the banks are pretty, but don't get too excited about them. These particular grapes are pressed into grape juice, not into wine. Tastes all right, but there's not one high in a barrel."

Our lead, after the Elmira series, had extended to five and a half games over Little Falls. Except for Sheffield, the players' mood was bright. They applauded Braun's announcement and Gattis said, "Give 'em more, Joe. They're here to learn."

Braun talked about geologic faults and glaciers carving lakes and valleys among the hills. I looked at Sheffield. He was disconnected from the rest of us, staring out a window, a lone black kid sitting in silent distress.

When we arrived at Geneva a few hours early, Braun parked the bus near a rocky little beach on the narrow shore of Lake Seneca. The beach was deserted. Willie

Finnegan stripped off his clothes and splashed into the lake. Three others joined him. They churned like small boys at camp in the summer afternoon heat.

I was sitting on a bench with Mike Zamba when Sheffield joined us. For a moment Sheffield was silent, perhaps embarrassed by the presence of Zamba, who was hardnosed, politically conservative and at the same time believed that minor league players should form a union.

"I'm still thinking maybe I ought to go home," Sheffield said.

"You're okay with the manager now, Ralph," I said. "We're not even going to fine you, because you can't afford a fine. Would you mind telling me how you're going to make your decision?"

"I'll call my Dad," Sheffield said. "He drives a truck, but he's a real smart man."

Beyond us Finnegan swam with a strong Australian crawl.

"Then your Dad will tell you not to throw away your career. And when you're done talking to him, ask him to call me if he has any questions. Collect. You're not getting fined and your Dad's phone call is on the club. I'm beginning to think we're too good to you."

"Sheffield," Zamba barked, "how old are you?"

"Twenty-two."

"Well, I'm twenty-four," Zamba said, "and let me tell you, there's a lot of difference." (Advancing toward my fifty-sixth birthday, I had thought that twenty-two and twenty-four were just about the same.)

"When I was your age," Zamba said, "I was just as arrogant as you. I told everybody that I didn't need baseball. Baseball needed me. Then a bad thing happened. The Pirates dropped me from their organization. I can do other things. I write for a baseball magazine. I've got some skills. But now it's March and I'm out of the game. Now it's April and nobody's asking me to pitch. Now it's *May*.

I got so I couldn't look at myself in a mirror. Hell, I wasn't good enough to be a pro. I couldn't even look at my wife, who's damn pretty. That's how bad I felt about myself.'' Then, in sudden tenderness, Zamba said, ''Ralph, at your age you need baseball. Don't cut your own throat. Don't break you own heart.''

I knew how it would end. Sheffield stayed with the team, vowing that for all eternity he would keep track of the number of outs. The group that was the Blue Sox accepted his return but only in a limited way. He would remain a fringe character, sitting by himself on bus rides, pounding his portable radio and saying, half seriously, half in a new self-mockery: ''Soul music, come in. Where are you, soul? Don't black people have radios around here?''

We swept two games from Geneva, a last-place club, but Little Falls kept winning and our lead did not grow. Then we lost two straight games to the Newark Orioles at Colburn Field. Newark was developing into the strongest team in the Western Division of the league. (At the end, they won their division by ten games.) Gattis told the players furiously that they had to beat good teams as well as bad ones if they expected to finish first, and then he shouted at them in general frustration. Little Falls kept winning. When we left Newark on August 5, our lead was down to a mere three and a half. There was still almost a month to go. Our lead was no longer large enough to make anybody truly comfortable.

The players met among themselves. They barred Gattis, Veale, myself and everyone else. They voiced gripes about the manager but choked others down before the meeting deteriorated. They decided finally, Zamba reported, that ''the most important thing is to worry about winning our games, instead of worrying what the hell Little Falls is doing someplace else.''

The times were tense, but I had another promotion that

could briefly relieve stress. On August 6, before a home game against Little Falls, five young women wearing white bathing suits, high heels and brightly colored capes gathered at home plate for the finals of the Miss Utica Blue Sox contest. After Fred Snyder announced the names, each girl spoke briefly on why she wanted to be Miss Utica Blue Sox and told a little about herself. Then she dropped the cape and walked to first base in skimpy bathing suit and skin past whistling fans and smiling judges: Jimmy Tompkins, Don Jacoby, Gattis and myself. Gattis insisted on being a judge. So did I.

We put out a statement that contestants would be judged on poise, personality, appearance and intelligence. We needed every fan we could get, including the feminists. But it was, to put matters delicately, a legs contest. An attractive brunette named Sabrina Hofstra won. She had a nice smile and nicer legs.

There had been some lobbying for Sabrina, notably by Jacoby, and a little research revealed why. All the other candidates Joanne had interviewed were less than eighteen years old. That meant, as Brian Robinson put it, that they weren't "fair game." Sabrina, nineteen, was legally an adult.

I handed her a tiara and a fifty-dollar check, for which she would have to come to the rest of our home games as a hostess, look decorative and smile some more. She did her job cheerfully and well, but whenever Sabrina appeared at Murnane her mother walked at her side as a duenna. Sabrina was pleasant to the athletes, but with Mom so close she was not approachable for serious propositioning. "Might as well have voted for a sixteen-year-old," Jacoby complained.

The contest beautified barren Murnane, but when it was over Little Falls pounded us, 10–3. Our lead shrank to two and a half games. Neither player meetings nor fierce speeches from the manager seemed able to stop our steady, infuriating slide toward second place. We had now lost another three in a row, and nine of our previous sixteen games. The mood within the team was grim and prickly. Gattis fumed alternately at the players and at the front office. He claimed that Joanne was so cheap she'd given him waterlogged balls for batting practice. The extended family was squabbling in whiny ways. The team had lost its winning touch. And now Roy Moretti began to talk about packing up and going home.

Back in Victoria, British Columbia, Moretti was, he said, a sales manager in a Chevrolet agency. He was obscure but made a comfortable living. Here in Utica he was a superb right-handed pitcher, nicknamed "The Canadian Goose," idolized, famous and underpaid. When Roy was right, which was most of the time, we needed only to carry a lead into the eighth inning. Then he'd come in and save the game. He was the linchpin of the pitching staff, confident, always ready to work, uncomplaining and proud without being haughty. He was a good pitcher who knew that he was good. But he was also a husband in a troubled marriage.

"I wouldn't say," Alissa remarked at home one night, "that Roy has as good a body as Barry does, but Roy's so charming."

I blinked. I may have blanched. My sixteen-year-old daughter was remarking on male bodies, even as I, at sixteen, had remarked on female bodies at a summer lake alive with pretty girls in Lastex bathing suits. (I would rate them, in quiet tones, from A to C, for my friend Frank Wolf, never imagining, even for an instant, that the girls might be rating us on a similar scale.) But when Alissa spoke of masculine bodies, another chink was knocked from my shell of chauvinism.

After we had beaten Watertown, 6–2, on August 7, maintaining our lead at two and a half games, Moretti told me at the beer bar that he felt he had to return to Victoria.

I dropped Alissa at the Bradford Avenue house and drove Roy to a lounge at the Ramada Inn. It was a Sunday night, which meant that a modest free buffet would be set out at the Ramada; management was content one night a week to make its money on drinks. The lounge was dark and loud with rock music, but Roy liked the place and I wanted him to be comfortable.

He'd been playing baseball for a long time, Moretti said above the raucous, pounding noise of rock. In fact, when he was small, he had cracked the Little League at seven, by lying about his age. The rules said that you had to be eight. Now, twenty years later, he was wondering if his life in baseball would lead him anywhere but to divorce court. His wife, Heather, was a registered nurse, with a wide circle of friends. "They ask her what she's doing with a man who leaves a good job in the summer to play a kids' game in a town they don't know for a team they never heard of, and for $500 a month." Utica heroics meant little, if anything, in the Canadian West. Our greatest games, Roy's greatest games, were festive occasions in Utica but generally unnoticed in the national media. Roy had reached an age where a man is expected to get serious and Heather Moretti and her friends, three thousand miles away, hardly regarded pitching for the Blue Sox as a serious endeavor.

"We can win the pennant, Roy," I said. "You want to be with a pennant winner, don't you?"

He nodded, but said, "I kind of get the feeling my marriage ought to come first."

"Has she said, 'Come home or we're through'?"

"Not in those words. She's very lonely. She hasn't used those words yet."

"The team can give you a hand in flying her into Utica."

"She can't get away from her work as a nurse."

Moretti was one of nine children. Although his father

left his mother, Enid, when Roy was young, Moretti described his life in Victoria as generally free of stress. "It's real laid back," he said. "There's not a lot of crime or anything like that. It's an easier life than you find in the States."

"But you like to win," I said. "You like competition." He was sipping Irish whiskey. He shrugged. He didn't know what to do, he said.

"You love Heather?" I asked.

"A lot," Moretti said.

Then I didn't know what to do. Could I argue that he should stay and risk divorce, with all its torment, self-doubt, loneliness and lawyers? Not very convincingly. Should I tell him that he had already done a great deal for the Blue Sox and that he should fly to Heather, without guilt, without worrying about his teammates and with my blessing? I didn't want to say that either.

I said, "The whole team looks up to you, Roy."

"I know that. I appreciate that."

"Even Alissa is fond of you."

Moretti gave me a small grin over his glass. "You've got a fine daughter there, Rog."

"I want this pennant badly, just as badly as Gattis," I said, "but I can't tell you to stay and lose your marriage. I can't say that."

Roy nodded and tapped me on the shoulder in a gentle gesture of affection. We exchanged troubled looks and, in Robert Frost's phrase, we were men together.

On August 8 Roy saved a victory over Watertown, keeping our lead at two and a half games, stayed up most of the night making farewells to other players. On August 9 he flew home to Victoria.

I thought, in a spasm, There goes the pennant. And after all the work that all of us had done. But part of my job as president was to absorb pain silently and to keep my doubts and anxieties to myself.

"Come on, Jimmy," I said to Gattis. "We're gonna make it without him."

"Bet your butt we are," Gattis said.

Our eyes met, full of apprehension.

Like the existence of many other wanderers, a minor league ball player's life is touched with schizophrenia. He leaves his home environment, his family, his friends and sets forth to play baseball with strangers. He can win fame, glory (although not much money) far from home, but when he returns no one knows what he has done. Stories about the Blue Sox in the *Times, People* and *USA Today* pleased most of the players. "Now when I get back to Austin," Jimmy Tompkins said, "I won't have people asking me, 'What's a Blue Sox?' " But where the high deeds of major leaguers sound and resound in the press and on television, a minor leaguer's triumphs and disasters usually draw local attention but no more. After an exhilarating pennant race, full of crackling ball games and ovations, minor leaguers go home to an empty greeting. "Say, where have you been for the last few months?"

Without Moretti, the relief burden switched to Tompkins and several others, who performed well. We hit hard and we played hard and we did not collapse. Instead, we played .500 ball. So, fortunately for our side, did Little Falls. We held our narrow lead. Nobody talked about Moretti. Like combat pilots, the players did not dwell on those who were missing. That would have depressed us all.

On August 16 we defeated Elmira, 23–4, establishing our lead at an even three games. Early that evening my telephone rang. Moretti was calling from Victoria. "It's okay now with me and Heather," he said. "I can come back now, if you want me.

"If you come back, Roy, I'll personally chauffeur you in from the airport."

He would return on August 18. When he left, our lead had been two and a half games. By the time he rejoined us the lead was two. The Blue Sox had survived his absence. His marriage, Moretti reported cheerfully, was surviving the season.

The other players arranged an impressive greeting. They took strips of white tape from the trainer's room and pasted the tape to Moretti's locker. Then they wrote messages in heavy black ink.

Rag Arm.

We Got Rid of Mark (I Won't Run) Smith. Get Rid of Moretti.

We're Still in First Place. Go Back!

Who Needs a Prima Donna, Anyway?

Go Home. Finnegan Needs the Work.

Mix in a Whole Season For Once.

Stick With Car Sales.

Nice Disappearing Act. Join the Circus.

Roy Who?

When Moretti walked into the locker room the next day he surveyed the signs and grinned. He sat down and lit a cigarette and he continued to smile. Then, whistling, he set about removing the tape from his locker.

For the first time I felt solidly confident that we would win the pennant.

6

Pennant Race

On August 12, with Moretti still among the missing, we mounted a silver Birnie coach for the pleasant seventy-mile ride south and east to Oneonta. The roads run from the foothills of the Adirondacks to the foothills of the Catskills past upland meadows and tidy working farms. Although it was cool and drizzly, I decided to turn this trip into an outing.

Oneonta, by tradition a feared and mighty power in the New York-Penn League, was struggling through its worst season in memory. Before a few of our earlier games, Bill Livesey, once farm director for the entire Yankee organization and now a manager in the obscurity of the Penn League, muttered to me: "Well, let's see what my incompetents have in store for me tonight."

Errors. Base-running mistakes. Pop flies in clutch situations. That's what the Yankees usually had in store for patient, poised Bill Livesey, a white-haired and substantial baseball man.

"People ask," he said, "if I'm going to take the players to Horseshoe Falls, when we go to play in Niagara. I tell them no. Then they ask me if that's because I'm afraid I might jump. Hell, no. If I got this ball club standing near the falls, I'd be tempted to push every one of them over."

We liked to play Oneonta, because when we concentrated on business we could beat them. As a diversion on August 12, I scheduled a side trip to Cooperstown. That way all of our players could get into the Hall of Fame, if only for a day.

This being 1983, the Baseball Museum contained television monitors, which show classic major league ball games on repeating loops of videotape. Beyond the screens you can find the cornerstone of Ebbets Field—oh, hallowed rock—a lifelike statue of Roberto Clemente, and, amid a cornucopia of memorabilia, a double locker adorned with possessions that once belonged to John McGraw and Christy Mathewson.

Although my father, as a native Brooklynite, rooted for weak Dodger teams in patient melancholy, Mathewson, the great New York Giant right-hander, was the particular favorite of his own boyhood. Early in life I heard, over and over, stories of Matty's grit and of his fadeaway, the pitch now prosaically called a screwball. Mathewson was a college graduate (Bucknell) when few other ball players were and, in my father's memory, he never lost his gentlemanly bearing, never gave up any runs until the Giants had scored first and, quite apart from baseball, was a phenomenon at the game of checkers. According to my father, Mathewson could don a blindfold, then play a dozen simultaneous checker games, holding the picture of all those red and black boards so clearly in his mind that he would win every match. To this day, I can look at a portrait of Mathewson for a long time, seeking out the secrets of majesty.

To my delight, the twin locker at Cooperstown contained not only John McGraw's flannel uniform—it must have felt like one huge hair shirt in summer heat—but also a neat leather box holding Mathewson's own personal set of checkers. Beside that rested Mathewson's Bible. The book was open to Amos and the long-dead hand of Matty had marked a passage in the margin:

"For thus saith the Lord unto the house of Israel, Seek ye me, and ye shall live."

I stood in gaping wonder. Your father's heroes are ever mightier than your own.

Some of the players asked Bob Veale to walk into the Hall of Fame and tell them about any members he had known. He talked about Clemente, with whom he had played for seven years in Pittsburgh. "Clemente always used to say he wasn't playing only for himself. He was playing for all the kids in Latin America. He wanted to show everyone that Latins were good, tough ball players, not hot dogs."

The Blue Sox, who were admitted free as working professional athletes, mingled with civilians and enjoyed themselves, but coolly. There were no gasps or cries of awe. Indeed, even in the Hall, I heard a ball player grousing. "It's cold and rainy," Jimmy Tompkins said, "and we get taken here to look at things and here are all these souvenirs. But it's just three days before payday. We're all so broke we can't buy a damn thing."

Ball players generally find a way to complain, even when there is nothing to complain about. But here I thought Jim Tompkins had a case. It is awkward to stand and gaze at plaques of the greatest ball players who ever lived, supported only by a Class Single A wallet.

The rain persisted in Oneonta, where at seven o'clock it was obvious that we would not be able to play. "We'll make this one up on August 26," announced Sam Nader, a short, genial but businesslike man who was the owner of the Oneonta Yankees and a longtime friend of Vince McNamara, the league president.

According to the rules of the New York-Penn League,

rained-out games were to be rescheduled for the next available date. We were due back in Oneonta the following night. I told Nader that we would prefer to play the doubleheader tomorrow.

With our lead over Little Falls so narrow, I didn't want doubleheaders backing up on us during the last week of the season. The league had installed a so-called experimental rule calling for games that were stopped by rain to be resumed from the point of the interruption. McNamara had just written me that a game with Watertown, called after three innings on August 8, would have to be resumed on August 29. If I went along with Nader and his August 26 date, we would have, in effect, two doubleheaders within four days close to the end of the season. Nader said that was my problem, not his. He had scheduled "an important promotion" for the next night, selling all his tickets, at reduced rates, to a machine tool company. He had announced that the game would start at seven-thirty and, since a doubleheader would obviously have to start earlier, he was opposed to my suggestion. The machine tool promotion had been set for weeks. It was too late now, he said, to jiggle starting times.

I found a league constitution in the press box. "It says next available date very clearly," I told Gattis. "I think I'll carry this to the league office right now."

"Good," Gattis said, "but you're gonna lose. The league always takes Oneonta's side. They're the Yankees. We're the independents. Believe me. I've been through this before."

"Maybe we'll lose, but at least we'll fight, Jim. Come into Nader's office with me. I'll telephone Vince McNamara. I think we'll get a fair hearing and I want you there."

From his home in Buffalo, McNamara asked me to state my position first. It was a simple position and I said dryly that I'd just reread the league constitution. Tomorrow was the next available date. We wanted to follow the constitution and play two in Oneonta then.

Nader's turn. Sam described the promotion at great length and even with emotion. He spoke about all the new fans machine tool night was certain to create for New York-Penn League baseball. This promotion would benefit *everyone* for years. It would build a bigger base for the Oneonta ball club. Changing tomorrow's starting time would ruin everything.

My turn at the telephone. "I'm going to rule for Sam," McNamara said. "You play two against them August 26."

"Vince," I said, "you're letting a promotion take precedence over the pennant race."

When McNamara spoke again, his genial tone had vanished. He sounded like a traffic court judge challenged by a drunken driver. "Oh, is that what I'm doing?" he said. "Well, you've certainly been in this league for a long time, haven't you? I'm really glad to learn from you what I'm doing."

"Oneonta isn't in the pennant race," I said, "but the Blue Sox are. Sam can rearrange his promotion and get the newspaper to announce the new starting time. Vince, you're putting us in a position where we'll get so backed up by doubleheaders, we may run out of decent starting pitchers."

"I understand now," McNamara said. "You're the only man in the league with a pitching staff. The only man in the league who can have pitching problems. I've made my ruling. One game tomorrow. Two on August 26."

I might as well have been the drunken driver arguing against the sober judge.

I didn't like McNamara's decision, but Nader had been more passionate and eloquent than I. As Joc Braun started the bus toward the hills to the north, I said to Gattis, "Damn, but I should have made a better presentation. I should have gone to that phone prepared with notes. Next time, if there is one, I'll hit McNamara with the Gettysburg Address, if that's what it takes to win a ruling."

"Hey," Gattis said with unusual calm, "I want you to know I appreciate that you tried."

"The league doesn't like us," Moss said.

"It used to make me crazy," Gattis said. "Now I try to accept it. You can't do any more than what you did."

The year before Gattis had gone wild on at least two occasions when he felt umpires were weighting their decisions against the Blue Sox. After a fiery protest got him nowhere one night, he uprooted second base at Murnane Field, and, as I mentioned, walked out to right field and scaled the bag over the wall. On another protest, he walked to second base, took off his spikes and pretended they were hand grenades. Biting off an imaginary firing pin, he hurled the spikes in the general direction of the umpires. McNamara, that blustery judge (and former umpire), was, underneath, a gentle sort of autocrat. He didn't like to fine or suspend anybody. But Gattis' behavior in 1982 forced his hand. The fierce Utica grenade thrower was given a week of enforced rest. Gattis had to sit in the stands for days while Moss managed the club.

Rain tapped at the windows of the bus. "I think Mac made a wrong decision," I told Gattis, "but I don't believe it was prejudiced against Utica. Just wrong."

"The whole league is prejudiced against Utica," Gattis insisted. "They're all organization types. Conformists. We're the independents, the freethinkers. We do things our own way. They can't stand that. The New York-Penn League does not want an independent team to win the pennant."

"Vince McNamara is an extraordinary old warrior, Jim. He's kept the league afloat for thirty years, and you know how many minor leagues have folded. Now he's seventy-two and his health isn't the best and this league, this little New York-Penn League, is like a child to him. McNamara is not going to attack the integrity of that child any more than I'd attack the integrity of Alissa.''

Gattis' chin went out and he assumed a stubborn look. "What you're saying sounds good, but it isn't true. The whole league, including the president, wants us to lose.''

We were fielding a team that was a year or two older than the general average. This irritated the other owners and, I suspect, touched them with envy. But, as far as I could tell, McNamara made his official league rulings impartially.

After the so-called brawl at Erie, Paul Mangiardi wrote angrily that I had contributed to the shoving matches and further that I was trying to impose my conditions on the league and should be reprimanded. McNamara found for Utica. He threw out Mangiardi's letter. After the Utica blackout, a number of people tried to goad McNamara into issuing some sort of directive aimed at me. Vince declined, saying, ''It's his first year in the league and he's entitled to a few mistakes.'' I could agree or disagree with the president of the league, but I never questioned his ruling sense of fairness. He called 'em as he saw 'em, like Bill Klem.

But beyond McNamara, and essentially out of sight, there did exist a powerful group who wanted us to lose. This consisted of the eleven major league farm directors, who had stocked the other teams in the Penn League. We were winning with more than a dozen players these farm directors had released. Seitz was cut by Atlanta. The Pirates dropped Zamba. Don Jacoby, who was hitting almost .400, had been released by the Cardinals. The farm directors were annoyed and sometimes furious to find us winning with ball players they had discarded. Probably the farm bosses were called in by their superiors to explain why the discards fared so well. Farm directors do not want to bury their mistakes. They simply want to see them pumping diesel at truck stops, rather than surviving in baseball to hit home runs or win eight ball games in a row for Utica. Our success created nagging questions about the farm directors' omniscience.

There was also a venal element to this situation. Farm directors, like most front office personnel in baseball, are poorly paid. I know one who supervises a minor league network, six teams, 175 players, and earns only $22,000 a year. He works fourteen-hour days, contends with the egos of six managers and watches over all those ball players, who are prey to slumps, torn muscles, hubris and despair, for take-home pay of less than $400 a week.

The man is serious and ambitious. "I know baseball is supposed to be glamour," he says, "and I know that if I quit there'd be fifty people lined up for my job. But I have to make more money and I've got a plan. You can make decent bucks, $50,000 or more, as a major league general manager. The quickest way for me to move up is to have all my farm teams win pennants. With that on my résumé I can go ahead and become a general manager. Then I'd make a real living and stop driving a 1971 car." He despised the Blue Sox, this man told me, because we might be costing *his* New York-Penn League entry a pennant. That would deface his job résumé.

Gattis and Moss believed that farm directors dictated policy to McNamara. I did not. The question remained unsettled. Even when an important late-season decision went against us, nothing was proven. Several hours before that decision, Gattis had humiliated the umpire who made it in the presence of the umpire's date. Pique or policy? We would never know.

Gattis worked with another theory that he propounded like a fundamentalist zealot. We won, he said, because we played the most intense baseball in the league. "I want you guys," he told the athletes night after night, "ready to play and ready to win. I don't want just one guy on deck swinging a bat. I want four guys lined up swinging. Let that pitcher know you can't wait to hit. Take out the second baseman on the double play. Run over the catcher at home. You know what will happen? The other teams will start to say, 'Uh oh. We got to play the Blue Sox. And we don't want to play the Blue Sox. They're too tough.'"

With Moretti still away, Gattis ran his long-promised intensity poll. "We're getting forms printed up in the front office," he announced at a meeting in the red brick clubhouse. "Everybody has to vote. Just list in order the other players you think give a hundred percent of themselves a hundred percent of the time. You know what I mean by intensity. An absolute hundred percent. And everybody has to vote—you *have* to vote—except you can't vote for yourself."

To my surprise, Larry Lee, our smooth-faced Prince Valiant at second base, finished first. Larry wanted to be known as "Spike" but nobody called him anything but Larry. He didn't look rugged enough to be a Spike. He was neither voluble nor demonstrative. He made occasional mistakes. He played hard quiet baseball every day. That won him first place with twenty-one votes.

Rocky Coyle, Bible reader and holler guy, finished second with nineteen. Coyle charged at every ball game, on good nights and bad ones. One incident at Auburn exemplified his mixture of Christian puritanism and baseball toughness. Coyle was in center field when someone lined a sharp single directly at him. The ball took an erratic bounce and struck him in the groin. Down Coyle went, quivering and making high-pitched sounds of pain.

Danny Gazzilli, the trainer, ran to center field as quickly as he could. But Doc was sixty-two and portly. No sprinter. By the time Gazzilli reached Coyle the pain had subsided sufficiently for the outfielder to speak.

"Doc," Coyle said, still writhing, "it caught me bad.

Right at the tip of my pecker. But do me a favor, Doc. Rub my shoulder. I don't want the fans to know where I got hit."

"You ought to wear a cup," Gazzilli said.

"Nah," Coyle said, recovering rapidly now. "I'm pretty rugged."

Joe Picchioni, the first-base coach, finished third, although he almost never played. Picchioni was the son of a Tucson college instructor, and he was rumored to have worked briefly as an erotic dancer in a distaff "B" bar. He had fine reflexes and good rhythms to his movements, "for a white guy," Sheffield pointed out. Pic could not hit New York-Penn League pitching. Still he was out every afternoon at two, working on his swing or volunteering to throw batting practice for better hitters. The players noticed.

We had a three-way tie for third: Krynitsky, our strong, assertive catcher; Moss and Steve Sproesser, a backup catcher who played as rarely as Picchioni but worked with verve and drive, warming up relievers in the bull pen. Again the players noticed. In fact the pitchers, taken separately from the position players, voted Sproesser the most intense of all the Blue Sox.

Next came Bob Merenda, a reserve outfielder, who helped the regular outfielders warm up between innings. He never complained and seldom played. Jay Acton, reserved and unemotional when working at literary law, pleaded achingly on his visits to Utica for a chance to throw some batting practice to the professionals.

I enlisted Bob Merenda in a cabal. "You see that tall white-haired man," I said to Bobby. "I'm going to let him pitch to you and I want you to hit the longest home run of your life."

"Isn't that Mr. Acton?" Merenda said. "You told me he was a stockholder. If I hit him hard he may get sore."

"He's a stockholder, but I'm the president, Bobby. Take him as deep as you can."

Jay warmed up throwing to me in sunlight for several minutes. He showed good velocity for a literary lawyer, plus a high school curve.

When Jay was ready, Merenda grabbed a bat and hit one of the hardest line smashes I have seen. It looked more like a two-iron shot in golf than a baseball drive. The ball rocketed from the bat, climbed the air and rose screaming into the summer sky. It landed in another neighborhood.

"Damn," Merenda said to me. "Now I'm in trouble." He spun out of the batting cage and whispered, "I shouldn't have hit him that hard."

Acton's usually serious face bore a wide, bright grin. He had never known he could throw a baseball for such distance: 60 feet from his arm to home plate and 420 feet from Merenda's bat. That was Bobby, more intense and kindly than talented. Real pitching always seemed to stop him. (And *that* concluded Acton's fantasy that he could get professional batters out with his high school stuff.)

The intensity list trailed on: Brian Robinson and Shawn Barton, our two shortstops, down to Wolfe and Hendershot, down further to Ralph (Walkabout) Sheffield, who got one vote, and Daryl (Alimony) Pitts, who got none.

Baseball is a harder game to learn and in many ways a more difficult game to play than, say, football or basketball. If I could teach an African rhinoceros to cradle a football between its horns I would at once have a running back strong enough to break every record in the National Football League.

RHINO RUNS FOR 1,860 YARDS;
TRAMPLES DALLAS LINEBACKERS

A giraffe, properly coached, could deflect more jump shots with its chin than Kareem Abdul-Jabbar does with both huge hands. But neither animal could play shortstop, a position that demands quickness, speed, mobility, gamesmanship and a good throwing arm. Baseball requires highly developed human skills and human intelligence.

The nature of the game is so complex that players reach their peaks relatively slowly. Some batters do not crest until they are thirty years old. Certain pitchers enter their primes even later. Unlike football or basketball, baseball often seems to be a game played best by men on the brink of middle age.

Almost nobody proceeds from college ball to the major leagues. Why? A youngster's bat is quick. A young pitcher's arm literally throbs with strength.

The answer, it seems to me, takes us into the intellectual nature of playing baseball. Not intellectual in the scholarly sense but intellectual in that a good ball player has to be able to think, reason and react and do all those things both wisely and quickly. Even though eight-year-olds can play a primitive version of the sport, baseball is a damn hard game to master. Hitting, which may appear to be a matter of reflexes, requires memory, anticipation and elements of shrewdness. A good batter always remembers who is pitching to him. What stuff does this particular pitcher have? What did he throw me last pitch? Last time at bat? Last week? What is he likely to throw me now? A written description tends to diminish a real action, but learning *how* to hit—as opposed to swinging hard and hoping— took such extraordinary talents as Mickey Mantle and Willie Mays many years to develop. Similarly, a pitcher works not simply with power but with guile. His art is never higher than when he fools a hitter. In the field, you have to position yourself correctly and constantly remain aware of the game situation. Who is on what base? How many out? What's the score? You want to decide what you're going to do with the ball *before* it is hit to you. And even something as deceptively easy as running the bases can be a humiliation—as Ralph Sheffield found out—if you forget to think. Unlike my fullback rhinoceros, a baseball player canot simply trample the opposition.

The Blue Sox knew how to play baseball and how to think. Gattis' speeches, whether mild or diatribal, reminded the Sox to play intelligent and intense baseball. It was important, even essential, to keep reminding them. Minds can wander amazing distances over a game and over a season. But because the Blue Sox were a year or two older than any other team, the players already knew better than most what they had to do. That knowledge, that experience, as much as our four hitters at the ready on deck, grinding their teeth and pumping their bats impatiently, was why we reached the middle of August in first placc.

Some of the players resented the persistent reminders— and, to be sure, Gattis' manner. Willie Finnegan, our fast, wild, beer-guzzling right-hander, went to epic lengths (for baseball) in illustrating that point. He composed a long narrative poem, the Beowulf of the Blue Sox, which built through stanza after stanza to this end:

Now Jimmy Gattis is the one who manages this crew,
And he don't like it when we go and drink and
    smoke and screw.
But when we win our games each day,
Then what the fuck can Jimmy say?
It makes a feller proud to be a Blue Sox.

Willie recited the verse to ball players, front office people, groupies, anyone who would listen, always with what Gattis wanted—intensity.

* * *

One still hot August afternoon I heard my name called with great urgency. It was Gattis, who said he was worried because the team was unresponsive to his latest assortment of fight speeches. "I'm gonna do something now that will set fire to this team's butt. I guarantee it. I'm gonna activate myself as a player. I'm gonna pinch-hit in rough spots. I may not run good anymore, but I still know how to hit."

"With intensity," I said.

"I'm not kidding. Could you do that for me? Fill out the papers or whatever. I want to get in this pennant race with my bat."

"Well, sure, Jim, and good luck."

Before the season ended, Gattis inserted himself into the lineup five times. He did not hit safely once. I remember thinking that intensity alone was not enough. Then I resolved to give the word "intensity" a good long rest over the winter.

With Moretti's return on August 18, with our manager ready to take on the best pitchers in the league and our lead holding at two and a half games, our mood was cheerful, almost manic, despite a gray, damp day. Moss walked about smiling. Veale sang to himself. The pitchers neglected to complain about having to run. Coyle and Jacoby staged an impromptu wrestling match back of second base, two strong young bodies tussling until Gattis told them to stop. "Fun is fine," he said, "but we don't need anybody getting hurt."

August 18 was a Thursday. By Sunday, August 21, we had fallen into second place for the first time since July 2.

Our slide down the mountain began in a persistent, seemingly harmless drizzle. We were to play Elmira, no better than a .500 club, and as the rain soaked Murnane, Gattis fretted. "I hate rainouts," he said, "particularly at home. I just hate 'em. I hate missing a game when I've got the team ready to play. Then I hate the make-up double-headers.''

One of the multitudinous drawbacks to Murnane Field was the quality of the soil that was the playing surface. A number of varieties of infield earth look good and drain well, notably the reddish composition called New Jersey clay. Little Falls played on New Jersey clay and the mixture of a golf-green lawn and tinted earth made for that handsome summer aspect. Murnane did not have New Jersey clay. We had no-name dirt, dusty in the wind. When it rained, we had plain Utica mud.

Different ball fields absorb rainfall at different rates. Modern stadia with plastic grass—I wonder if a plastic earthworm is now evolving—dry quickly, helped by tractors equipped with vacuum nozzles. For all its historic wonders, the old Polo Grounds was set lower than the water level of the nearby Harlem River. A downpour at 10 A.M. meant no game at one-thirty for the Giants.

Murnane drained about as well as a malarial swamp. Rain sat in stagnant pools in the outfield and turned the infield into a small tidal basin. On several occasions we could not get in a home game while Little Falls, with similar weather thirty miles away, was playing in tolerable conditions.

There are three ways to dry a soggy field and we used all of them August 18. A chemical compound, with the trade name of Diamond Dry, looks something like sawdust. It mixes well with wet dirt and absorbs water. Then there is a technique, which Gattis enjoyed and the Utica fire department despised, of fighting the water with flame. Pour gasoline over the wet spots and set fire to the gasoline. Among the smoky black fumes, some of the water boils away. Finally, you can hire a helicopter to hover. The big blades create a drying wind.

At six o'clock Gattis dispatched a half dozen ball players to carry bags of Diamond Dry to the worst spots on the field. Then I sent one of the ground crew to a gasoline station with orders to buy three gallons. Not always confident of the ground crews' thinking, I felt compelled to add: "Buy regular now. We don't need super unleaded to burn the field."

Joanne Gerace assigned Alissa to call the media and report that a helicopter soon would be hovering over second base. I eavesdropped on Alissa's debut as a publicity person and heard her doing fine. "Hello, *Observer-Dispatch?* This is the Utica Blue Sox. We're going to have a helicopter drying out Murnane Field and we think that's a good picture possibility for you. Yes, a helicopter. The pilot's name is Harold Lennon. How does it work? The blades spin and that makes a wind that dries the puddles."

I paused amid all the activity. "Liss, would you like to be executive vice-president for media relations?"

"Be careful," Joanne said.

"I'd love to," Alissa said.

"Good," I said, "but remember, Liss, the Blue Sox policy is this: the more exalted your title, the smaller your paycheck."

Gattis poured gasoline near the right-field wall and threw a match. The stuff caught with a loud whoosh. Black smoke curled upward. Flames jumped close to the right-field wall, which was made of wood. Veale, our fire control officer, sprayed the wall with a hose. There was no damage, but we had just added as much water to the field as we had removed. Later Gattis lit four less menacing fires.

By nine o'clock the drizzle had stopped. The field looked messy but playable, and the crowd, about 2,000 people, was making noises of impatience. "No game," announced Jim Jurasin, a husky Kentuckian who was the senior umpire. "The field is too slippery. Someone might get hurt."

Our three hours of work had come to nothing. "When

did you ever hear of a ball player hurting himself on a wet field?'' Gattis shouted.

"No game," Jurasin repeated and, as McNamara instructed all his umpires to do, he walked away from Gattis and the site of the argument.

"He's wrong, dead wrong," Gattis told me. "We've played in worse conditions than this."

"I think he's wrong, Jim, but it's an umpire's judgment call. I'm not going to protest a rain-out."

"After all we've done on this field," Gattis said. "If they didn't hate Utica they'd let us play, I guarantee it." The big jaw jutted. "I'm not going to forget it. I'm going to shove it right up that umpire's ass."

He tried. He called a batting practice for the whole team, which lasted from nine o'clock to ten-fifteen. And he led off the batting practice himself. Moss shook his head but assumed an impassive look. A few of the players fumed. "He's putting on a show for himself," one said. "He's got an audience so he's gotta take his swings." Jimmy Tompkins said the manager was "short on brains."

Gattis was making a point. If the field was dry enough for batting practice and shagging fly balls—and it was—it was also dry enough for Utica and Elmira to play.

But right though this was, clear though this was, Gattis chose an incredibly contentious way to make a point. Jurasin had made his ruling. Now Jim was showing up the umpire—showing him up to the players and to the crowd. Gattis could well be making the Blue Sox an enemy for the balance of the season. I thought of Moss's dictum: "Whether you like the man or not, the umpire is your friend. Treat him as a friend or he may take the close calls away from you."

Jurasin, an assertive and competent sort, would surely share the story of this abrasive batting practice with other umpires and they, too, could mark the Blue Sox as contentious. Managing, as John McGraw is supposed to have said, is not a popularity contest. It doesn't have to be an unpopularity contest, either

Since we had no more home dates scheduled with Elmira, we had to make up the game away the next night, as part of a doubleheader at Beautiful Dunn Field. (Direction signs in Elmira announced the way to "Beautiful Dunn Field," as though the adjective were a part of the ball park's name. Dunn had covered grandstands and reasonable dimensions, making it a Vale of Kashmir in contrast to Murnane, but beautiful seemed excessive. Sabrina Hofstra, Miss Utica Blue Sox, was beautiful. Dunn Field was a pleasant place to watch a game.)

Our enforced nine o'clock batting practice, which set the players grumbling at the manager, had no discernible positive effect the next day. Following the three-hour bus ride to Elmira, our hitters could not get untracked. Elmira swept us, 5–1 and 2–1.

After the first game Gattis reached a peak of fury. He marched into the clubhouse and called for the team's attention. Then he announced, hoarse with anger, "Fuck all of you." After that he left the clubhouse, slamming the door.

I collared him and said, "Jim, they didn't mean to lose. Go on back in there and say some positive things." If he heard me, he made no sign. His jaw was set and his blue eyes focused on something far away. Jungle Jim looked like a man obsessed. He was damned if he'd take guidance or direction from anyone.

I talked to some of the players individually. Most were simmering but controlled. Typically they shrugged and said, "He don't bother me none." Moss was tight-lipped and disturbed. He said he felt sorry for what the pressure was doing to Gattis. Jimmy Tompkins, shaking his head, asked me seriously if I believed that Gattis was sane.

Our lead, after the two losses and the dumbest fight speech I have ever heard, shrank to a game and a half.

We fell out of first place on the sunny afternoon of Sunday, August 21, losing a tense and exciting game to Little Falls on the manicured grass and New Jersey clay of Veterans' Memorial Park. In an early inning, Don Jacoby tried to throw out Stanley Jefferson, at home. Jefferson, the fastest player in the league, made a good slide, but an accurate throw from third base would have nailed him. Jacoby threw high and Jefferson was safe. That was one run we should not have allowed.

In the seventh inning, as we came back from a four-run deficit, Larry Lee singled and took second when Bob Hendershot pinch-hit safely. Rocky Coyle singled sharply to left and the outfield throw was very high—like Jacoby's earlier throw from third—making the Mets' catcher, Gene Hawkins, reach upward. It also made Hawkins a perfect target for a hard, low slide that would have taken his thin legs out from under him.

For reasons that neither discussion nor argument ever clarified, Lee did not slide into Hawkins. Instead the winner of the Blue Sox intensity poll tried literally to tiptoe around the catcher, extending one toe toward home plate in a misbegotten parody of ballet. Hawkins kept his footing and the ball. Lee missed the plate. Hawkins turned around and tagged him out. There was a run we should have scored but lost on a play that was as inept as it was inexplicable. The final score was 6–4 against us. The two plays at home plate made all the difference in the result.

Two minutes after the game ended, with Daryl Pitts taking a called third strike, I found Gattis sitting alone in the visiting team's dugout. "Stay with me," he said. "You better stay with me for a little while."

"Sure, Jim. But why?"

"Because if I get close to that Larry Lee now I'm going to hit him."

Pain rather than anger ruled his tone. The cords in Gattis' neck stood out and his face was pale and he inhaled with gulping, snorting sounds.

"Jim," I said, "try to breathe normally. Take three deep breaths. Take them slow and easy."

"I don't fucking feel slow and easy. Just sit here, would ya? Okay? Thanks."

He had suffered a nightmare while wide awake in the afternoon. Larry Lee had made a critical mistake that was at best foolish and at worst cowardly. Lee had shunned contact with the Little Falls catcher, whom he might have, should have, knocked flat. Here was Jim Gattis, tough, committed Jim Gattis, and his team, his emblem and his pride, losing and looking tentative and frightened. And with that the Sox had fallen into second.

"That fucking Larry Lee," Gattis said, "never plays another game for me. Fire me if you want, but as long as I'm here, Larry Lee sits."

"Keep breathing," I said. "If they took your blood pressure now you'd break the gauge."

"But did you see that?" Gattis said. "He didn't fucking slide. We give the guy [Lee] a break. We sign him out of Pepperdine. Nobody drafted Larry Lee. Nobody else wanted him. We give him a break and he doesn't even slide."

I was not feeling much more cheerful than Gattis myself and I wished wildly that we'd had Jackie Robinson in there, running for Larry Lee. Jack would have scored with a thunderous slide and kept the rally alive. Afterward they would have had to put Gene Hawkins back together with Scotch tape. But we didn't have Jack, we had Class A ball players, and if we'd fallen to second place, at least we ought to do it with professional dignity. I remembered Billy Martin trying to punch Reggie Jackson—the late Elston Howard stepped between them—and how afterward I thought

Martin, for that moment, was closer to hysteria than to leadership. (Later that day Jackson would weep in his hotel room.) Managers don't hit their players. Functioning managers don't. Corporal punishment among muscular adults can lead to a riot. Besides that, it doesn't work.

"You're going to breathe normally, Jim," I said, "and you're going to start feeling better."

"We're out of first place."

"The season isn't over. We get Little Falls at home on Tuesday night. We can beat them. We can catch them. *They* caught us. And tomorrow, when you're feeling better, you'll sit with Larry Lee. I'll sit there too, if you want. And we'll figure out what went wrong."

I looked about for Veale, but he was absent. Since Bob had concluded that Gattis was courting a possible coronary—both Jim's own and one he might trigger in others—the pitching coach tended to withdraw from moments that he felt were overly charged. Moss asked what I thought of Veale's periodic aloofness, and I said I didn't like it any more than I liked Gattis' rages. But in the practicalities of Class A baseball, where everyone worked as much for passion as for money and the whole run of a season was only twelve weeks, I was not likely to change the ways of a thirty-one-year-old manager, to whom macho victory was all, or a forty-nine-year-old pitching coach who had survived three decades of pennant races with remarkable cheer. The applicable doctrine is called the limits of power.

Gattis was calmer now. "We'll have some scotch in Utica," I said.

"That would be good."

"And just don't talk to Lee. Don't say anything to him until tomorrow."

"You may be right," Gattis said, "but don't you agree with me that he made a horseshit play?"

"Everybody in the ball park would agree with you."

He nodded. I touched his arm. "You all right?"

"I will be."

I wandered off and passed a plaque, inscribed when Veterans' Memorial Park was opened in 1953:

> So near is grandeur to our dust,
>   So near is God to man,
> When Duty whispers low, *Thou must*,
>   The youth replies, *I can*.

Emerson. How in the world would you encounter Ralph Waldo Emerson on an afternoon like this?

I wondered if Larry Lee had seen the inscription.

Although my joint role as club president and therapist had drained me, my labors for that afternoon were not yet done. John Pitarresi, the black-mustached young reporter for the Gannett newspapers in Utica, usually wrote upbeat stories about the Blue Sox. Scott Pitoniak, the other regular baseball writer, sometimes invoked sarcasm, but Pitarresi exulted when we won and wrote tolerant pieces when we were beaten. Now John approached Gattis as the manager walked toward a yellow school bus crammed with slouching, silent Blue Sox ball players.

"Can I ask a couple questions, Jim? Do you think you can come back and catch Little Falls?"

"Fuck off," Gattis said. He kept walking.

Pitarresi looked as though he had been stabbed by a close friend. Add a toga and you would have had a stricken, mustached Caesar. Pitarresi turned to me and repeated his exchange with Gattis.

I said that the hot words were unfortunate but impersonal. "In Jim's mood, you might have been a tree."

"Well, I'm not a tree," Pitarresi said. "I've covered this club fairly. I've even given the Blue Sox some breaks. You remember when I ran that correction for John Seitz."

"I appreciate your work," I said, "and most of the

players do too. You just caught a losing manager at the wrong time."

"But he abused me."

"And he was wrong to abuse you, but abuse goes with a franchise to write baseball. Stengel got abusive. Billy Martin threatened to punch a columnist. Happens."

Ed Ruffing, an experienced Utica police reporter who sometimes worked the finicky scoreboard at Murnane Field, swelled our group to three. "Ed," I said, "have you ever taken abuse from a cop?"

"Sure," Ruffing said. "They're under pressure. They've snapped at me a hundred times."

"Come on, John," I said. "What do you think journalism is? Dan Rather smiling at a camera, with his million-dollar contract in a bank vault? That's show business. You're a journalist."

"And what the hell is Gattis?" Pitarresi said.

"As far as you're concerned, just one more manager with a temper."

Twenty-eight summers earlier I had learned most pointedly that a hide of tank armor is a suitable exterior for a sportswriter. I was about Pitarresi's age, equally sensitive, equally indignant, but without the mustache.

Bob Cooke, of the *Herald Tribune,* had decided that I should spend the summer of 1955 covering the New York Giants. I was young, newly confident and rising. The *Tribune* was paying me $10,000 a year, an extraordinary newspaper salary for that period; it was more than many major league ball players earned.

Regardless of the wages, I did not want to cover the Giants. They were not as exciting a group as the Dodgers of Robinson, Pee Wee Reese and Duke Snider (and therefore not as good a continuing story) and they were managed by Leo Durocher, who was something other than one more manager with a temper. Durocher was the most manipulative, vexing, mercurial character in baseball.

Difficult as Gattis became under the strains of a pennant race, he remained fundamentally straight, a man doing his job honestly according to his lights, dim though those lights sometimes became. On every day but August 21, Jim answered questions for as long as reporters wanted to ask them. I think any manager, like any President, should be forgiven at least one snarl at the press per season.

Durocher, who traveled paths of corkscrew turnings, had Hall of Fame talent at snarling and also possessed a glaring Hollywood charm that he turned on and off at will, like a spotlight. Charming, he convinced men that he was their best friend and women that he had spent all his life waiting for a single night of their love. Snarling, he could frighten a lion tamer.

The reporters covering the Giants had been dominated and co-opted by Durocher long before I arrived at the Polo Grounds. He was said to have lent money to one impecunious writer with the comment: "Knock me in the paper and I'll call my note." As a joke, a dominating joke, he set fire to a reporter's story while the reporter was diligently typing the lower half of a page. Durocher sneaked up to the typewriter, whipped out a cigarette lighter and, *violà!* Sparks flew from the prose of a weary hack.

His favorite device was to use the press as an adjunct to his team in a clever and wholly cynical way. He'd call in a reporter and say: "I'm going to tell you something you can use for a story. I'm gonna help you. But if you ever say you got this from me I'm gonna call you a lying son of a bitch."

Excited by the idea of an exclusive, members of the weak press corps around the Giants accepted these demeaning terms. After that Durocher made his thrust: "Sal Maglie isn't really putting out. He's loafing."

The writer then composed an essay on Maglie's supposed indolence. The pitcher read the piece, fumed and went to the manager to complain. "Yeah," Durocher would say, "you can't trust these newspaper bastards. They're out to screw you any way they can. But you want to show them up tonight? Go out there and pitch a shutout. You'll make the writers look as dumb as they are."

As a newspaperman, I did not write all that I saw and heard. If a married player sat in a bar, stroking the thigh of a cocktail waitress, that was lust, not news. I wouldn't report it. Even when a player ventilated emotions about a manager or management, I sometimes protected him from himself. As Cooke pointed out accurately, no one story was worth jeopardizing a source.

But I had separate rules for Durocher. If he was going to spend his summer manipulating me, I was not going to spend my summer protecting him, letting him use my columns to his own ends, behind the camouflage of anonymity. "You didn't get this from me."

The 1955 Giants, champions of the baseball world, got off to a stuttering start and Durocher snarled more often than he charmed. One afternoon, when the Giants had a day off to travel by train to Chicago, Cooke said, "We need a lead story. Maybe you can get Durocher to sound off."

The team was in fifth place (and would finish a distant third). I telephoned Leo, who ranted about Maglie, a favorite target.

"But it isn't just Sal," I said.

"Damn right it isn't. That feller in right field [Don Mueller] don't move off his ass. The guy at third . . ." And so on for a good ten minutes. Durocher concluded that "this team's spirit is shot." It was May, a bit early to surrender. I had the lead story Bob Cooke wanted.

I flew to Chicago the next morning and when I reached Wrigley Field someone showed me a copy of the *Sun-Times*. My story, which had been syndicated, was featured on the back page of the tabloid, next to a counterstory by Jerome Holtzman. In Holtzman's piece, Durocher denied all the things that he had told me and added, "The guy that wrote it is a liar and when he comes on the field I'm gonna tell him so to his face."

Durocher was famous for fast hands in physical combat. He had once literally shoved Babe Ruth into a locker at Ebbets Field. But honor won a narrow decision over nerves and I walked onto the field. Durocher did not call me a liar, nor did I challenge him to a duel. He did, however, stop speaking to me, which made it difficult to find out who was pitching the next day.

After four days of Durocher's silence, I called Bob Cooke. He directed me to write a letter to Horace Stoneham, the president of the Giants, "because Horace is a good guy. He'll get this thing resolved." I did as I was bidden, concluding to Stoneham that I thought an apology was in order.

Back in New York, Cooke reported that Stoneham had gotten my letter, understood the situation and that an apology was indeed in order. I was to apologize to Durocher.

I shook my head. This was the *Tribune*, a paper with a hard-earned reputation for integrity on all matters but presidential elections, where the Republican candidate—Dewey, Eisenhower—invariably appeared in print as a faultless knight.

"I was sitting at the telephone next to my typewriter," I said. "While Leo talked, I typed his words. I got it right."

Cooke, a decent man but an inexperienced editor, grimaced. "The point," he said, "is that in my job I have to worry about our over-all relations with the Giants. An apology won't hurt and Leo will start talking to you again."

I said first that I would not apologize and second that I couldn't travel with the Giants again because Durocher's silence effectively cut me off from whatever news he might make for rival newspapers. Cooke said I would continue to cover the Giants or I would be assigned to the copy desk, where I would edit harness racing results and write headlines very late at night. My resignation took the form of a letter to the managing editor, and Red Smith later wrote that the *Herald Tribune* had fired me "for quoting Leo Durocher accurately."

At the time I felt a certain relief. I would now be able to concentrate on magazine articles and books. But as John Pitarresi complained to me at the Little Falls ball park, I remembered the sting of Durocher's abuse and the pain of being called a liar in print.

"I'm so upset at Gattis," Pitarresi said, "I'm not even sure I want my job anymore."

I thought of buying him a soothing drink. Then I thought, No, let him learn the way I did. Covering a baseball team, particularly a team in a tight pennant race, is fun, but also rugged. It in no way compares to a senior seminar on the Lake poets. Left on his own, Pitarresi began to like his job again in a few days, partly because Gattis, at my urging, went a bit out of his way to be pleasant. However, as in my adventure with Durocher, the incident ran its course without anybody apologizing to anybody else.

"Damn," Gattis said to me in a Utica saloon, "doesn't that kid Pitarresi realize the pressure we're under? And damn that Larry Lee."

We were sipping scotch. We felt a little more relaxed. I said reporters weren't employed to worry about other people's stress. "He had his own problem. A deadline."

"You straighten that one out," Gattis said. "John is a nice feller. I'll go have a talk with Lee at the ball park tomorrow. Him and me, alone, with the door closed."

"Just as long as you promise not to hit him," I said.

"Hey," Gattis said. "I was just talking. I've never hit one of my ball players in my life." That made me laugh and mutter, "Congratulations."

*   *   *

Gattis met with Lee in the large bare manager's office within the red brick clubhouse the next day. Both later recounted versions of a charged discussion and each version worked to confirm the other.

Gattis insisted that Lee had made a gutless play.

Lee said it was a dumb play. He admitted that. But it wasn't gutless.

Gattis said that he himself couldn't remember making a play that horrible, even in high school. It was gutless and chicken, but Lee was right on one point. It was also dumb.

Lee said, "Well, if you want, I'll just take my .320 batting average and go back home to San Luis Obispo."

Gattis thought, but did not say, that a wide generation gap stretched between the thirty-year-old group—himself, Moss, Moretti—and the twenty-year-olds—Lee and Sheffield. The younger players lacked a primal hunger for victory.

Both men stayed with their points, but Gattis conceded that he wanted Lee and his .320 batting average to remain in Utica. Lee stopped talking about going home. He had not been rugged enough to take out the Little Falls catcher, but he was rugged enough to stand up to Gattis.

Lee remained with the team and was benched for a few days. The Horrible Play Affair concluded like the Pitarresi Putdown: with no apologies but at least a viable truce.

After a hard rain postponed a game with Oneonta, adding to our dog-day doubleheaders, Little Falls rode into Murnane on August 23. The Mets still held first place but only by half a game. It was a cool, blue late summer dusk that would be illuminated with a soft orange sunset, glowing in the western sky beyond left field, a lovely incongruous backdrop for the disharmony that followed.

Gattis had moved Don Jacoby to Lee's position at second. (He would eventually install Lee in Jacoby's position at third.) Some of the players said Jacoby should have been moved earlier; that it was typical of Gattis' hardhead-edness to use a man out of position for most of the season. It hurt the team, they said, and all those hard smashes whizzing past him embarrassed Jacoby, who was popular because he seldom complained and usually hit. The players were agitated by the tension of the pennant race and by the explosive situation with Lee. Closed-door meetings between a player and a manager have a way of becoming public information on a ball club in a matter of hours. The Blue Sox gossip mill worked with great efficiency and now in the clubhouse three pitchers and two position players were debating whether it was right to bench Lee, much less to accuse him of cowardice. They had picked up Gattis' comment that he had not "made a play that horrible even in high school," and they laughed at it.

"We've all made horrible plays in high school," someone said. "If Gattis denies that he did, he's blowing smoke."

"Even Reggie Jackson musta made horrible plays in high school," someone else said.

"He made some for the Yankees," I said.

"You know," Jimmy Tompkins said, "there are only three ways for a baseball team to play: for the manager; in spite of the manager; or you can be so fucked up by a manager that you can't do *anything*. That's what's happening to us."

"If he just won't get so damn mad all the time," Daryl Pitts said. "It's like he don't believe we're trying."

"Come on, guys," I said. "You're trying and so is Gattis. Be professional. Would you rather play for a manager who didn't care?"

Pitts responded to my pep talk with a two-syllable word: "Shee-yit."

"Hey," Mike Zamba said to me, "I been with the guys all afternoon. The team was real nervous in Little Falls the other day, but now they're just sounding off. Underneath everybody is laid back just right."

Ball players complain about their managers routinely, as schoolchildren complain about their teachers. But there were, I felt, questions here that were more than routine. They could be answered only when the pennant race had run its course. Was this simply standard griping? Or, as Tompkins suggested, was Gattis' chronic rage demoralizing the team? (Or, to give Gattis his due, was that chronic rage the spur, the repeating 120-volt shock that kept the Blue Sox playing as hard as they played?)

Max Patkin, an experienced and accomplished baseball clown, had been booked into Murnane Field for the evening to attract and amuse our fans. It turned out to be a sour night for comedy.

I'd met the estimable Max decades earlier in the lobby of a Philadelphia hotel where he broke into an impromptu act for a small gathering of Brooklyn Dodgers. Max was tall, skinny, fast-talking and he seemed to be double-jointed, even at the hips. "Hey," Patkin said, "when I was in service I had to hit against Hugh Casey. You guys remember him." Casey was a strong, hard-drinking relief pitcher with a good fast ball, a superb curve and unbridled hostility toward hitters. "I know that I can't *hit* this guy," Patkin said, "so I decide to go for a walk. I get into my crouch." Patkin bent forward so far that his long chin approached his toenails.

"Naturally, Casey doesn't like this. He shouts, 'Hey, Jew! Straighten up before I stick a fast ball in your ear.'

"All right. I was scared." Patkin straightened and stood on tiptoes, creating an enormous strike zone. " 'Anything you say, Mr. Casey.' And he strikes me out."

The Dodgers laughed and even Jackie Robinson, who despised ethnic remarks, could not suppress a giggle. Max was a funny man with a funny body.

Now, at the age of sixty-three, Patkin was still riding

the circuits, coaching first base for a few innings in a shabby uniform, playing pantomime and bellowing one-liners to the crowd and to the ball players.

Moss came to bat in the first inning with Rocky Coyle at second and missed a hard slider, low and inside.

"Hey," Patkin yelled from the first-base box. "What time do the hitters show up?"

Moss backed out and glared at Patkin. Then he singled Coyle to third. The tension of the night enveloped Max and affected his act. Despite Zamba's claim that the team was "laid back," the players were tense and somber. Patkin was rather like a clown at an execution.

"This was the big one," John Pitarresi wrote in the *Observer-Dispatch*. "It's Utica against 'The Valley Town,' big versus little, the All-American Boys [the Mets] versus the dirty old men .us, that beautiful ball park down in Little Falls versus ramshackle Murnane Field. The contrast between Patkin's act and the mood of the Blue Sox couldn't have been sharper."

The mood lightened when Coyle scored on an infield out and Jacoby pulled a long home run to right, giving us a 3–1 lead. But Little Falls tied the score in the fourth inning. Then in the eighth, on a critical play, fortune abandoned our side.

Moretti was warming up, which was customary in the late innings of close and important games. At about the same time a baseball Roy threw got loose in the bull pen, rolling onto the field, and Eddie Wolfe ripped a home run over the center-field wall.

As soon as the extra ball appeared, Jim Jurasin, umpiring at first base, yelled, "Time." He was, of course, the umpire Gattis had tried to humiliate with that dubious session of nighttime batting practice. I don't imagine that Jurasin loved us, but his call was clear and honest. You can't play the game with two baseballs on the field.

We argued that the pitch was thrown before the time-out

call, but we didn't argue with much fervor. We knew that Jurasin was right. So in a tie game, with first place in the balance, on a grim and ferociously competitive night that began with a clown, we lost a home run that would have given us a lead.

Fans shouted at Wolfe, "Do it again, Eddie." He could not. He took a called third strike and, still tied, we went into the ninth.

It was an unusual night when Moretti had nothing, but this was an unusual night. The Mets pounded him. Roy hit a batter. Before the half inning ended, the Mets had scored four runs.

Even in the face of wretched luck, the Blue Sox did not die. Jacoby singled, Pitts walked, Sheffield singled, and Larry Lee, recalled from the frosts of Thule, came in and pinch-hit a clutch single to center. That gave us two runs and hope, but there the rally ended. Little Falls won, 7–5, and took a one-and-a-half-game lead.

Referring to the called-back home run, a reporter asked James Wright, a tall, morose right-hander from New Jersey, "Is God against the Blue Sox?"

"You can't say that," Wright answered. "God's the only one Who knows where He stands."

Ridiculous question. Sensible answer. Jupiter Pluvius, I thought, in irritation. Will the press kindly spare us from theology.

"It ain't over till the fat lady sings," Willie Finnegan shouted in the clubhouse, "and she ain't sung a fucking note yet."

Moretti sat in front of his locker with his head in his hands for a long time. Then this composed and polished veteran picked up a bat and beat it against his locker door, making a nasty, clangorous sound and leaving the metal bent and ugly.

I thanked Patkin for his efforts in my trailer office.

"Boy," Max said, "your kids were tight. The mood wasn't right for my act."

"We were playing for first place, Max."

"I always like to go into the clubhouse afterward," Patkin said, "and tell the players good-bye. But not tonight. They won't want to see me. I've been doing my act for more than thirty years and there were only seven times before, in all those years, that it was like this. Wrong mood to say good-bye. Seven times before. This is the eighth."

Max seemed relieved to escape the funereal Blue Sox atmosphere. I sat alone. If ever a team seemed down, that time was now and that team was the Utica Blue Sox. Then the next day we traveled to Little Falls and blew away the Mets, 13–1.

Mike Zamba won it, going the first six innings. Moretti pitched the last three powerfully. According to the standings, Little Falls' percentage was .646. Ours was .645. We might win or we might lose. We weren't quitting.

The trouble with doubleheaders, most winning managers tell you, is that you tend to split them. One victory. One loss. No progress. After our brave triumph at Little Falls, we faced successive doubleheaders against Oneonta and, true to managerial intuition, or dread, we split them both, playing neither very well nor very badly.

The first split, at home on August 25, turned into something more than a split. It became a schism, dividing the team from one member of management and drawing quite clearly the fissure that was spreading between Gattis and the players.

After we beat Oneonta, 6–1, we played uncertainly and got ourselves defeated, 6–4. This was not driving, pennant-winning baseball, but fortunately Little Falls lost its game. At 11:25 P.M., on the night of Thursday, August 25, the Blue Sox were back in a tie for first place.

Somewhat wearily—the season without a day off was

grinding at all of us—I repaired to the free beer bar while Joanne and an assistant counted the receipts from a crowd of almost 2,000 fans. The team had at last caught on solidly in Utica. People were clicking off their television sets, where the New York Mets and the New York Yankees performed via the cable company, to travel to Murnane and watch us play. This had not happened in Utica during any other year in recent memory.

At the bar I found the now familiar crowd: Jimmy Tompkins, Willie Finnegan, Brian Robinson, John Seitz, Don Jacoby, Daryl Pitts, Roy Moretti, Mark Krynitsky and a few others. They seemed generally disappointed by the split but also generally relaxed. Fine, I thought. Linger at the Blue Sox beergarden for a bit and keep talking baseball.

That was not a unanimous view. In the clubhouse Veale said something about closing the bar tonight so the players "wouldn't be hung over tomorrow." This message got around and was eventually relayed to me by someone at another level of management.

I was glad then that I had been around, had some experience with athletes and beer. In Veale's time in the major leagues, managers set down rules and, since athletes had not then been liberated, the rules had to be followed under the threat of a fine. Today, through their union, the major league players can appeal fines from almost any ruling that they regard as unreasonable. Veale, essentially a conservative man, came from the old autocratic tradition.

But his point did not seem notably reasonable to me. Young men can certainly drink a few beers on the night of August 25 and recover entirely by the night of August 26. As Stengel put it, "The young ones always come back good, if they only remember to get a little sleep."

Quite beyond that, closing the beer bar would not necessarily eliminate drinking. Anyone, including the players, could find an all-night supermarket two blocks from

Murnane, its shelves beckoning with six-packs. I remembered a talk once with Fred Shero, a cerebral and successful hockey coach, on a similar issue.

Certain coaches and managers, concerned with a team's image, order athletes on the road not to drink in the bar of the hotel where the team is staying. "And that's plain silly," Shero said. "I encourage them to drink at the hotel. That way maybe they'll stop at one or two. If I say no, and they have to take a cab to a bar and maybe spend seven dollars, I know they'll never stop at one or two. They've traveled a good way and they want to get their cab fare back. So they go right on drinking."

I kept the beer bar open for a reasonable length of time, despite some shouting at me to close the place, and then drove off to Spilka's for a nightcap with Joanne, Veale and some others.

Alissa was waiting up for me at the house on Bradford Avenue. "You just left me at Murnane," she said. "Doc Gazzilli had to drive me home."

"I knew you were with friends."

"But you just left me." Then, flirtatiously, "You forgot your only daughter, Dad."

"I guess I did for a moment. The whole night was somewhat crazy."

Alissa was sitting on a beige couch, the secondhand beige couch, looking remarkably grown up in jeans and earrings and a gray knitted blouse. "Someone"—she mentioned a man connected with the Blue Sox—"keeps making a joke. The first Blue Sox who gets me—if you know what I mean."

"I know what you mean."

"Well, this person says the first Blue Sox who gets me wins a hundred-dollar bonus. That's not funny, Dad."

I looked at my sixteen-year-old. She did not appear grown up any more.

Baseball needling tends to be heavily ethnic and smut-

tily sexual. Often it is also funny. But sometimes somebody crosses a line and, as in this case, offers a comment
that is every bit as droll as child abuse. That is part of the
nature of baseball, if not a part that the game's shiny new
Commissioner would like to advertise.

In fact, I have known only one ball club where a
hierarchy of ball players actually worked to keep needling
within civilized boundaries.

That hierarchy consisted of Jackie Robinson and Pee
Wee Reese. In another book, I called that team "The Boys
of Summer."

On August 26 we split another doubleheader with
Oneonta. The Mets won a single game, which bumped us
back into second place by half a game. Then, granted as
much mercy as the late-season schedule allows, we were
able to ride away from some of the tension and play a
two-game series at Niagara Falls.

The bus trip, 222 droning miles, would take us far from
Murnane Field, which some of the players were coming to
associate with stress. A change of scene was welcome,
particularly because we were traveling to an area where I
insisted we mix sight-seeing with baseball. It was my
reading that the team needed relaxation more than another
brace of fight speeches. Indolence was no longer a problem, if it ever had been. I was more afraid of burnout than
of lethargy.

Mike Zalewski, our rotund, romantic statistician, informed Moss and myself that he had fallen in love with
such a crashing passion that he was inviting his new friend
to join him on the trip. The girl, thrilled, according to
Zalewski, would drive them both to Niagara Falls in her
own car.

"Are her eyes all right?" Moss said.

"Sure. Blue. Beautiful. She's a beautiful European girl
with blue eyes. Why?"

"You haven't shaved in three days, Mike."

Zalewski scratched his belly. "Listen, Moss. You know what I told her? She's had the rest. Now try the best."

"Be sure to bring a toothbrush," Barry said. "And toothpaste."

Zalewski grinned wildly. He had thought of a favorite riposte. "Moss, your next single will be your three thousandth minor league hit."

Zalewski trotted away in high excitement. "Where do you think he finds them?" I said to Barry.

"In Utica bars," Moss said. "You know he can be charming, almost smooth." Moss's face brightened. Then he feigned seriousness. "I suppose what he *really* tells them is that he's president of the Utica Blue Sox."

Zalewski's romance would be ardent and brief. The girl tended toward wine and whiskey and when she wasn't drinking—by Zalewski's account—she was ordering steaks. She ran up a bill of $250 in two days at the Red Jacket Inn, a pleasant tourist hotel that rose beside the wide Niagara River. Love was important to Zalewski, but not so important as a threat of bankruptcy. After he paid the European girl's bill and rode back to Utica with her, he broke off the romance. "She was probably dipping into Mike's private beer budget," Moss concluded.

The ball park at Niagara Falls is called Sal Maglie Field, after the famous Giant pitcher who knocked down hitters with more menacing guile than anyone I've seen. Maglie was called "The Barber" because, supposedly, he could trim a batter's chin whiskers with his fast ball. Despite Durocher's complaints, Maglie was one of the great, glowering, major league competitors of the 1950s. Now in Niagara Falls, his hometown, where they had named a ball park for him, Sal was soft-voiced and congenial, no more menacing than a grandfather in a sentimental Hollywood movie. He was completing his successful recovery from a stroke. He didn't go to many ball games any more, Maglie told me on the telephone. He needed a good deal of rest. But he wished me and the Blue Sox well.

"If you can still throw," I said, "you start tonight, Sal. Doubleheaders have been chewing up our pitchers."

An old man's voice came back. "I can just about throw across my living room."

It started to drizzle shortly before game time and the players, full of nervous energy, began to run the bases in the rain. An umpire appeared to inspect the field. James Wright rushed from third base toward the plate, finishing with a hard, sloppy slide. The umpire, joining the silly, nervous game, called Wright out.

The rain increased and a nasty wind began. We retreated to the dugout. Water trickled over the steps. "Once I was playing in Arizona," Ed Wolfe said, "and the wind got so bad we had to call the game. A wind-out."

"I was playing somewhere," Moretti said, "and the wind blew so much sand, we had to stop that one. A sand-out."

By now water was rushing down the dugout steps in unpleasant, muddy curtains. We backed into the clubhouse, a small shed directly behind the dugout. This was not much better. In the clubhouse water rushed up through a flooded drain in a persistent geyser.

Rain soaked the flag and the wind blew the wet flag so sharply that the metal flagpole hinged halfway up. The upper portion of the pole drooped at a 45-degree angle. (The players related this to Zalewski's virility.) Another rain-out meant another doubleheader, our third in four days. Sure enough, this angry summer storm, which would have been picturesque observed through a large, wide window, blew away our game.

By way of keeping spirits up, I arranged for the bus to journey into Canada next morning for tourism and a trip to Horseshoe Falls. Joe Braun had taken tourists on the trip before and warned the ball players not to joke with the

Canadian immigration inspectors. "Don't talk," Braun said. "Don't volunteer anything. Just answer what they ask you, and answer straight."

In the Blue Sox' present mood, Braun might as well have warned kindergartners to remain silent. Before we crossed the International Bridge a French-Canadian inspector boarded the bus and started asking where people were born.

"I ain't tellin'," Finnegan said. He was led away to an office for more questioning. "Russia," said Bob Merenda. He joined Finnegan in the interrogation room. Now we had to sit for half an hour while Finnegan and Merenda showed drivers' licenses and explained that they were American-born, nonsubversive and carrying no drugs. When Finnegan and Merenda finally were released, they drew sustained booing from their teammates. Then, as we started off, Sheffield called in a rash and risky try at humor, "They missed the cocaine."

"Shut up," Braun ordered in real anger, "unless you want to spend a month in jail."

In Canada we had to walk down a long asphalt slope to reach a little dockside where the famous, fragile putt-putt boat called *Maid of the Mist* sails out toward the water that roars over Horseshoe Falls. We broke into small groups and put on black slickers. The spray from the falls drives at you like hard rain.

I stood with Alissa, who was wide-eyed with delight finally to be making a real trip with the team. Joanne, Alissa's roommate at the Red Carpet, was suitably maternal, but as the *Maid of the Mist* plowed into turbulent water Alissa leaned toward Ralph Sheffield. All you could see of either of them, in their slickers, was a round face framed in a black monk's hood.

The falls welcomes you with unearthly thunder. The noise grows louder as the little boat approaches. You feel a drenching, driving spray and see, closer, always closer, a massive, unending, cascading waterfall that is all at once beckoning and frightening.

"Hey, Prez," Sheffield said as the boat bobbed in swirling currents. "We got better falls than this in Africa."

"What might those be, Sheff?"

"Famous place," Sheffield said. "In Tanganyika. You musta heard of it. Soul Falls."

It was a merry day, but then we split another double-header, falling a full game behind Little Falls as we did.

Afterward Alissa and Joanne departed in Joanne's ancient red Volkswagen. (The team bus remained a male redoubt.) Zalewski vanished with a hangdog look and his costly love. The rest of us boarded the bus for a long and rather difficult trip home.

I sent someone to fetch a small bottle of scotch—for staff morale, I said—and to buy cases of beer for the players. Gattis and I worked on the scotch until it seemed that we had won three doubleheaders, not split them; until it seemed that we still owned first place. This was the night a few athletes smoked pot, while others urgently told them to open some windows so that management—Gattis, Moss, myself—did not catch a whiff of the stuff in our seats up front. We never noticed.

This night, on this long bus ride, the team's anger at the way Gattis had treated them erupted in a song, composed and sung by Jimmy Tompkins, the bard of Austin. Tompkins called the song "Ode to Jim Gattis," and based the words and melody on Bob Dylan's "Don't Think Twice. It's All Right."

Gattis was sleepy with scotch as the bus rolled along the New York Thruway, but I could hear Tompkins' lyrics perfectly clearly.

"Well, there ain't no use in calling out my name, Jim.
'Cause I ain't gonna pitch today.
No, there ain't no use in calling out my name, Jim.
'Cause this middle relief won't pay my way.
I can't get a win. I can't get a save.
All that goes up is my damn E.R.A.
I ain't gonna see that ole Double A.
But don't think twice. It's all right.

"There ain't no use in screamin' on the bus, Jim,
When we lose another game.
No, there ain't no use in screamin' on the bus, Jim,
'Cause we can't hear what you say.
You are a psycho and no friend of Larry Lee.
You have no class, no originality.
One more week, this will all be history.
But don't think twice. It's all right.

"Well, there ain't no use in drinkin' that ole
    scotch, Jim,
When you are in second place.
No, there ain't no use in drinkin' that ole
    scotch, Jim.
It's something you'll just have to face.
Let me buy you a drink. Say, this one's on me.
One thing you can bet that you ain't gonna see,
    Except in your dreams, is the ole major leagues.
But don't think twice. It's all right.

"Well, so long, Jimmy babe,
Where you're bound only time can tell.
Good-bye is too good a word,
So we'll just say, "Go to hell."
Soon, very soon, you'll be part of our past.
You can have your ball club and that lousy
    Murnane grass
And take Texas Star Baseball and shove it up your ass.
But don't think twice. It's all right."

Jimmy Don Tompkins was somewhat angrier (and certainly more eloquent) than most of the Blue Sox. He had come from poor beginnings and had fought his way into the University of Texas on good intelligence and a fast ball swift enough to win him an athletic scholarship. His father ran a gasoline station in Austin. Jimmy wanted to pitch in the major leagues.

He was having a decent year at Utica, with an earned run average slightly higher than 3.30, but he was also twenty-four years old. A decent year, as opposed to a great year, in the New York-Penn League portends journey's end for a twenty-four-year-old ball player. Tompkins was a good pitcher, a gutsy pitcher, but when I told that to scouts who visited Murnane, their answers always ran in a pattern: "Pitchers younger than Tompkins are already in the major leagues." When I reminded them that Sandy Koufax, Whitlow Wyatt, Dazzy Vance, Sal Maglie had needed many, many years to master major league finesse, they told me never mind. That was time past. We live in an era of organizations with rules and policies and research studies and fiats. One unbreakable rule holds that a twenty-four-year-old minor league pitcher is geriatric.

Tompkins' "Ode to Jim Gattis" contained more than his personal dismay. It represented the thinking of a substantial number of Blue Sox who believed, right or wrong, that Gattis' abuse was muddying their outlook, spoiling their prospects, dirtying their dreams.

The bus continued to journey along the thruway. The pot smoking subsided. Almost everyone went to sleep. I remembered the poignant joy of the earlier night when Tompkins sang, after we had beaten Little Falls and our spirits soared into flight. I could hear Bill Veeck's strong voice reminding me, "The game is supposed to be fun."

It was less fun now than it had been. Some nights were hard and stony grinds. Oh, the magic was still there. The Froebel days and Dodger years lingered with me. But stress—the unrelenting stress of a close pennant race and the bumpy stress of egos in collision—was crowding fun out of the game. The stresses worked on Gattis and the different players in different ways, so we had silly jokes and somber songs. Some players like Tompkins had bet their futures and their most desperate dreams on twelve baseball weeks in Utica. Not every dream was coming to a happy pass.

Gattis was harsh, but Stengel had been harsh and Durocher had been harsh and McGraw was harsh before any of them.

Rolling somewhere east of Rochester and west of Syracuse at 3 A.M., I concluded that the game is supposed to be fun *for the fans*.

Seen from within, lived from within, a pennant race that slashes about you like the boiling, misty river under Niagara Falls, where everyone wants to win and only a few can be winners, is something else.

For all its glories, baseball is a brutal business.

7

Denouement

Certain baseball mirages were fading. Friends who were fans telephoned from New York, inquiring about the pennant race, and when I reported that we were just about tied for first, with one week remaining, they suggested that my mood must be beyond joy and approaching ecstasy. Never explain and never complain. The fans imagined the Blue Sox as a gallant band of brothers, everyone supporting everybody else, smiling and heroic in the shared bounty of the glory. The Rover Boys Go to a Pennant Race. Once—as a nine-year-old right fielder—I would have imagined that myself.

The reality of the Blue Sox, as pressure increased and the season waned, when any mistake could be our undoing, when rival egos clashed with clangor and shouts, when everyone felt that his manhood lay on the line with each night's game, when the terror of a misplay loomed as large as hope of victory, was too much to explain to civilians, even if they had wanted to hear it, which they did not. Imagine telling a lawyer, who has worked until midnight preparing a brief for a fractious client, that guiding a baseball team through an obscure minor league season was taking all my strength and poise and verve and self-control. The response, after a dry, lawyerly laugh, would have been: "Come on. You're having the summer of your life." (Perhaps I was.)

But the Blue Sox obsession, that we *had* to win, infected me as surely as it dominated Jim Gattis. I noted that a Korean passenger plane, Flight 007, had been shot down over Russian airspace, killing everyone aboard. I thought, One more move in the nuclear chess game that the United States and the Soviet Union play each day. That stress would pass. The *real* game was here at Murnane Field, which had become the center of my world. The *great* issue was whether the Blue Sox won or lost. If that makes little sense in retrospect, it still was so for most of us during the final week of the season. We didn't want World War III to break out just then because it would have disrupted the pennant race.

According to farm directors in the major leagues, the primary purpose of minor league teams is to develop talent. Typically, a pitcher may be worked not purely toward victory but toward a preset number of pitches for the night. After, say, a hundred pitches, he may be taken out regardless of the score. Managers are ordered, on pain of firing, to bring along their charges slowly. You don't overuse Dwight Gooden in the New York-Penn League. His efforts there are only schooling for his major league career. The majority of ball players whom the big organizations assign to minor league clubs are supposed to be allowed to grow in a protected environment, like so many minnows on a trout farm. (This is, at least, the theory. In practice, the demands of competition sometimes overcome the trout-farm approach.)

For an independent team like the 1983 Blue Sox, teaching was at best secondary. You want to win. If you develop major league prospects in the process of winning, so much the better. But that is not why we played ball in Utica. We played to win.

Now, in the fading season, we really had a chance to upset all the carefully chosen and higher-priced talent placed in the league by eleven major league farm directors. They forgot their trout-farm theories and fumed. One even tried to have Barry Moss disqualified for arcane reasons. (He failed.) All this was heady stuff, Hippocrene with beaded bubbles winking at the brim. It made me muse on the irony of things. Within, at most, ten days the Blue Sox would disband forever. Our enlarged, battling, volatile family would disperse and never come together again, not even at Christmas. Vital and vibrant though our ball club was, its life span was a mere twelve weeks, barely longer than the span of summer butterflies. But how we performd in these final, heated, desperate days—how we performed in the last batch of games—would live in memory and define one portion of our self-esteem for all the rest of our lives.

I thought of Henry V addressing his troops on the eve of Agincourt. As I heard him, the king spoke in Shakespeare's words and Laurence Olivier's diction. For a giddy moment I considered trying a Shakespearean speech to rally our troops, who had mastered, damn it, the knack of splitting doubleheaders. Then, falling back to earth, I remembered my previous invocation of Shakespeare: lines from *The Merchant* in defense of Alissa Kahn. The borrowed eloquence had proven ineffective. The little redhead was convicted. Besides, it was Hollywood stuff—one more vanished mirage—that a torrent of words could further rouse the team. Hell, the players knew what they had to do on the field. Base hits, rather than iambs, were the order of the times.

For the rest of the season, the five nights from August 29 through September 2, we would play all our games against the Watertown Pirates. The Pirates were a young team, which had started abysmally, but by this point they were learning how to win. Twenty-one-year-old ball players, if they are any good at all, can improve quickly. By the end of August, Watertown had become tougher, sounder, more aggressive.

Further, their manager, Bill Bryk, had once run a team at Gray's Harbor, Washington, a rainy seaport town represented in the Northwest League. When Bryk won a pennant there in 1978, his slugging third baseman was a strong-jawed character named Jim Gattis. Bryk was bluff and hearty, a good fellow who had given Gattis a sack of batting-practice baseballs back in June. "I know you're independent, Jim," he said, "and I know independents don't have any money." But, with *this* pennant in the balance, Bryk had more to show than friendship. He wanted to demonstrate his integrity by knocking the Blue Sox and his old buddy Gattis out of the race. We might have had a less demanding final set of games playing a team managed by a stranger who at this stage was anxious mostly to go home.

Alissa was a cheering, lively housemate in my squat white clapboard home on Bradford Avenue. She was working as hard at her jobs as I was at mine and it pleased me to see her perform as program salesperson, sometime media assistant and occasional usherette. In the last capacity, she had a final encounter with Utica lust. One languorous late summer night she was directing a fan toward a box seat when, seized by passion, emboldened by beer, the man leaned forward and bit Alissa on the shoulder. She was learning too. She walked away. "Better to be desired than ignored," I offered in cold comfort.

"But he *bit* me, Dad."

"It's a good thing he didn't break the skin, or you probably would need a tetanus shot."

"Or maybe rabies," Alissa said, wincing.

She had become too sophisticated in the ways of baseball to ask any longer if I thought we'd win the pennant.
She recognized that I knew no more than she. Rather, she
directed her questions toward life within the sanctums of
the team. "Dad, what do you and Barry talk about on the
road?"

"In our room? We talk seriously about serious things.
Sometimes we joke."

"Girls, Dad. Does Barry ever talk about girls?"

"From time to time."

"Do you, Dad?"

"Only when Barry forces me to."

Because so many visiting clubhouses were cramped, or
had inadequate shower facilities, or both, the team usually
dressed in a motel. Moss donned his uniform slowly,
adjusting his stirrups over his white inner socks with care
and making sure that the knee fold in each knicker was
even. Our uniforms were four seasons old and Barry reminded me of a man fussing over the fit of a pawnshop
suit. But one day he said with complete seriousness, "You
know, no matter how many times I've done it before,
putting on a baseball uniform gives me a thrill." He then
swung his bat a few times in front of a mirror, checking
the position of his hands and elbows, making sure that his
swing retained all of its swift smoothness.

After the games, sometimes we replayed important moments. I needed a scorebook to keep track of matters.
Barry could carry an entire ball game in his head. On other
nights, having had our fill of a game, we deliberately
talked about other things, far from Utica. Barry recalled a
trip to Denmark he had made with his father. The elder
Moss lectured on new techniques in laser surgery. Dr.
Moss, Barry said without sadness but matter-of-factly, had
very little interest in baseball.

I remembered my own father hitting ground balls for
hours on a tidy diamond in Queens. He told me: "Look

the ball into your glove. The ball won't bite you." (No, it won't. It sure as hell can nibble at you, though.) When a grounder hopped high and I grabbed it at eye level, my father called: "L. H. Kahn."

"L.H.? What's the L.H. for?"

"Lucky hop," my father would say, grinning.

Without this kind of support, Barry went about teaching himself the game. Gattis, who knew Moss in childhood, insisted that he did not have outstanding innate ability. But Barry worked so hard and learned so well that he won a scholarship to Pepperdine and a fine, though minor league, professional career.

It was his mother who was the household fan. Once or twice Barry asked me to mail good Utica newspaper stories to her in California, if I spotted any. "She likes to collect my clippings," he said.

"And after nights when you don't get any hits?"

"Send nothing," Barry said, deadpan.

I showed him a powerful passage from Harry Stein's first novel, *Hoopla,* which focused on Ty Cobb, who seized an era with his furies, spikes and bat. After relating certain incidents of Cobb's behavior and imagining others, Stein built the section toward a question: Was Cobb deranged?

Barry usually played with great concentration and control, but flames of competitive fire sometimes burst through. One night, late in the season, he lifted a soft pop fly toward first base and ran into the infielder who was trying to catch the ball. An umpire declared him out for interference and ejected Moss for "attempting to injure another player." I was sorry to lose Barry's bat. Ty Cobb would have approved.

At long last we had come to the part of the season in which, Gattis said, the ball players could be left alone to motivate themselves. Under the master plan that Jim tried to follow—and did when he could keep his emotions in check—the daily routine would now be free of harangues. "If the ball players can't get themselves up and do it every night," he said, "with a possible pennant less than a week away, then they aren't real ball players. I guarantee it."

Indeed, our manager became more quiet and less visible, except for one afternoon when he suddenly began to throw handfuls of Murnane Field rocks toward an umpire.

Everybody felt drained and strained by the pace of a season with no days off and the demands of this particular pennant race. Some of our players lost weight. I developed the first paunch of my life on an abominable dinner diet of ball park hot dogs, sausage sandwiches and something called tomato pie, which is pizza without cheese served cold. (The Revenge of Benito Mussolini.) Other players developed miscellaneous minor infections and upset stomachs. A sore throat began to bother me. We were a portable laboratory of psychosomatic disease.

Countering the ailments was the reality that a pennant actually was possible, which charged everybody with enthusiasm. We were a great mix of infirmity and energy, which is typical of ball clubs in a tight race. On a major league level, arrays of team physicians treat everything from tension to hangnails with a reasonable degree of technical proficiency. The Blue Sox medical staff consisted of Danny Gazzilli, whose unswerving approach to problems was ice—and possibly vitamin pills—now; heat later. I ministered to the sore throat myself with Dewar's White Label (to make the microbes woozy) and lemon twist (for essential vitamin C).

The Sox were still not a completely set team, as, say, the 1927 Yankees or the 1976 Cincinnati Reds, were wholly set. But Jacoby was performing adequately at second base, turning a number of smooth double plays. He did not resemble that most graceful of second basemen, Charlie Gehringer, but he did look professional, which was all we needed. Lee, now shuttled in and out of the lineup, was reliable at third and kept his batting average close to .320. Indeed, at the end of August our *team* batting average was .316, by far the highest anywhere in professional baseball. Detractors attributed this entirely to the short right-field fence at Murnane Field. Nonsense. We could hit just about any pitching in the league.

Ed Wolfe was consistent, though unspectacular, at first base. Ralph Sheffield was spectacular, though inconsistent, in center field. Moss was clearly the best designated hitter in the league and Rocky Coyle, the Bible-reading outfielder, was pushing his average toward .380. We were a better-looking ball club than I'd imagined I could find anywhere in Class Single A.

But the doubleheaders chewed up our pitching rotation. We carried ten pitchers, but having to play six games in four days—from August 25 to August 28—left the staff overworked and, in Gattis' term, ragged. Then, on Monday, August 29, we had to play a kind of semi-doubleheader against Watertown, finishing an earlier suspended contest before the regular game. "I'm telling you," Gattis said, "that the league is trying to bury us, with the schedule or any other way they can."

John Seitz worked a strong five innings in the suspended game and we walked off with an 8–2 victory over Watertown. Gattis then went to Roy Moretti, who had relieved in thirty-seven previous games. "Can you start this one for us, Roy? We need the win."

"Sure," Moretti said, affecting his clipped John Wayne style.

"Your arm isn't tired, Roy?" I said.

He shook his head and said, "Fine."

That was Roy's manner whenever he was asked about pitching. "Yep." Or at the most a three-word sentence. Roy was our Cy Young, our Christy Mathewson, and he knew perfectly well how good he was. Alissa had a name for men who acted in John Wayne movie-time style. She'd call the man a "Macho Studley." I never found out where she learned the phrase. Moretti, I hoped before the second game began, was one Macho Studley who could carry off his terse, swaggering confidence.

In the first inning he struck out four men and yielded a run. He got Todd Davidson, Watertown's leadoff hitter, with a biting overhand curve that hit the dirt and skipped past Mark Krynitsky. It was a strikeout and it became a wild pitch when Davidson beat Krynitsky's throw to first. While fanning one Modesto Martinez, Moretti bounced another curve and Davidson advanced to second. Fred Yoder, Watertown's designated hitter, lined a fast ball safely to left, scoring Davidson. Then Moretti struck out Mike Berger, a dangerous hitter, and Ron DeLucchi, who was the prize of all the Pirate prospects at Watertown. I had not seen four men struck out in one inning before, much less four strikeouts leading to a run. It was a fascinating, miserable half inning.

But we came back with two runs in the bottom of the first and after that Moretti showed us what a splendid starting pitcher he could be. He had a buzzing, moving fast ball which tore the air at slightly more than ninety miles an hour. He had that sharp, down-breaking curve and he knew how to mix the pitches so that he was either overpowering the hitter or catching him off stride. He also threw a slider and he could throw a spitball, "which I'm not using because I don't have to."

"Hell," Bob Veale said. "He ain't using the wet one because he's afraid he'll get caught."

I suspect he was using it, but even within the intimacy of the Blue Sox organization discretion was not always out of place. As a lady remarked to me once in a somewhat different context, "I don't have to tell you *everything.*"

Moretti breezed through the second inning, adding another strikeout. He yielded a pair of two-out singles in the third, then struck out Mike Berger for the second time. In the fourth we scored two more runs, building our lead to 4–1.

My hands would actually grow cold from the tension of these late-season games, and I retreated to my trailer office to warm my hands and ease my sore throat with a modest scotch. "If Roy's arm holds," I told Joanne, "we're safe."

"No, we're not," she said, looking young and stricken. "I've made a terrible mistake. We only have sixteen baseballs left. I'm sorry. But if they hit a lot of fouls, we don't have enough balls to finish the game. I don't know how this happened, but . . ."

"I don't care how this happened," I said. "If we run out of balls, Moretti misses a victory because we lose the game on a forfeit. Do you know what that means?"

"Second place," Joanne said in a tiny voice.

"Call every sporting goods dealer in town. Call them at home, damn it. Wake them up. We've got to get balls."

She found a gentleman named Monk, proprietor of Sam Montana's Sports Shop, at rest in his living room before a television set. Monk pulled on his shoes, opened the store and sold us two dozen official New York-Penn League baseballs. My throat was aching again by the time the balls arrived.

"No more of this," I told Joanne.

"I'm tryin'," she said. "You know how hard I'm tryin'? I've worn the same dress for three days because there's no time to go to the cleaners. You've noticed—don't tell me you haven't noticed—I haven't had a chance to get my hair done in three weeks. I feel so messy. What must you think of me?" (I needed a haircut myself.)

I looked at the two boxes of Wilson A 1010 baseballs as a prospector might gaze at a pan of gold. I gave Joanne an embrace and she brightened. "Don't tell the guys on the team about this, okay?"

"Okay, and tomorrow pick up three dozen baseballs for

every home game we have left. Do we have enough bats?''

"Yes. Yes, we do. Don't get on me, please. I'm working as hard as I can.''

Alissa joined me when I returned to the presidential box behind home plate. She looked neither tired nor frayed. Ah, the dazzling country of youth. Moretti struck out six more— that made twelve for the night—and Liss commented knowledgeably on the way he mixed his pitches. "I'd like to try to swing a bat myself,'' she said, "but not against Roy. He's too good. Anyway, the trouble is, when I swing, I don't know whether to watch the ball or my bat.''

"Watch the game for now,'' I suggested.

We won it, 5–1, and Moretti's wonderful performance, plus the beneficence of Sam Montana's Sports Shop, put us back in first place by half a game. "Utica,'' Scott Pitoniak wrote in the *Daily Press*, "has a 45–25 record, while the Little Falls Mets are 45–26. Each team has four games remaining before the playoff. The Blue Sox once again control their own destiny. Should they win all their remaining games, they will clinch the title and meet the Newark Orioles, who have already clinched the Western Division [by ten games].''

There it was. If we played well enough we were only four games distant from champagne.

Watertown played hard and skillfully the next night and we went into the ninth inning with some problems. Little Falls had already won its game, defeating Batavia, 8–7. Fred Snyder announced the score over the public address system. Watertown was beating us, 5–2. Another damnable fall from first place loomed, with subsequent disorder, recrimination and sorrow. But desire, in powder-blue uniforms, never burned more brightly under the Murnane lights than it did in the ninth inning that evening.

We came back, as much by will as by skill. Our players' drive to win, their stout refusal to be defeated, was almost tangible. You could feel it rising from the field into the steep, bare bleachers. We were, and would remain, essentially in a half-game situation. For most of the four remaining days we would either lead by a half—an extra game that Little Falls had played and lost—or trail by a half. That is about as close as both the mathematics and the climate of a pennant race ever becomes.

With one out, Daryl Pitts walked. Ralph Sheffield was safe on an error. Sheffield's great speed to first base caused rival infielders to hurry their plays and make mistakes. Moss lashed at a breaking ball and drove it on a line off the wall in deep right center. Two runs scored. We trailed by one. Ed Wolfe bounced out, but the next two hitters, waiting for a good pitch, exercising tight control, walked. That loaded the bases. Larry (Clutch) Lee lined a sharp single to left. Moss scored the tying run, but Ron DeLucchi, the Pirates' fine prospect, threw out Don Jacoby at the plate. Tie score. Extra innings.

As it began to drizzle in the bottom of the tenth, we pressed our attack and loaded the bases with two out. Ed Wolfe walked toward the batter's box. The skies opened. Deluge. The umpires met in the downpour and called time. Despite Gattis' conviction that New York-Penn League umpires were storm troopers in blue, he didn't argue. It was raining that hard.

We sat in the clubhouse abusing the cumulonimbus clouds. They lingered heedless overhead. No one said much to Ed Wolfe. He walked about in nervousness for a few minutes and then clutched his portable radio and played rock music, escaping as best he could, into cacophony. The downpour never let up and umpire Jake Falvey informed me that he was suspending the game and that we'd have to resume it from the precise point where rain had stopped us, as part of a semi-doubleheader the next day. We ended the evening essentially tied for first.

Bad as another doubleheader might be for our pitching staff, we would end up with something even worse and almost without precedent. No games the next night and a semi-tripleheader at Watertown on September 1.

The weather began to clear late the next morning, but the field at Murnane retained the consistency of thick soup. We hired a machine called a Scavenger that sucks up water with a vacuum system. Murnane defied technology; we might as well have tried to drain the Mississippi. We skipped practice and searched for wheelbarrows. The players pitched in, moving loads of dirt to the worst spots, raking and shoveling furiously. The Blue Sox assumed the look of a chain gang; volunteers, to be sure, in their jeans or uniform pants, but a chain gang still.

At about three-thirty Jay Acton rushed into my office, his usual calm manner displaced by incredulity and distress. "Your manager," he said, "is throwing rocks at an umpire."

"No manager would do that. Not even Gattis."

Jay then described a scene. Falvey had been watching our ball players toil, in the company of a girl friend under intermittent sunshine. Gattis spotted the couple in the stands and began to throw stones. "Not as hard as he can throw," Acton said. (Under the extraordinary circumstances, this was a blessing. Gattis still possessed a third baseman's mighty arm.) "He's kind of lobbing them," Acton said, "but one of the rocks came so close to hitting the girl that Falvey had to block it with his hand."

"Is Jake sore?"

"Very sore."

I sought out Gattis and asked him what on earth he thought he was doing, and did he want every close call to go against us tonight? "It was a joke," Gattis said. "Falvey knows it was a joke. He and I get along."

"Just don't do it any more, Jim. Okay?" Gattis looked past me and began directing Jerry Moore, a left-handed pitcher, who was shoving a wheelbarrow full of dirt.

I approached Falvey in the almost empty bleachers. He was a stocky man, with a thick upper body, and he told me he had played linebacker at a high school in Massachusetts. "I've been in fights and I'd fight your son-of-a-bitch manager. I'd take him on. But, damn it, an umpire can't get into a fight with a manager during the season. You just tell Gattis to stick around *after* the season. I'll meet him any place, any time. With my fists."

"I'm not a fight promoter, Jake. I came over to apologize on behalf of the Blue Sox."

"I don't notice Gattis apologizing," Falvey said.

"His head is so caught up in the pennant race, he doesn't know what he's doing."

"Well, a manager is supposed to know what he's doing, same as an umpire."

"Right, Jake. You're right. I just want to ask you not to take this out on our kids. They're playing their hearts out."

Falvey stood up. "Never. I'd never make your kids victims." He cleared his throat and said distinctly, "I have my integrity."

Gattis could never explain to me why he had thrown rocks at Falvey and, as I kept reminding myself, we were running a ball club, not a program of group therapy. To this day his strange conduct leaves me bewildered. Jim was a man of high intelligence and resolute, sometimes pigheaded resistance to authority. All I can conclude is that on this late summer afternoon the pighead factor blotted out his intelligence like an eclipse.

*   *   *

A large and excited crowd began walking through our gates at six-thirty that night, August 31. This was our final regular-season home game and our enthusiasts crowded the bleachers and milled about the beer stand in good spirits. The players continued to work on the muddy field.

I telephoned Vince McNamara at his home in Buffalo and asked if he would speak to Falvey and the other umpire, a pleasant black-haired Cuban émigré named B. B. Gutierrez. "It's a big night for us, Vince, and we're getting a tremendous crowd. I wish you'd tell the umpires how important it is to get in these two games. Finish the suspended game and play the other."

"First, they already know that," McNamara said. "Second, I talked to them this morning and made the point."

The rock throwing still bothered me. I didn't doubt Jake Falvey's intended fairness, but if a narrow decision had to be made on playing these games, would he give Gattis and our side the break? Even Lincoln had moments of partiality.

"Vince, it wouldn't hurt if you told them one more time for emphasis."

McNamara's tone turned harsh. "Will you let me run this league? I've been doing it since you were learning to button the fly on your knickers." There was no way to press further. I retreated, thanking McNamara for his time.

Acton and I, Gattis and Veale, Falvey and Gutierrez moved about for several hours studying the condition of the field. Our side saw dry spots. Bill Bryk of Watertown saw swamps. The umpires kept their perceptions to themselves. Falvey did not appear to be angry, just businesslike, but Gattis *had* embarrassed him in front of his girl. Scheduled game time came and went. We tramped about. The fans began a chant: "Start the game." I pointed out the size of the crowd to Gutierrez. I was staying away from Falvey. Right field still looked soggy. The area behind the pitcher's mound stayed wet and slippery. At 9:30 P.M. —some fans had been in the ball park for three hours—

Falvey spoke softly to Gutierrez, after which both umpires began to shake their heads. The games were postponed. I glared at Gattis. He who throws stones in the afternoon gets to sit on a spear at night.

I called McNamara. Since no more home games were scheduled, we could not issue rain checks. We were going to have to refund $5,000. "Vince," I said, "can we play the two here tomorrow afternoon, the suspended game and the one we just lost? The weather forecast is good. Then the teams can take buses to Watertown for the single game that's scheduled there tomorrow night."

"That's stupid," McNamara said. "We don't change the rules as we go along. Here's what we'll do. You go to Watertown tomorrow, finish the suspended game and then play two. At the Watertown park. It's their home date, not yours." Then, more kindly, "I'm sorry you lost your gate."

"You mean you want us to play three in one night. A tripleheader?"

"It's not really three. One is only completing a suspension, which according to our rules you've got to do."

"It isn't *only* a suspension. The tie game could go on for ten more innings. If it looks like a tripleheader, lasts like a tripleheader, grinds down our pitchers like a tripleheader, then it is a tripleheader."

"Very funny. You still play three. That's my decision."

What the hell. *Toujours gai*. It was only one more disruption of the pitching rotation Gattis and Veale had worked so carefully to build. It was only $5,000 wiped out of the income of a marginal operation. *Toujours gai*. It was only a mild incitement of our fans to riot. But what can you expect out of a day when your manager turns Viet Cong and bombards an umpire? I wondered whether Gattis had read Shirley Jackson's classic *The Lottery* in English class. My phone rang. It was David Israel, Blue Sox director, sometime columnist and law aficionado, calling from Los Angeles with advice.

"Sue the league," Israel said.

"On what grounds?" I said.

"Prejudice against the Blue Sox. Diminishing the value of your investment. Someone just telephoned and told me what happened. Speaking for fifteen percent of Blue Sox stock, I'll support you if you sue the New York-Penn League."

"David, the constitution says that for the last twenty games the umpires, not the owner of the home club, determine whether field conditions are good enough for a game to start. I don't like it. You don't like it. But the umpires made their decision. It's a judgment call."

"That's not the point," Israel said. "The point is I want you to sue the league."

"And the league's defense is that I agreed to abide by the rules, including umpires' judgment calls, freely and openly, as the lawyers say, when I bought into the franchise. Do you seriously expect me to argue against that in court?"

"Al Davis sued Pete Rozelle," Israel said, referring to an irrelevant case in which the multimillion-dollar Oakland Raiders took on the megamillion-dollar National Football League. It was irrelevant because, among other factors, the Blue Sox assets would not carry us through the first day in court.

Israel continued to prattle until I turned him over to Acton, who placated Israel by pretending to take him seriously. "You mean," I said to Acton, "you wouldn't take a case we can't win, and that could drag on for months, on a contingency basis?"

"No," Acton said, "and it wouldn't drag on for months. We'd be thrown out of court in ten minutes."

Now Scott Pitoniak of the *Daily Press* bounded up, holding his reporter's pad, asking if I thought McNamara and the league were prejudiced. "That's really why the games were called," he said, "isn't it?" I didn't want to say anything to the press, something I accomplished by offering a flabby paragraph of no comment. There was no need to get everybody madder at us than they were. But someone else climbed a soapbox. "Calling off the games was gutless," he declaimed on the record. "This is about the thirtieth in a series of decisions that have gone against us because we're an independent team with no affiliation. The field was perfectly playable." It was not. At best the field was imperfectly playable. Nor was the decision—made against the home team and the home crowd—gutless. It was courageous, which is not to say that it was right.

Years before, in a brilliant little book called *Sports Page*, Stanley Woodward, the storied newspaper editor, described a favorite reporting technique. Get someone angry. Get someone angry at somebody else. Then read the first party's quotes to the party of the second part, who has been attacked. You usually draw an explosion and a nice windy piece.

In my Dodger years, the device wasn't necessary on days when there were games to cover. But I sometimes used it to fill columns when there was nothing to report but a postponement. Pee Wee Reese, a quiet, tolerant observer of the American press, used to say, "Watch out for them rainy days."

Pitoniak, employing the Woodward technique, telephoned McNamara with a verbatim recitation of the accusatory remarks.

"That," Vince said, "is one hundred percent incorrect. I know these games are critical. I talked to the umpires and told them to do everything in their power to get the games in. People in Utica making these accusations are just unhappy because things aren't going their way. [True.] You're just making an issue out of this because you want to sell newspapers. [Probable.] What did you say your name was?"

"Scott Pitoniak."

"Are you a Catholic, Scott?"

"Yes, sir, I am."

"Then I'm going to light a candle for you in church, son," said the president of the New York-Penn League. "I'll pray that you stop making all this trouble."

Beyond my office the fans at Murnane fed one another's fury. They didn't want their refunds. They wanted ball games. It wasn't raining. It hadn't rained for hours. Why weren't the Blue Sox out there playing?

Fred Snyder's announcement that the umpires had called the game "on account of wet grounds" drew extended booing. A blue-collar sort, bearing a child on his shoulders and speaking in a Slavic accent, told Gattis: "I come to game at six o'clock. Travel forty miles. I bring my boy. What is this stuff, no game?"

"It's not us," Gattis said. "It's the damn umpires." (Jim was now, and I hoped forever, a retired rock thrower.) He chattered at the child to cheer the boy and mollify the father. "The guy had some pair of arms," Gattis told me later. "He could have torn me apart."

The fans formed a ragged, sullen line to get their money back. One man said to me, "You never intended to play tonight. You just wanted us in the ball park to sell us beer."

What could I say to a fan who was accusing me of turning a pennant race into a bunco operation? Nothing that I would not regret. I kept walking.

Little Falls played and won its game. The Mets' record became 47 and 26. We stayed at 45 and 25, which placed us half a game out of first place.

The night was getting cold. Tomorrow came September. I drove to Spilka's and played disc bowling with Joanne, Alissa and Veale. "You *got* to be more detached," Veale said. "Otherwise these nuts will eat you up."

I ordered a Remy Martin for my coach. I applied more Dewar's to my sore throat.

Since we now had to play three games on September 1 and another game on September 2, the final date of the regular season, we decided to spend the next night at the Ramada Inn at Watertown. That would keep the team together and tire the players less than a 190-mile commute on a hilly two-lane blacktop that twisted among poor dairy farms and poorer villages.

We had first-line if somewhat arm-weary pitching ready for the tripleheader. We would use Moretti to finish the suspended game, then start John Seitz and Mike Zamba in the other two. Little Falls would be playing the Oneonta Incompetents, so practically we felt we had to sweep the tripleheader. Of course, if Ed Wolfe singled in that suspended game we could conclude game one right there, possibly freeing Moretti to start one of the other two. But then whom could we start on the last night of the season? As I told Gattis, "The way things are going, we better just take it three games at a time."

In Watertown Wolfe told me that he had been unable to sleep the night before. "Coming into that bases-loaded situation," he said, "it all depends on me. I never been through anything like this before. I want a hit. I want to get it over. A single up the middle on the first pitch. Wouldn't that be nice?"

"It'll earn you beers," I said.

"But I'll take anything," Wolfe said. "Wild pitch. Passed ball. Please, just not an out."

Nobody needled Eddie. The bases were refilled, the game resumed and the whole team stood up and cheered when Wolfe walked in to hit. His face was pale. He fouled out to the right fielder.

Moretti, implacable, unflappable Mighty Mo, struck out two Pirates in each of his first two innings. Then, in the twelfth, Brian Robinson walked, Sheffield scratched a single and Moss walked, loading the bases again. Who was the hitter? Eddie (Bases Loaded) Wolfe. By this time color had returned to his face. He hit a sacrifice fly and we had won the first of three, by 6–5. We'd also had to work Moretti longer than we wanted.

Although Roy insisted that he was ready to start the second game, we elected to send him to the bull pen. We would save him for another short burst of power pitching should a suitable situation develop. It never did.

Seitz was not sharp in the second game. Watertown took a quick 3–0 lead and we never caught up. The Pirates beat us, 4–3. We had fallen a full game behind. If we were defeated in the third installment of McNamara's tripleheader, the pennant race would end right here.

With our defeat we had lost what Scott Pitoniak called "control of our own destiny." Even if we won game three and won again the following night, we would finish second unless Oneonta found a way to defeat Little Falls.

Gattis had nothing to say during the second intermission. The players were quiet, disappointed. Seitz walked in circles, highly agitated, shaking his head. If we were going to fold, this seemed to be the time and this slightly misshapen country ball park, called Alex Duffy Fairgrounds, seemed to be the place.

But Zamba pitched beautifully, keeping his slider low and away, and curbing the Pirates' enthusiasm to lean into it, with good inside fast balls. In the fourth inning of game three, Pitts, Wolfe and Jacoby all hit homers. We scored seven runs and won the ball game, 8–4. Taking two thirds of the McNamara tripleheader, we stayed half a game behind the Little Falls Mets.

That last performance was nothing less than gallant. "I don't want to hear," I said to Gattis, "that this team lacks courage or intensity."

"You won't hear it from me now," he said.

"This team has major league courage," I said.

"I know it," Jim said, "but we're still a half game out. I'll tell you this: if there's any justice in the world, any justice at all, we win this pennant tomorrow."

I agreed with him. I even felt that he was understating, which suggested that my own emotions, like his, were getting out of hand. Clinically, I knew that this was a low minor league pennant race, being played out in Jefferson County, an obscure and impoverished corner of New York State with no national media, no television cameramen paying attention. But I was stirred, as John Lardner used to put it, clear to my ganglia. Tomorrow I might find *myself* throwing rocks at an umpire.

I felt I had to get away from the team. I wanted to drive back to Utica, sink into my secondhand bed and read a nice bad book—the worse the better—on any subject other than baseball. I told Mike Zalewski I was leaving, for the night, and I instructed him to rearrange the rooming list.

Moss looked stricken. "You *can't* go," he said.

"I'm tired, Barry. My palms are still sweating and my throat hurts."

"We've been together all year."

"You hit like hell before I ever came along."

"If you go, Zalewski will put the trainer in with me and the trainer's assistant will sleep on the floor. They both snore. Why are you going? Why are you breaking up a winning combination?"

And so, to be sure, I had to stay.

A tall, drawling gumshoe, who identified himself as the Ramada Inn security officer, announced that I had to sign a form, accepting liabilities for all damages, before the motel would admit our players.

"Why is that?"

"In case they create disturbances or break up rooms."

"Now look, fella, we're here to win a pennant. Our

players are a fine bunch of people. I'm damned if I'll sign anything."

"It's hotel policy with ball clubs," the gumshoe said.

"Shove your policy," I said. "We've paid for our rooms. We've just played three ball games and we're tired. The club lawyer is here. Take your fucking policy to him."

I introduced the detective, a black-haired, stone-faced fellow, to Jay Acton. A few minutes later they were shouting at each other. All this in the motel lobby, crowded with athletes.

"What's the trouble?" Jim Gattis asked. When I told him, he said, "Why don't you or Jay just sign?"

"Jay may have legal reasons. But I won't have the ball club, and that includes you, Jim, treated like a gang of rowdy bums. I'm proud of every kid on the Blue Sox."

Jim laughed. For once I was more emotional than he. "I'll talk to the detective," Gattis said.

I called off Acton. By now Jay was ashen with anger and citing legal doctrines faster than the detective could assimilate them. We moved away, leaving this situation to Gattis. Jim never told me what he said, what moves he made. But ten minutes later the gumshoe sought me out again. "It's all right," he said. "You won't have to sign anything. Your manager is a gentleman, a real gentleman."

Amid our stress, Jungle Jim had vanished. Gentleman Jim, the Malibu charmer, had returned. "Hey, guys," I shouted at Jacoby, Wolfe and Lee. "When you get to your rooms, don't break all the lamps, the way you did the other time."

There had not been any other time. But the gumshoe looked aghast.

Joanne and Alissa, our women's liberation contingent, were assigned to room together, but Liss occupied herself first with some fans who had made the trip from Utica and were chattering about the tripleheader. They had never seen a tripleheader before. (Neither had I.) Joanne, as she later put it, "simply crashed." She pleaded exhaustion and the effects of mediocre red wine.

Barry and I sat on our beds. "You want to talk?" I said.

"Not much," Barry said. "Not much. We've got to win."

"Actually, it's a good thing the season is winding down," I said. "My hands are always cold. When I move I feel every nerve crackling."

"It's something, isn't it?" Barry said. "We've got to win."

"Well, whatever," I said, "you can be happy with the season you've given us. I never had a roommate who could play the game like you."

Barry nodded, embarrassed. He had a hard time accepting praise.

I went to sleep thinking of old Dodgers and young Blue Sox. Pee Wee Reese reminded me of Barry or, at this stage, Barry reminded me of Reese. There was a thoughtfulness to both men and intelligence, though when you burrowed deep you found an iron competitive core. Larry Lee was a compact Duke Snider. A marvelous clutch player, really, which you could miss because once in a while—in certain clutch situations—his concentration lapsed and he might stumble over a foul line. Gattis would be a variation on Durocher (who was a Dodger before he was a Giant). Both were unpredictable, fierce, stubborn, manipulative, charming, and wise in most of the ways of baseball. But Gattis was a tempered Durocher; tempered by education. When you probed Jim deeply, you found a wellspring of kindness. He talked for days about the Slavic fellow who had not been able to see a ball game with his son.

Moretti reminded me of no pitcher I had known; not Carl Erskine, not Don Newcombe, not Preacher Roe, not

Sandy Koufax. Roy was quiet, stylish, open, cordial and the one man you wanted most to throw the one pitch when you *had* to get an out. And after he had thrown that pitch and gotten that out, he withdrew into himself, seeming to need no approbation. The Camus of the mound. The deed was all.

At some black, threatening hour, between one o'clock and dawn, I became aware of a figure lowering itself onto my bed. I felt alarm, horror and then a mixture of both. I kept my eyes closed but knew I wasn't dreaming.

Moss and I were sharing a locked motel room. The figure pressing intimately toward me could only be our staunch designated hitter.

Damnation. Damn it to hell. And I'd believed I knew him well. What could Barry Moss want in my bed? A pause. A shudder. There was only one thing that he *could* want.

These wild amoral California kids. This must be misplaced lust. My designated hitter, the ultimate road roommate, was turning out to be a gay caballero.

I would sit up (I thought) and speak most sternly. I was old enough to be Moss's father. Or should I lecture him on classical romance? The world was full of beautiful women. Most were warm and receptive, if you approached them in a gentle way. Age could not wither them nor custom stale their infinite variety. Direct your passion, Moss, to those who are best equipped to receive it.

I opened my eyes wide. By the light of a clock dial, I saw Moss in his bed. He looked harmless, even vulnerable, in sleep.

The figure was not Barry. Relief touched me for a second and, jarringly awake now, I decided that the form was an intruder. The clock showed 3:01 A.M. I wrote a final headline in my mind:

Ball Player, Writer
Slain at Ramada Inn

Intruder and Numerous Credit Cards Still Sought

The bat! Barry had left his bat, number 22, leaning against the far wall. If I could break away and reach the bat, we would survive, unless the night intruder had a gun.

A high voice pierced my anxiety. "Dad, is it all right if I sleep in here with you and Barry?"

Alissa was the murderous intruder. I resumed breathing. "Sure, dear, but you'll have to take the floor."

When Joanne "crashed," she had locked herself and both keys within the motel room issued to her and Liss. Wine and fatigue, Joanne claimed, had put her so deeply under consciousness that she heard neither the telephone nor Alissa's tapping at the door. Liss wandered about with the Blue Sox fans. Someone found an all-night diner and bought her breakfast at 2:15 A.M. Then she had returned to the motel and, after failing to rouse Joanne, called my room. I stayed asleep. Barry answered the telephone. "I'll turn the bolt so the door stays open," he told Liss. "Then just come in and find a place to lie down. Be sure to lock the bolt behind you."

And that, Alissa can tell her grandchildren, is how she got to share a room with Barry Moss, the great designated hitter of the Utica Blue Sox, when she was just four months beyond her sixteenth birthday.

Considering the circumstances, the three of us slept well.

At 1 P.M. I found Gattis, dead-voiced and grim, trying to pencil a lineup. He sat alone at a table in the motel dining room. "It's not coming out right," he said as I joined him.

"Moretti pitches," I said.

"That's the easy part. They're using Rich Sauveur, a damn slick, skinny left-hander."

"Little Falls has to lose," I said.

"I got an intuition that they just might do that," Gattis said. "Hey, we're not the only guys who're feeling pressure."

Gattis would start an outfield of Coyle and Hendershot, both right-handed batters, with Moss in left. Although Barry was a left-handed hitter, on a good night he assaulted pitchers who threw from either side. Gattis penciled himself in as designated hitter. We would use Brian Robinson at shortstop, but third base continued to be a black hole. "If I play Lee at third," Gattis said, "we get our best defense, but I don't much like Lee against a left-hander. Sauveur could take his bat away. Jacoby . . ."

"Don't put Donny back at third," I said. "We've *got* to win this game. I see a slow hopper sliding off Jacoby's glove. Remember The Ugly Finder."

"I remember."

We sat silently. In essence Gattis was trying to create a flawless lineup out of a Class Single A roster. But every Class A roster is inherently flawed. The player you want the most always seems to have moved up to Double A. Strain twisted at Gattis' strong-featured face.

Moss took a seat opposite us, felt the tension and had the good sense to say nothing. At length Moretti appeared. "Hiya, fellers." Roy looked calm and enthusiastic. He tried twice to start conversations and when these efforts failed he picked up a Watertown newspaper and began to read the major league results.

From time to time Gattis repeated his new catch phrase: "If there is any justice in the world." Except for that we sat there like morticians in the presence of an affluent, bereaved family wondering how much to invest in a coffin. Long faces. Zero small talk.

Gattis finally decided to start Steve Sproesser, the

hardworking bull-pen catcher, at third base. A scouting report on Sproesser would read: "Excellent desire. Fearless. Good power. Low-percentage hitter. Will stop line drives with chest. May have to, considering limited talent."

Nothing we did would matter unless Little Falls got itself beaten. And the Mets were playing the Oneonta Yankees, the team so bad that its manager wanted to push the players over Niagara Falls.

It was going to be a long, long wait till game time.

The early evening air was cool and clear. It would get cold. I wrapped myself in my Sri Lanka Blue Sox jacket and took a seat just off the playing area, near the Utica dugout.

Rocky (Bible) Coyle led off with a line single to center. Coyle stole second. Gattis was batting in the second spot. He made a lunging swing and hit a bounder to the second baseman. Despite fading reflexes, Jim knew how to hit. By going to the right side, he advanced the runner. But Ed (Bases Loaded) Wolfe tapped to Rich Sauveur. Two out and a man on third. Then Barry cracked an outside breaking ball sharply down the third base line. The Watertown third baseman managed to stop the ball but he threw it away. The scorer ruled error. Coyle scored. We had a run.

Moretti struck out two Pirates in the first and another in the second, when he gave up a pop-fly single to left. Ball players used to call that kind of hit a "Texas Leaguer." Now it's a "flare." In baseball the language, like the faces, is always changing.

Moretti was commanding on the mound. He worked quickly in the urgent chill, as though he were impatient to dispose of this hitter and start devastating the next victim.

Brian Robinson led off the fourth inning with a single. He danced back and forth off first and drew a balk. An infield single moved him to third and Mark Krynitsky took an outside pitch into deep right. The sacrifice fly scored Brian. We had two runs, a 2–0 lead.

It is customary in the New York-Penn League (and all professional baseball) to announce or display the scores of other games. But when Steve Sayers, the bearded, lethargic general manager of the Pirates, heard that Oneonta had opened a lead over Little Falls, he forbade his public address man to announce the score. "It could encourage the Blue Sox," he said, "and make them play harder." (By the laws of physics, psychology and baseball, we could not be playing harder than we were.)

"Steve," I said, "in the major leagues the scoreboards show what's happening in all the games, regardless of the circumstances. If no one else, the fans have a right to be informed. I know you're in the bushes, but show some quality, Sayers. Act big league."

"I'm not going to do it." He pouted through his beard. "You aren't the boss tonight, I am."

I commissioned Mike Zalewski as our communicator. "Open a telephone line to Oneonta," I told him in the press box. "Keep it open all game long. That may take a little doing, so be polite to the operators. If you try to seduce one on the telephone, you're fired."

Zalewski did what he was told. (We had an operative at work in Oneonta. Catching the endemic paranoia, Jay Acton had driven there "just to make sure that nothing funny happens, that the league doesn't get a chance to job us.")

We dispatched a batboy to hurry from the dugout to the rooftop press box, like an Olympic torchbearer, and bring us back the news from Oneonta. Amazingly, the Yankees moved ahead of Little Falls, 6–1, after four innings. All these days, these weeks, these months, had come down to the fractions of two games.

Moretti was performing magnificently. Two more strikeouts in the fifth. He struck out the side in the sixth. Two more strikeouts in the eighth. Going into the ninth inning, Roy had himself a two-hit shutout and our 2–0 lead looked lovelier than spring.

Then Ron DeLucchi whipped his bat into a high fast ball and slammed it 400 feet over the center-field wall. There was a moment of shock. Our impervious pitcher had been scratched. Hercules was human. "Forget it, Roy," I bellowed. "All you gotta do is get the next man." That was roughly akin to reciting the alphabet to an English scholar. Moretti took three deep breaths, recovering. He got the final out on a grounder to Brian Robinson.

We had won another ball game that we could not afford to lose. Under pressure that would have flattened lesser teams, we had won five of our last six, including two out of three in that wretched tripleheader. But we had not won the divisional championship. Zalewski bellowed that Little Falls was coming back at Oneonta. I considered planting a spear in his right foot.

Still in his spikes, Gattis clattered to the press box and began to call the Little Falls game, batter by batter, down to the rest of us on the field. Doc Gazzilli and his assistant, the snorer, dragged out cases of champagne. We stood about, in Jefferson County cold, listening to Gattis' shouts and watching his hand signals.

"Nobody touch that champagne," I ordered, "until Onconta gets the final out. Anybody who jinxes us gets dismembered."

Oneonta had scored again, 7–1, but Little Falls came blazing back with four in the eighth. Our players were tramping in jittery circles. Steve Sayers kept the public address system alive and insisted on announcing inconsequential awards to his last-place ball players. *Mozart.* I was trying to hear Mozart. And this man kept playing Spike Jones.

With two men on base for Little Falls in the eighth inning, Acton later informed us, Stanley Jefferson, the all-star center fielder, had pulled a 390-foot drive that carried over the left-field fence, foul by a yard. I was thankful that I had not seen it. Then Jefferson popped out and Oneonta hung on. The Yankees won the game, 7–5. Up in the press box, Gattis threw both hands into the air in exultation.

Players erupted on the field. Champagne erupted on the field. Moss and Mark Krynitsky hoisted me to their shoulders. The players formed a circle and chanted my name. Even Bob Veale joined them. They chanted my name over and over and over.

I looked at the faces of my smiling, roaring summer friends.

I have known worse moments.

In the major leagues a party follows a championship, as surely as the ball is round. Then, after general roistering and two days of workouts, where the reporters outnumber the ball players logarithmically—the press grows in mysterious ways—the World Series begins. It was that way in 1903 and it is that way today.

In the New York-Penn League, what follows a championship is another ball game. The play-off opener to be sure, but another ball game. The low minors have no budget and little tolerance for waiting time. Economics 101. Unless you play, you don't draw gate receipts.

Amid the champagne joy of the bus ride home, I reminded Gattis that we had to play again in seventeen hours. "I know," he said. "I want to start Danny Roma."

"What I mean is we put a cap, an iron helmet, on partying. Tomorrow we go to work again."

"Right," Gattis said, "but the guys just won the division championship. You don't want me to tell them to go to bed right away. They wouldn't do it."

"I'm talking about us, Jim. You and me. I've had

enough champagne. I don't think we ought to mix in any scotch."

"The Waffle House," Gattis said. "I'll meet you there for coffee."

He seemed contained, happy, astonishingly calm. We had won. We had beaten the Mighty Mets and their organization. We'd won in the cold small hours of the last night of the season. We were urban fellows and we won in a farmers' town. Gattis disdained talk about justice on earth and leaned back in his bus seat and smiled. He was an amiable uncle at the reunion of a happy family to which everyone has brought the perfect gift.

The Waffle House is a small, all-night hole in a tenement on Genesee Street. It offers glaring ceiling lights and uncertain food. When I walked in, a stranger was abusing an off-duty Utica policeman, daring the cop to arrest him. The cop turned away from the drunk. He wanted to finish his coffee and go to bed. "But ya better cool it right now, guy. You don't want to get me mad."

"Cops just wanna push people around," the drunk told me.

"Slow down, tiger," I said.

Gattis, Veale and Moss arrived, creating a contrapuntal scene. We balanced on backless stools at the counter.

Suddenly, beyond the window, Gattis' small blue Honda, on loan from Carbone Pontiac, began rolling down Genesee Street. It picked up speed. The curb was free of other people's cars. We rushed out of the Waffle House in time to see the empty Honda collide, nose first, with a telephone pole. The pole stood straight. The Honda's neat blue hood buckled into an asymmetric hump.

"You know what I musta done," Gattis said, grimacing. "I was so excited that we won the division, I left the car in neutral. And I forgot to put on the handbrake. I'm sober. Right? I'm sober. Two, maybe three cups of champagne. Now everybody will think I smashed the car when I was drunk.''

He was both sober and remorseful. When we got to the Honda, it steered and started without problems. But it looked like a teenager's disaster.

Gattis cursed himself.

"Jim," Veale said, "the company that gave it to you got to have insurance for this kind of thing. What's it gonna cost you? The deductible. Maybe $250.''

Gattis turned to me. "You want to help me through the play-offs," he said. "I know you do. I guarantee it. All right. Call the people at the car company when the play-offs are over. Tell 'em I'm sorry. Will you do that for me?''

"I will," I said, "if you give me the $250.''

"Damn," said the manager who had just won the Yawkey Division championship. "How could I do this? Yeah, I'll give you the $250 as soon as I get my last paycheck. Tell 'em, will ya, that I'm a responsible guy. I'm sorry. And most of all, tell 'em I was sober.''

The front office staff was variously manic and hung over when I assembled them for a final meeting at 11 A.M. on Saturday, September 3. We were to play the Newark Orioles, who had won the Yawkey Division title by ten games, for the championship of the league in a best-two-out-of-three series that would start at Murnane Field. After we opened at home, the series would shift to Colburn Field in Newark, the smallest of the twelve New York-Penn ball parks, but the only one that offered video games for fans whose baseball attention lapsed.

"This is our World Series," I began, "and I want everything handled in a major league manner." I looked about my tiny office. Joanne, her brother Rocco, Penny Lacey and Alissa had wedged themselves into what had been designed to be a mobile bedroom.

"We won," Joanne said gaily.

"I know we won. The score was 2–1. Now we have to win two more." I then outlined what was ahead and work I wanted done. Vince McNamara was coming for pregame ceremonies. I wanted McNamara soothed and pampered, not irritated. Congressman Sherwood Boehlert had come to at least ten games with his family, each time insisting on paying for his tickets. We would reward Boehlert by letting him throw out the first ball. Gattis and I would offer a few brief remarks and we would certainly thank our fans. One of our stockholders was intent on making a victory speech of his own. I did not look forward to letting him loose with a microphone in his hand, but short of spoiling the day with an unpleasant confrontation, there was no way to keep him quiet. We would try to suffer him gladly.

Rocco Gerace, as director of stadium operations, would have to follow a specific checklist. He was to get on the ground crew. I wanted Murnane looking as neat as a botanic garden. I liked the image but it was wasted. Rocco had never seen a botanic garden. He was to run every scoreboard number from zero through nine, making certain that all the bulbs lit and all the wire connections were secure. Bathrooms. I never seemed able to get over what Walter O'Malley had told me about the quintessential importance of tidy bathrooms. "I want someone in the men's room," I told Rocco, "and someone in the ladies' room. Flush every john and make sure that it works. And make certain there are enough towels and tissues."

I could barely believe what I was saying. We had just won our divisional championship and I was conducting a seminar on toilet paper.

"Concessions. Figure a crowd of 2,500 to 3,000 and order accordingly. Make sure the seats behind the backstop are dry. I'll be sitting there with Mr. McNamara. Liss, move back there when you're finished selling programs

and see if he wants a hot dog or a Coke. I call him Vince.
You call him Mr. McNamara.''

"Okay," Alissa said. "I can take his order.''

"We ought to prepare a program insert that thanks the
fans," Joanne said.

"Right. We ought to thank everybody there that you can
think of. Win with a grin.''

Joanne found thirteen individuals and organizations worthy of thanks, including Sabrina Hofstra, Miss Utica Blue
Sox, and "The Utica Firefighters Association for Blue Sox
exposure on the public service announcements concerning
arson." I let her sentence structure stand. If the Blue Sox
were consistent on one point all year it was this: we were
unshakably opposed to arson.

I disbanded the meeting and told them all: "The players
have done their job. Now it's up to you to do yours.''

September 3 gave us a warm and pleasant Saturday
night. Fortunate with the weather, we hit turbulence in the
pregame ceremonies.

A small group—the stockholder, Gattis, Vince McNamara, Veale and I—stood in an uneven line on the first-
base side of home plate. Fred Snyder introduced the
stockholder, and speaking without notes, he began to attack the league yet one more time. "A lot of decisions
went against us," he said. "The league didn't want us to
win . . .''

"If this shit continues," McNamara said to me, "I'm
walking right off this field." The league president had
driven a long way to present us with the Yawkey Trophy,
a handsome silver-plated bowl, "emblematic," as he would
say, "of winning the Eastern Division championship.''

"A president of a league should not have to put up with
this," McNamara said. "When you were in Brooklyn, did
they dare abuse Warren Giles [the late president of the
National League]?''

"Not publicly," I said. I began to tell McNamara meandering stories about Giles, so that it would be difficult for him to hear (and react to) the abuse. By the time I had told one and a half stories, it had subsided.

McNamara, introduced next, was booed. He set his teeth and handed me the Yawkey Trophy.

"Thank you, Vince," I said, "not only for the trophy but for your efforts all year." When you win, you can *afford* to be gracious. I held the bowl high over my head. The crowd cheered. "I accept this," I said, "but the players won it." I looked into our dugout. "I thank you fellers from the heart." I turned to the crowd. "You hear despair words about American youth, but if you could know these young Blue Sox players as I do, you'd feel better about the future of the country. And not to slight Roy Moretti, our great right-hander from British Columbia, you'd feel better about the future of Canada, too."

I heard a healthy round of cheers. Some of our players applauded Roy. We later counted the crowd at 2,624. Then Fred Snyder introduced both starting lineups and Congressman Boehlert threw out the first ball, from the mound to Mark Krynitsky. Sherry was feeling excited. He wound up carefully but threw a high change-up, a simply gorgeous pitch to hit.

"Now," Snyder said, "let's all join Robert Merrill in singing our national anthem."

A dreadful, crackling sound scraped from the loudspeakers. Someone turned down the volume and we had silence. Going beyond my checklist, Rocco Gerace had borrowed a "new, high-quality cassette player" and the damn thing wasn't working. Tokyo's best was failing us in Utica. I thought of another song: "Let's Remember Pearl Harbor."

"Bob," I said, handing Veale the microphone, "you sing. The crowd will join in."

"I'll help you," Gattis said.

"Cain't," Veale said.

"Why can't you?"

"Got a plug." That meant he had a chunk of chewing tobacco comfortably wedged between his front teeth and his lower lip.

"Spit it out," I said. "Then sing."

"Won't," Veale said. "It's a *good* plug."

"Come on," I said.

"Can I spit into that silver Yawkey Bowl?"

"Sure."

Veale spat and hit the center of the bowl. He started to sing the national anthem in his strong, deep voice and the crowd began to join him. The voices from the stands grew louder. A breeze stirred the flag that we still flew in honor of Utica boys and men killed in Vietnam. The voices and the flag and the soft September breeze surely moved us all.

> "O'er the land of the free
> And the home of the brave."

Veale reached into the silver Yawkey Trophy, recaptured his tobacco plug and shoved it back into his mouth.

The silver bowl was soiled with a dark circle of tobacco juice. Still, we had won it.

In our noble, staggering march across the summer of '83, we had to proceed directly from the Battle of Little Falls, which we won at Watertown, to the Battle of Newark, New York, that obscure village east of Rochester, which people confused with Newark, New Jersey, a site of great Yankee farm teams five decades ago. Without a sufficient time break, none of us was fully prepared for the transition.

Gattis had run a quiet team meeting. He congratulated the players and said they all knew what they had to do. "Play hard. You want to win the league. I want to win the league."

"And you can win the league," Veale said. "That'll be something you'll always remember."

The spirit was mild and gentle. We took the field curiously casual, not really ready to play another game. Gattis started Steve Sproesser at third base again and in the third inning Sproesser plucked a grounder and threw it into the seats back of first, where the baseball hit a seven-year-old child named Sherri Hockenberry. It was the same kind of night for the Sox as it was for Sherri, who needed treatment at a hospital before she was well enough to go home. Unpleasant.

Newark scored two in the third. We came back and tied it, but Newark scored another two in the fourth when we made two more errors. In the seventh, when we were still being beaten, 4–2, Moss, Coyle and Wolfe banged out hits and we had a run. Then we loaded the bases with nobody out. We seemed about to break another game apart. But Sheffield forced Coyle at the plate and Larry Lee, who had been delivering so many clutch hits for us, came off the bench to bat for Sproesser and bounced into a double play. When we made another error in the eighth inning, Newark scored two more. The Orioles defeated us, 6–3.

Gattis was controlled, disappointed and soft-voiced in the clubhouse. "You had your chances. They didn't work out. Five errors. You made five errors. If you play that way in Newark tomorrow, we all go home."

Players nodded and looked at their spikes. "Mike Zamba starts and, if we win, which we damn well better do, we'll stay overnight in Newark for the final game. All those errors probably mean you weren't ready to play. Well, Newark is gonna be ready. They'll be pumped up. If you guys aren't ready, you'll have a lot of time to think about it because you won't have to play any more this year."

Nobody else said much. A clubhouse after a losing play-off game has all the cheer and brightness of a sepulchre. In our final effort at home before a huge (for Utica) and loudly cheering crowd, we had failed.

The sense of a ball player in that circumstance is to flee the scene of failure, to find a few drinks and perhaps to seek the pulsing counterpoint of female comfort, until curfew and beyond.

Labor Day weekend was upon us. People were leaving Utica to fish and camp and watch their children gambol in the Adirondacks. Tim Birnie, the bus contractor, reported that all his air-conditioned coaches were committed to tours. We would have to make the three-and-a-half-hour ride to Newark in an old yellow school bus.

"That'll look great," Willie Finnegan said, "goin' into their yard in a kiddie car. We'll look like some fucking high school team."

I thought to tease Willie by saying that I could have argued for a Birnie coach if we'd won the play-off opener. A look at Finnegan's face, drawn and concerned, censored the joke. A play-off series is not much of a time for comedy.

If we lost now, we would not be disgraced. We had prevailed over the ragtag label and a season full of taunts that our athletes were geriatric rejects. We had beaten five expensively financed farm teams for the Yawkey Trophy. We had demonstrated that, in an era notable for computers and conformity, an independent club, free spirits, could win a divisional championship. Computers! The Mets' organization people were forever talking about computers and how they helped Mets' ball clubs win. Well, our high-technology equipment consisted of one electric wall clock (broken) and one portable electric typewriter and we had snatched a championship from the Mets of Little Falls. Let them program *that* into the computers at Shea Stadium. Nice guys may or may not finish last. Computers had just finished second.

But now Newark had stung us. It was time to forget the Mets. The opening loss completed a transition in my own concentration from pennant race to play-off. I half suspected, half hoped the same thing had happened to the team.

After we reached Colburn Field in Newark, I sought out Art Mazmanian, the guileful, white-haired baseball veteran who managed the Orioles, and said, "I'm here to wish you and your players all the luck in the world, starting in about three days."

Mazmanian grinned from the bull-pen bench where he sat. We shook and Mazmanian said, "Your hand is cold."

"Damn right."

"Why might that be?"

"I believe the psychological term is nerves."

Mazmanian held his foxy grin and insisted that he was not nervous himself. I thought, Art Mazmanian, white-haired, Macho Studley fox, if you're *not* nervous before a play-off game, what on earth are you doing in baseball? I wanted to take his pulse rate but moved on.

Vince McNamara spoke again at the Oriole ceremonies and presented the silver Wrigley Trophy to Newark officials. Nobody here needled the president of the league. Nobody spat into the Wrigley bowl. The cassette player bringing the national anthem to life worked perfectly. The proceedings were organizational, smooth and dull.

We then proceeded to mess ourselves up in the first inning. With Sheffield at third base and Rocky Coyle at first, Gattis called for a double steal, a good aggressive tactic for the situation. Both teams were tense. The steals could work. Or a Newark athlete could throw the ball away. But our timing was off. Coyle got himself thrown out at second. Then Sheffield, who broke late, got *himself* thrown out at home. We had double stolen into a double play.

"That was not in our game plan," I remarked to Jay Acton.

He nodded tightly.

"You fellas ought to relax and enjoy the game," Vince McNamara said. "That's what we're here for. To enjoy the game."

"I'm here to win," I said.

"All right," McNamara said. "You've got a chance."

Zamba, working with two days' rest, looked uncomfortable on the mound. Mike was a smart, consistent pitcher, not simply a fast-ball thrower, but even the smartest pitcher needs some snap on his stuff. This evening Zamba had little. He was just about pitched out. He gave up a double and a homer in the bottom of the first and, that quickly, we fell two runs behind.

Yet, once more, the Blue Sox would not quit. Moss pounded a long double to left center, igniting a two-run rally and, *that* quickly, we were tied. Then Zamba, tightroping with a bad fast ball and an uncertain slider, scrambled through the second and the third, holding the tie until the fourth when two Orioles reached base with one man out.

It can be troubling, even painful to watch a fine pitcher work when he doesn't have much left in his arm. Gattis had seen enough. He sprang out of the dugout and marched to the mound, waving in Roy Moretti. We were replacing a man, working on two days' rest, with a man coming in on *one* day's rest. I said quietly to Acton, "I guess now is the time we thank McNamara for all the doubleheaders and the tripleheader."

On the mound, Gattis reminded Moretti that Newark had runners on first and third and that an outfield fly would cost a run and the tie. Moretti already knew those things. He nodded, loosened up with eight warm-up pitches and struck out Newark's shortstop, Gerry Barragan, with a low inside slider. Then he got an infield out. We had escaped.

Roy would again become the centerpiece of a most magnificent game. Newark's pitcher, Rich Rice, had been well rested by Mazmanian and we couldn't crack the good hard stuff he threw us. Moretti did not have good hard stuff. He had left his best fast ball in the cold of Watertown two nights before.

What Roy did was show the Orioles fast balls. That is, he threw them high, wide, out of the strike zone. He didn't have enough speed to overpower the batters and he recognized that and worked accordingly. He showed the fast ball and mixed in sliders, inside, outside, but always low where a good slider is particularly difficult to hit.

There are only two ways to make a batter miss a baseball. Get him to swing on the wrong plane, or get him to swing at the wrong time. Moretti, without the usual Moretti fast ball, was doing both. Watching him, I remembered old Branch Rickey preaching on the wonders of "variable velocity."

Roy picked up more strikeouts in the fifth, and in the sixth and seventh and eighth. The fast ball out of the strike zone had just enough speed to upset the Orioles' timing. The down-breaking slider at the knees had them swinging over the ball. And Roy was accomplishing all this with an arm that I'd have thought was so overworked that it must be ready for taxidermy.

These were two very fine baseball clubs, Newark perhaps a shade more talented, the Blue Sox a bit more baseball wise. Contests like this have a way of establishing their own rhythm, which is mystic and dominates the night. Here, after the misbegotten double steal, we'd seen two flurries of scoring in which runs appeared to come easily. Then we reached the 2–2 tie. After that no runs came at all. The teams were pressing each other in ferocious battle—the hand-to-hand combat of baseball—pressing, pressing, pressing until the weaker team cried out, so to speak, and collapsed. I had a sense that whichever team scored next would win the game.

We reached Rich Rice for base hits in the sixth, the seventh and the eighth, but each time the Newark pitcher and the Newark defense held us off. I sat with Acton, McNamara and my still sore throat, a silent, wet-palmed watcher. How long could Moretti keep going? There had to be a limit to endurance, even for Roy.

Larry Lee opened the ninth inning by lining a single to right center field. Gattis, whose managerial courage was extraordinary, continued to play aggressively. He flashed a steal sign and Lee slid safely into second base. Now Gattis called for a sacrifice bunt, to move the tie-breaking run to third.

Krit bunted up the left side and Rice raced in for the ball and threw to third. The throw was low. Lee and the baseball arrived at the same instant. Under all that pressure Jeff Doerr, the Newark third baseman, could not make the big play and rescue an imperfect throw. The ball skipped past him and carried deep into left field, toward the bull-pen bench where Mazmanian had sat in pseudo calm, three hours earlier.

Lee regained his feet and sped home. We had our run. Krynitsky kept going and made it all the way to third. When Ralph Sheffield lifted a fly to right field, we scored our second run. Then, in the bottom of the ninth, with an arm that belonged in the Museum of Natural History, Moretti struck out the side. The hand-to-hand combat was over. Newark had cracked. We had won the game, 4–2. The play-off series was even.

I looked down at my scorebook. In five and two thirds innings, Moretti had struck out eight Orioles. He had not given up a hit. *Without a fast ball*. I ran onto the field where our players were milling in a merry circle. I found Moretti and embraced him. John Wayne had vanished.

Roy was one happy kid. "Every spot," he said breathlessly. "I hit every spot I wanted to hit all night."

I found Mazmanian. "Ya got me," he said. *"My* hands are a little cold right now."

A curious grouping of characters developed at midnight in the lounge of the Sheraton Hotel, where we were staying. Officials of the Newark Orioles stood against the bar, drinking and muttering that we'd been lucky. (Luck had nothing to do with our victory.) Then, as whiskey mellowed them, they sent drinks to the table where I sat with Acton, Alissa and Joanne.

Moretti was sitting at the adjoining table by himself. He knew what he had done and he didn't want to dilute his accomplishment with nonstop chatter. He also did not want to be alone. So he sat by himself, where he could hear the sound of voices.

I approached him, took his hand and said, "You know you didn't give up any hits?"

A small grin. "I sorta suspected."

"What can I do for you, Roy? What can the Blue Sox do for you?"

"Bailey's Irish Cream," Moretti said.

I let him run a tab until the bar closed.

Now there was only one more game to play, one more game to win.

"Who's pitching?" I asked Gattis at breakfast, "and, by the way, you managed one hell of a game."

"Thanks. It could be Seitz. It could be James Wright. It could be Finnegan. I've got some ideas I want to play with."

This was Labor Day and the village of Newark was shuttered for the summer-ending holiday. The shops were shut and most of the restaurants were shut and the Internal Revenue Office, across the street from the Sheraton, was closed, with all its ominous secrets locked within.

"I'd assumed you'd go with Seitz [whose record was 12 and 3]."

"Maybe, but he hasn't been that effective lately and something happened yesterday that bothers me." Then Gattis described an incident in the hotel lobby after Moretti's victory.

Seitz approached him and asked who would pitch the final game.

Gattis said he wasn't sure.

"I want to know," Seitz said, "because I want to know what frame of mind to be in."

"Get into a frame of mind to get people out."

"I'll tell you one thing," Seitz said. "Tomorrow one team is going to win the championship and one team is going to lose it. Tonight I'll pray it's us that wins, but if we don't win, well, that's what happens. I won't let it affect the rest of my life."

"I'm disappointed in you," Gattis said.

At breakfast Gattis concluded: "I've got to think he's moving into a mind set where he feels he can afford to lose. Anyway, that's what I'm afraid of with Seitzie."

This was not a created anxiety but a real one. I couldn't imagine Moretti making mental preparations for defeat. "I've called a meeting with the pitchers for three o'clock in the hotel parking lot," Gattis said. "I should have my mind made up by then."

And that was where we gathered, on a concrete parking lot under the still warm sun, the young pitchers standing there, in sneakers, jeans, T-shirts and tension, while most of Newark slumbered through the holiday. Gattis was charged with nervous energy, but contained.

"I'm starting James Wright," he said, "and, James, I just want you to go as hard as you can. If you give us three good innings, that could be enough." Then—to Willie Finnegan—"I want you ready, Finny."

"I'll break their bats in their fucking hands," said Willie the indomitable.

Seitz's face looked long and mournful. "Then you, John," Gattis said. "You'll go in there to finish up."

The pitchers listened seriously, silently. "We've come a long way," Gattis said. "Now you guys do your jobs and we'll go all the way."

"I can give you a few more innings," Moretti said.

"I hope you don't have to," Gattis said. "And listen up. I'm saying I want Wright, Finny and Seitz ready, but I mean I want *everybody* ready. We can win this thing. We gotta win it.

"Questions?"

There were none.

The large round form of Michael Zalewski approached me in the lobby. "Can I buy you a drink?" he said. "This waiting gets on my nerves."

"And my nerves, too, Michael, but it's Labor Day and Newark, New York, is closed."

"No. I know a bar that's open, on a corner, half a block away. Except maybe we don't want to go there. I hear a motorcycle gang is in there drinking."

"I suppose," I said, "we can always walk in and if we see men swinging chains we can always walk out."

There were no motorcycle hoodlums in the little corner tavern, only a few disheveled Newark residents, drinking beer and playing a video game. I sat and sipped, listening to Zalewski's gabble, which was punctuated by electronic booms and squeaks as somebody destroyed another space invader.

"Why do you think he's starting Wright?" Zalewski said.

"Wright has a pretty good low slider. You saw what Roy did with low sliders last night."

"But Wright isn't Moretti," Zalewski said.

"And I'm not the manager. The manager and Bob Veale pick the starters. They've been doing it all year. I'm not changing that for the final game."

"You ought to overrule Gattis," Zalewski said. "Overrule him and order him to start Seitz."

The door opened and John Seitz walked directly to our table. "I'm a team man," Seitz said to me, "but don't you think that I should start tonight?"

"It doesn't matter what I think, John. The manager picks the pitchers."

"But you can order him," Seitz said. "He works for you. You can order him to start me."

"I could, but I won't. He's managed the team this far. He gets to manage all the way."

"But you know my record. I've won twelve games. Don't you think that I deserve to start?"

"It isn't a question of who deserves what. We're professionals. It's a question of what Gattis thinks will work."

"That's not fair," Seitz said. Tears showed in his dark eyes. "If I can't start, I'm just going home." As if to emphasize the point, he swung the small overnight bag he was carrying.

"Then it will be on your basebll record that you jumped the club."

"Oh, damn," Seitz said.

"John, if you never get to throw a ball tonight, we could never have come this far without you. I know that. Gattis knows that. The whole team knows that. John, do not jump this club."

He struggled for control. "I guess you're right." He seized control. "I guess I just wanted to mouth off to somebody."

"And you did, Seitzie, and you're entitled to do that."

"Don't mention this to Gattis."

"Of course not."

"I appreciate your listening. I guess I kinda wish you were the manager." John Seitz wheeled and he was gone.

"Thank you," I said to Zalewski.

"For what?"

"For keeping your mouth closed, Michael."

*   *   *

In the early evening a Newark official sullenly informed Joanne that we would all have to sit far down the right-field line for the final game. He was sorry, but that was the best that he could do. He said that he was under a lot of pressure for good seats. Actually, he was simply being difficult.

Incredibly (to me) the game attracted only 663 paying customers to Colburn Field. Still, that crowd included Congressman and Mrs. Sherwood Boehlert, who had made the long drive west from Utica. This was sheer, naked fandom. Newark lay outside Boehlert's congressional district. There was not one vote to be mined where we were. Boehlert was rapidly becoming my favorite politician since Gene McCarthy stood up against the Vietnam War.

I sought out Vince McNamara and said that the Blue Sox always reserved seats behind home plate for officials from visiting clubs and that Newark ought to show us reciprocal courtesy.

"They're just mad at you because of the guy with the slider. What's his name?"

"Moretti."

"And anyway, don't worry about it. I want Jay and you sitting with me again." (That worked out, but Joanne and Alissa were required to sit in Siberia. Sportsmanship, thou art a sometime thing.)

When Acton and I reached McNamara's box, on the third-base side of home plate, James Wright was warming up and Vince eased into an expansive mood.

"I've been running this league for almost forty years," he said. He looked natty in a fitted sports jacket, tie and slacks. "You know I'd been an umpire in the league and then I went into service and just before I was supposed to be discharged I got sick and I had to go into the infirmary at Fort Dix. I was a whippersnapper then, but I wanted my old job back and I called the league president, Robert Stedler, from the hospital. He told me to get better and that when I got home to Buffalo he'd have good news for me. The good news was that Mr. Stedler was appointing me league president.''

McNamara clutched my arm. "Forty years," he said, in a spasm of melancholy wonder. "Forty years and it seems like the blink of an eye. Where did all the years go, Roger?''

I remembered one favorite metaphor for life: a constantly accelerating express train, the years passing evermore quickly beyond the windows of the train that will not stop.

"I feel it, too, Vince, but look ahead. We have a fine warm evening and possibly a lovely ball game.''

From a baseball viewpoint it was not a lovely game. We scored one run in the first inning; four more in the fifth when Coyle tripled and Jacoby and Moss banged runs home, and two more in the sixth when Coyle homered. We had worn Newark down. Buckling before pressure and the Blue Sox, the Orioles made five errors.

Gattis' intricate pitching tactics became superfluous after he sent James Wright to start. Working with low sliders and off-speed stuff, Wright gave us the three good innings Gattis wanted. Then another three. Then three more after that. He pitched a five-hit shutout. The final score was 7–0. At precisely 10:15 P.M. on September 5, 1983, the Utica Blue Sox became champions of the New York-Penn League.

Most of the tiny crowd filed silently out of Colburn Park and headed into Newark, which was closed. About two dozen Utica fans rushed onto the field and tried to embrace our ball players, who were jumping up and down and embracing one another.

I finally got to Gattis, who was making sounds like a yodeler. "Jim. Come over to home plate with me. We've got to accept some more trophies from Vince McNamara.''

"I'm feeling very happy," Gattis said.

"Help me collect the trophies and you'll be happier.''

"Impossible," Gattis said. "I can't be any happier than I am."

Looking toward a blur of empty seats, McNamara handed us another silver bowl, "emblematic of the league championship," and then two heavy wood and metal pieces, the Governor's Trophy and the Senator's Trophy. The pennant itself, a large red and dark blue banner, shortly would be delivered to Murnane.

Moss arrived to help us tote our hard-won hardware. The other players did not seem to notice. They were busy leaping and hugging and squirting one another with champagne.

That we had won, that we had *really* won, did not hit me for three hours. Then I began making yodeler's sounds myself.

Almost a thousand people were waiting for us near the Murnane clubhouse when the yellow school bus pulled in sometime after one o'clock. The people cheered and shouted and called the names of all our athletes as each man stepped grinning off the bus. Gattis made a speech. I made a speech. The crowd continued to cheer and shout and the players continued to douse themselves with champagne, until the champagne ran out and they had only beer to toss about.

Marianne Boehlert, the congressman's wife, is a bright, attractive lady who usually limits herself to two manhattan cocktails for an evening. This night Marianne drank enough champagne to let her natural enthusiasm bubble through. She hugged Barry Moss. "You're my favorite Blue Sox," she announced.

Later she hugged Roy Moretti. "You're my favorite Blue Sox, Roy."

Then Don Jacoby. "You're my favorite, Donny."

According to Boehlert, who says he kept count, Marianne found seven favorite Blue Sox in half an hour.

The crowd mixed with our players and the champions mixed with the fans, which is how it should always be in baseball triumphs, heroes and admirers mingling in rough-and-tumble tumult. I recall noise, merriment and Roy Moretti putting a box of Wilson baseballs under one arm. "Aren't those balls club property?" some bluenose asked me.

"Mr. Moretti can take anything he wants."

At 5 A.M. I gathered Alissa and went home. When I arose to go to work at ten, on my first day as president of the *championship* Utica Blue Sox, I swallowed and noted in pleasure that my sore throat had healed.

Prescription: champagne to excess, insufficient sleep, victory.

And then, quite suddenly, too suddenly for everything but memory, it was done. The mayor of Utica offered us a parade down Genesee Street "in a few days." That wouldn't work. We had won on a Monday night. Players began to leave town Tuesday morning.

Gattis appeared in a van with his belongings. "Got to catch a plane for Tucson," he said.

"Well, I haven't always agreed with you . . ."

"And I haven't always agreed with *you* . . ."

"Right, but I'm sorry it's time to say good-bye."

"Don't be sorry," he said. "We're saying good-bye on the right note. You'll take care of that deal with my Honda?" He handed me $250 in bills.

I nodded and Manager Jim Gattis, that earth force lightly filtered through a personality, disappeared into someone else's car.

I telephoned Carbone Pontiac-Honda and told the dealer about the humpbacked hood. He had one question: "Is it so bad we can't hide it with our bodies?"

"No, it's not that bad. Why?"

"Honda prints this newsletter for dealers around the country. If the two of us stand in front of the car, holding some Blue Sox trophies, I can maybe get my picture into the newsletter." (We posed, but he still accepted the $250.)

Mark Krynitsky was using Joanne's telephone. I heard him say, "Hi, Mom. How's Dad? How was the picnic?" When he finished talking I said to our staunch, muscled catcher, "Krit, I never knew you were so soft and tender."

He smiled. "I'm always soft and tender, except between the lines."

I wandered outside and surveyed morning-after litter. Veale was looking at five hundred trampled beer cups. "Musta been a party here," he said.

When I returned to my office fifteen minutes later, a liter of scotch stood on my desk. "Joanne," I said, "who put that there?"

"Bob Veale. He said you bought him a lot of Remy Martin and he wanted to thank you."

"Big guy couldn't tell *me*," I said. "Underneath he's too shy to linger around for proper thanks."

Good-bye to Jungle Jim, the summer warrior.

Good-bye to Big Bob, philosopher and friend.

Good-bye to Don Jacoby, Italian-Jewish Cobra.

Good-bye to Larry Lee, Prince Valiant as clutch hitter.

Good-bye, Zam. Good-bye, Sheff. Good-bye, Seitzie. Good-bye, Roy, our Mighty Mo.

See you again at some ball park somewhere. We'll stay in touch. I'll catch you later.

You say those things. You never do.

The championship, the pennant and the rituals of farewell were coming so close, one on the other, that no one knew whether to laugh or cry.

Good Lord, we'd had a summer. We'd fought and scrambled with others and among ourselves and now we had beaten everybody, which was why we journeyed to Utica in the beginning.

Alissa was finished packing when I returned to 1917 Bradford Avenue. I was to drive to Albany where her mother had agreed to meet her. "Want to say some good-byes?'' I said. ''Want to see Murnane one more time before school starts?''

She nodded with great seriousness. ''Dad,'' she said, ''we won.''

''The players won,'' I said. ''We surely helped them.''

''I don't know if I can get *through* a lot of good-byes,'' she said. The runaway express train rumbles, even when you're sixteen years old.

''Let's try,'' I said.

She nodded again.

Barry Moss stood near the trailer. He wore designer jeans, a red polo shirt, sunglasses and an uneven little smile. ''Alissa,'' he said, ''don't let Dad poor-mouth you now. Have him bring you out to California so we can see each other again.''

''Right, Barry.''

Moss gave her a light embrace. I took his hand. What a gentleman. What a ball player. ''See ya,'' was all my roomie said.

I drove from Murnane barely conscious of the emotions within the alert redhead sitting beside me. ''Should we stop and get some gum for the ride?'' I said.

''Yes, please.''

I pulled in close to a drugstore and handed her a dollar. ''You get it,'' Alissa said. By the time I returned she had broken.

The elation of victory and the sorrow of farewell had caught up with her all at once. This magical, conquering team was suddenly history.

Two large drops ran down Alissa's cheeks as she offered the Blue Sox the benediction of her tears.

The nine-year-old right fielder, now Macho Studley, the president of the champions, felt joyous and bereft, but he was dry-eyed. He placed both hands on the wheel and watched the road.

Acknowledgments

Barry Moss conducted numerous background interviews with Blue Sox personnel, adding reporter to his other roles as coach and designated hitter. Further research assistance was provided at different points in the season by John Perritano, Paul Lomeo, and Elli Wohlgelernter. All have my thanks.

I was blessed with consistent support and encouragement from three editors: Samuel S. Vaughan and Paul Aron of Doubleday and Hugh O'Neill, formerly of Doubleday. Their enthusiasm for the book and the team makes each of them an Honorary Utican. Thank you, gentlemen.

Edward J. Acton, batting practice pitcher, agent, friend, originally suggested that I buy a minor league team. He then followed through with suggestions and assistance, even to covering a critical game (Little Falls vs. Oneonta) on my behalf. My debt to him exceeds by many measures the usual debt of author to agent. When crises came—and the Blue Sox seemed to have a crisis a day—Jay Acton was always there to help.

Thanks also to my fellow Blue Sox stockholders, besides Jay: Keith Barish; Craig Baumgarten; Larry and Luise Cancro; L. Dean Cobb; Marvin Goldklang; Joseph Helyar; Barry Hirsch; David Israel; Nicholas Kralj; Joe K. Longely;

Bill Murray; Mark Rothbaum; Sanford Schlesinger; Evander Schley; Edwin Shrake, Jr.; Thomas Weinberg; William D. Wittliff; and Miles Wolff.

I hope the book makes thanks to the Blue Sox players and Manager Jim Gattis superfluous. Go have a great life, guys.

R.K.

Ø

Super Sports Books from SIGNET

**Buy them at your local
bookstore or use coupon
on next page for ordering.**

Super Football Books from SIGNET

(0451)

☐ **SEMI-TOUGH by Dan Jenkins.** This superb bestseller, the prequel to *Life Its Ownself,* is "Funny, marvelous, outrageous . . . Dan Jenkins has written a book about sports, but not about sports . . . It mocks contemporary American values, Madison Avenue, racial attitudes, writers like me . . . Women abound. I loved it." David Halberstram, *The New York times Book Review* (137930—$3.95)*

☐ **INSTANT REPLAY: THE GREEN BAY DIARY OF JERRY KRAMER edited by Dick Schaap.** From the locker room to the goal line, from the training field to the Super Bowl, this is the inside story of a great pro football team . . . "The best behind-the-scenes glimpse of pro football ever produced."—*The New York Times* (138457—$3.50)*

☐ **EVEN BIG GUYS CRY by Alex Karras with Herb Gluck.** The nationwide bestseller by the former Detroit Lions tackle who's big enough to tell it like it really was. "Marvelous . . . one of the best!"—*Los Angeles Times* (125290—$2.95)

☐ **NORTH DALLAS FORTY by Peter Gent.** Eight days in the life of a football player. Eight days that take you into the heart of a man, a team, a sport, a game, and the raw power and violence that is America itself. "The only novel written from this deep inside pro football. I strongly recommend it."—Edwin Shrake, *Sport Illustrated* (089065—$2.50)

☐ **HE AIN'T NO BUM by O. A. "Bum" Phillips and Ray Buck.** Foreword by Paul "Bear" Bryant. The wit and wisdom of the N.F.L. supercoach who proves that nice guys can finish first. (095405—$1.95)

*Prices higher in Canada

Buy them at your local bookstore or use this convenient coupon for ordering.

NEW AMERICAN LIBRARY,
P.O. Box 999, Bergenfield, New Jersey 07621

Please send me the books I have checked above. I am enclosing $_____
(please add $1.00 to this order to cover postage and handling). Send check or money order—no cash or C.O.D.'s. Prices and numbers are subject to change without notice.

Name _____

Address_____

City_____State_____Zip Code_____
Allow 4-6 weeks for delivery
This offer is subject to withdrawal without notice